MW01225047

HISTORICAL DICTIONARIES OF
INTERNATIONAL ORGANIZATIONS SERIES
Edited by Jon Woronoff

1. *European Community*, by Desmond Dinan. 1993
2. *International Monetary Fund*, by Norman K. Humphreys. 1993. *Out of print. See No. 17*
3. *International Organizations in Sub-Saharan Africa*, by Mark W. DeLancey and Terry M. Mays. 1994. *Out of print. See No. 21*
4. *European Organizations*, by Derek W. Urwin. 1994
5. *International Tribunals*, by Boleslaw Adam Boczek. 1994
6. *International Food Agencies: FAO, WFP, WFC, IFAD*, by Ross B. Talbot. 1994
7. *Refugee and Disaster Relief Organizations*, by Robert F. Gorman. 1994. *Out of print. See No. 18*
8. *United Nations*, by A. LeRoy Bennett. 1995
9. *Multinational Peacekeeping*, by Terry Mays. 1996. *Out of Print. See No. 22*
10. *Aid and Development Organizations*, by Guy Arnold. 1996
11. *World Bank*, by Anne C. M. Salda. 1997
12. *Human Rights and Humanitarian Organizations*, by Robert F. Gorman and Edward S. Mihalkanin. 1997
13. *United Nations Educational, Scientific and Cultural Organization (UNESCO)*, by Seth Spaulding and Lin Lin. 1997
14. *Inter-American Organizations*, by Larman C. Wilson and David W. Dent. 1997
15. *World Health Organization*, by Kelley Lee. 1998
16. *International Organizations*, by Michael G. Schechter. 1998
17. *International Monetary Fund*, 2nd Edition, by Norman K. Humphreys. 1999
18. *Refugee and Disaster Relief Organizations, 2nd Edition*, by Robert F. Gorman. 2000
19. *Arab and Islamic Organizations*, by Frank A. Clements. 2001
20. *International Organizations in Asia and the Pacific*, by Derek McDougall. 2002
21. *International Organizations in Sub-Saharan Africa, 2nd Edition*, by Terry M. Mays and Mark W. DeLancey. 2002
22. *Multinational Peacekeeping, Second Edition*, by Terry M. Mays. 2004
23. *League of Nations*, by Anique H.M. van Ginneken. 2006
24. *European Union*, by Joaquín Roy and Aimee Kanner. 2006

Historical Dictionary of the European Union

Joaquín Roy
Aimee Kanner

Historical Dictionaries of
International Organizations, No. 24

FOR REFERENCE

NOT TO BE TAKEN FROM THE ROOM

The Scarecrow Press, Inc.
Lanham, Maryland • Toronto • Oxford
2006

SCARECROW PRESS, INC.

Published in the United States of America
by Scarecrow Press, Inc.
A wholly owned subsidary of
The Rowman & Littlefield Publishing Group, Inc.
4501 Forbes Boulevard, Suite 200, Lanham, Maryland 20706
www.scarecrowpress.com

PO Box 317
Oxford
OX2 9RU, UK

British Library Cataloguing in Publication Information Available

Library of Congress Cataloging-in-Publication Data

Roy, Joaquín, 1943–
    Historical dictionary of the European Union / Joaquín Roy, Aimee Kanner.
        p. cm. — (Historical dictionaries of international organizations series ;
no. 24)
    Includes bibliographical references.
    ISBN-13: 978-0-8108-5314-0 (hardcover : alk. paper)
    ISBN-10: 0-8108-5314-0 (hardcover : alk. paper)
    1. European communities—Dictionaries. 2. European Union—Dictionaries. I.
Kanner, Aimee. II. Title. III. Series.
JN15.R75 2006
341.242'203—dc22   2006002601

Contents

Editor's Foreword (Jon Woronoff)   vii

Acknowledgment   ix

Reader's Note   xi

Acronyms and Abbreviations   xiii

Maps   xix

Chronology   xxvii

Introduction   xli

THE DICTIONARY   1

Appendixes

  A European Union Member States and Candidate Countries   209

  B Presidents of the European Commission   211

  C Members of the European Commission, 2004–2009   213

  D Presidents of the European Parliament   215

  E European Parliament, 2004–2009   217

  F Presidents of the Court of Justice of the
    European Communities   219

  G Members of the Court of Justice of the
    European Communities, 2005   221

  H Select Regional Integration Associations around the World   223

Bibliography   225

About the Authors   259

v

Editor's Foreword

For over half a century, since it was created as a rather small and fairly specialized organization, the European Union has grown from the initial six member states to 25 at present and has increased its functions and powers, going from monitoring the coal and steel industries to managing the entire economies of member countries and even delving into social and cultural arenas, justice, defense, and foreign policy. This growth has not been slow and steady but rather in a series of bursts, and it was hoped that the most recent initiative, the constitutional treaty, would be well on its way to ratification by the time this book was completed. Rejection of this treaty in public referenda in France and The Netherlands, however, has stalled this process and made its future unclear. Thus the organization will have to carry on with its current rules and structure, but carry on it will. This setback, while a good opportunity for reflection, will not put an end to the processes of European integration.

The European Union is already the largest organization of its kind, with 25 member states and a population of 450 million. This *Historical Dictionary of the European Union* provides a glimpse of its history in the chronology, guidance through the maze of acronyms and abbreviations, and insight into its growth and operations in the introduction. The dictionary contains entries on constitutive treaties, constituent bodies, the EU's functions and powers, member states present and future, and important figures. The appendixes provide statistics on member states, commissions, and leaders, and the bibliography is an essential resource for those who want to know more.

This volume was written by Joaquín Roy and Aimee Kanner. Dr. Roy, Jean Monnet Professor of European Integration, is also the founding director of the European Union Research Institute and director of the European Union Center at the University of Miami. He has written numerous articles and 25 books, many of them on European integration. Dr. Kanner, assistant professor of political science at Florida Atlantic University, lectures on the politics of the European Union. She is the former associate director of the Miami European Union Center and has written extensively on the EU. Together, Drs. Roy and Kanner have collaborated on many projects and a number of books, but this is perhaps the most ambitious. It will certainly be of considerable use to their students, as well as the many others in need of information about this exceptional and thus far successful experiment in regional integration.

—Jon Woronoff, series editor

Acknowledgments

Without a number of individuals and institutions, the completion of this dictionary would not have been possible. To all of them, we would like to express our sincerest gratitude.

In particular, we would like to thank the European Commission for its grants and support of the Miami European Union Center and the Jean Monnet Chair, the European Union officials who have advised and supported us along the way, and those who have shared their expertise in locating resources in the libraries of the European Commission (Brussels), the Patronat Català Pro-Europa (Barcelona), and the Richter Library of the University of Miami (Coral Gables, Florida).

Several research assistants and colleagues have provided the following invaluable assistance: entry and bibliography suggestions from Nuray Ibryamova and Wendy Grenade; entry and bibliography suggestions and research from Markus Thiel; bibliography suggestions and organization from Roberto Domínguez; member state and candidate country research from Jaelle Thackoorie; research and bibliography organization from Melanie Mitchell; and entry suggestions, research, and editing from Eloisa Vladescu. Thank you.

To Valérie Panis, who works at the European Commission and is a former Commission USA Fellow at the University of Miami (Fall 2004), we could not have done this without you. Your untiring efforts to assist us with *all* aspects of this project, and the energy and dedication you not only inspired in us but demonstrated yourself, will always be appreciated.

We thank our editors for their patience and suggestions.

We extend a special thank-you to our respective families and friends, who consistently stand by us in all of our professional endeavors.

This being said, the views presented in this book are strictly those of the authors.

Reader's Note

European integration is a complex and evolving process, explained and clarified in this book. Since its beginning with the 9 May 1950 Schuman Declaration, there have been several official names associated with the project: the 1951 Treaty of Paris created the European Coal and Steel Community; the 1957 Treaties of Rome created the European Economic Community and the European Atomic Energy Community; after the 1967 Merger Treaty, they came to be known together as the European Communities and then the European Community; and the 1992 Treaty of Maastricht changed the name to European Union. European Community also refers to the first pillar of integrated competences as established in the Treaty on European Union.

Most of the name changes are accompanied by significant advances in the European integration process. On a practical level, the constant use of different names to refer to the same process during different stages in its development can be quite confusing. Therefore, the general guidelines we followed were to refer to the European integration process prior to 1992 as the European Community, and from 1992 on as the European Union. When describing an ongoing event, process, development, etc. that has spanned both periods, we use European Union. When referring to the European Community as the first pillar of the Maastricht Treaty, we use the term "Community."

Acronyms and Abbreviations

ACP	African–Caribbean–Pacific
AFL-CIO	American Federation of Labor and Congress of Industrial Organizations
ALADI	Latin American Integration Association
ALDE	Alliance of Liberals and Democrats for Europe
APEC	Asia-Pacific Economic Cooperation
ASEAN	Association of Southeast Asian Nations
ASEF	Asia-Europe Foundation
ASEM	Asia-Europe Meeting
BENELUX	Belgium, The Netherlands, and Luxembourg
BEPG	Broad Economic Policy Guidelines
BSE	Bovine Spongiform Encephalopathy (Mad Cow Disease)
CAP	Common Agricultural Policy
CARDS	Community Assistance for Reconstruction, Development, and Stability
CARICOM	Caribbean Community and Common Market
CCT	Common Customs Tariff
CEDEFOP	European Centre for the Development of Vocational Training
CEECs	Central and Eastern European Countries
CET	Common External Tariff
CFI	Court of First Instance
CFP	Common Fisheries Policy
CFSP	Common Foreign and Security Policy
CIS	Commonwealth of Independent States
COREPER	Committee of Permanent Representatives
CPVO	Community Plant Variety Office
CSCE	Conference on Security and Cooperation in Europe

EAGGF	European Agricultural Guidance and Guarantee Fund
EASA	European Aviation Safety Agency
EAW	European Arrest Warrant
EBRD	European Bank for Reconstruction and Development
EC	European Community
ECB	European Central Bank
ECCAS	Economic Community of Central African States
ECHO	European Community Humanitarian Aid Office
ECJ	European Court of Justice
ECOFIN	Economic and Finance Council
ECOWAS	Economic Community of West African States
ECSC	European Coal and Steel Community
ECU	European Currency Unit
EDC	European Defence Community
EDF	European Development Fund
EDPS	European Data Protection Supervisor
EEA	European Economic Area
EEA	European Environment Agency
EEC	European Economic Community
EESC	European Economic and Social Committee
EFSA	European Food Safety Authority
EFTA	European Free Trade Association
EIB	European Investment Bank
EIRO	European Industrial Relations Observatory
EMCC	European Monitoring Centre on Change
EMCDDA	European Monitoring Centre for Drugs and Drug Addiction
EMEA	European Medicines Agency
EMI	European Monetary Institute
EMS	European Monetary System
EMSA	European Maritime Safety Agency
EMU	Economic and Monetary Union
ENISA	European Network and Information Security Agency
ENP	European Neighborhood Policy
EP	European Parliament
EPAs	Economic Partnership Agreements
EPC	European Political Cooperation
EPP-ED	European People's Party (Christian Democrats) and European Democrats

EPU	European Political Union
ERDF	European Regional Development Fund
ERM	Exchange Rate Mechanism
ERM II	Exchange Rate Mechanism II
ESCB	European System of Central Banks
ESDI	European Security and Defence Identity
ESDP	European Security and Defence Policy
ESF	European Social Fund
ESPRIT	European Strategic Programme for Research and Development in Information and Technology
ETA	Euskadi ta Askatasuna
ETF	European Training Foundation
ETUCO	European Trade Union College
EU	European Union
EUISS	European Union Institute for Security Studies
EUMC	European Monitoring Centre on Racism and Xenophobia
EUMC	European Union Military Committee
EUMS	European Union Military Staff
EUPM	European Union Police Mission
EURATOM	European Atomic Energy Community
EUROPOL	European Police Office
EUSC	European Union Satellite Centre
EUSR	European Union Special Representation (for the Middle East Peace Process)
EWCO	European Working Conditions Observatory
FIFG	Financial Instrument for Fisheries Guidance
FVO	Food and Veterinary Office
FYROM	Former Yugoslav Republic of Macedonia
GAC	General Affairs Council
GATS	General Agreement on Trade in Services
GATT	General Agreement on Tariffs and Trade
GDP	Gross Domestic Product
GMOs	Genetically Modified Organisms
GNP	Gross National Product
GREENS/EFA	Group of the Greens/European Free Alliance
GUE/NGL	Confederal Group of the European United Left-Nordic Green Left
ICC	International Criminal Court

IGC	Intergovernmental Conference
IMF	International Monetary Fund
IMPs	Integrated Mediterranean Programmes
IND/DEM	Independence and Democracy Group of the European Parliament
ISPA	Instrument for Structural Policies for Pre-Accession
JHA	Justice and Home Affairs
MEP	Member of European Parliament
MEPP	Middle East Peace Process
MERCOSUR	Southern Cone Common Market
NAFTA	North American Free Trade Agreement
NATO	North Atlantic Treaty Organization
NIS	Newly Independent States
NTA	New Transatlantic Agenda
OAS	Organization of American States
OECD	Organization for Economic Cooperation and Development
OEEC	Organization for European Economic Cooperation
OHIM	Office for Harmonization in the Internal Market (trademarks and designs)
OLAF	European Anti-Fraud Office
OSCE	Organization for Security and Cooperation in Europe
PCA	Partnership and Cooperation Agreement
PES	Socialist Group in the European Parliament
PHARE	Poland and Hungary Assistance for the Reconstruction of the Economy
PSOE	Spanish Socialist Workers' Party
QMV	Qualified Majority Voting
RAXEN	European Information Network on Racism and Xenophobia
SAA	Stabilization and Association Agreement
SAP	Stabilization and Association Process
SAPARD	Special Accession Programme for Agriculture and Rural Development
SEA	Single European Act
SGP	Stability and Growth Pact
SIS	Schengen Information System
SIS II	Schengen Information System II

SPD	Social Democratic Party
TACIS	Technical Assistance for the Commonwealth of Independent States
TEIN	Trans-Eurasian Information Network
TEU	Treaty on European Union
TRIPS	Trade-Related Aspects of Intellectual Property Rights
UDF	Union for French Democracy
UEN	Union for Europe of the Nations
UK	United Kingdom
UMP	Union for a Popular Movement
UN	United Nations
UNESCO	United Nations Educational, Scientific, and Cultural Organization
UNFCCC	United Nations Framework Convention on Climate Change
UNICTY	United Nations International Criminal Tribunal for the Former Yugoslavia
UNMIK	United Nations Interim Administration in Kosovo
US	United States
VAT	Value-Added Tax
WEU	Western European Union
WTO	World Trade Organization

Maps

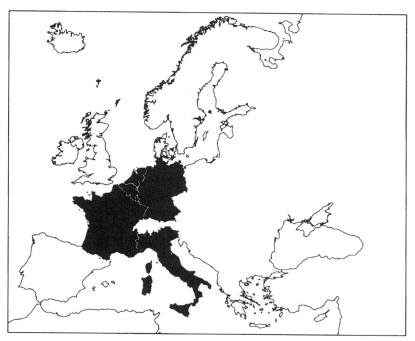

The founding members of the European Community: Belgium, France, West Germany, Italy, Luxembourg, and The Netherlands.

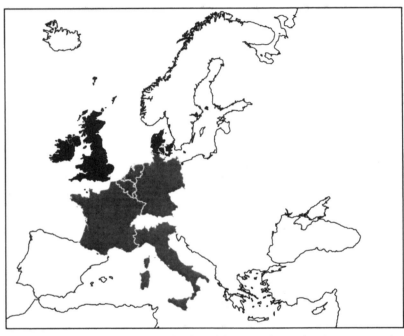

On 1 January 1973, Denmark, Ireland, and the United Kingdom became member states of the European Union.

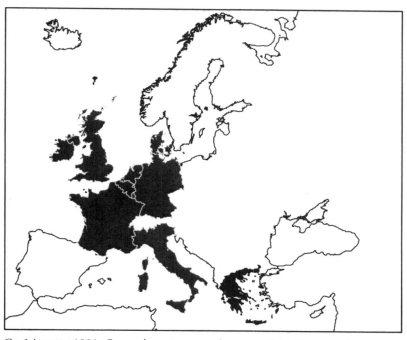

On 1 January 1981, Greece became a member state of the European Community.

On 1 January 1986, Portugal and Spain became member states of the European Community.

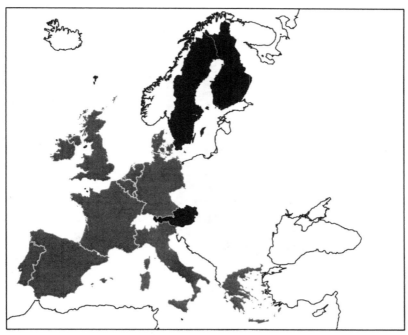

On 1 January 1995, Austria, Finland, and Sweden became member states of the European Union.

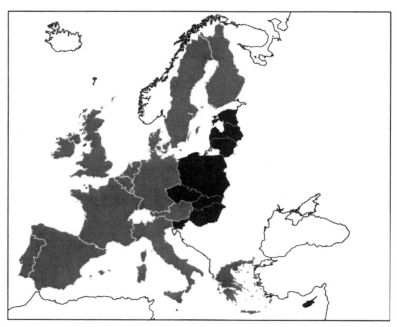

On 1 May 2004, Cyprus, the Czech Republic, Estonia, Hungary, Latvia, Lithuania, Malta, Poland, Slovakia, and Slovenia became member states of the European Union.

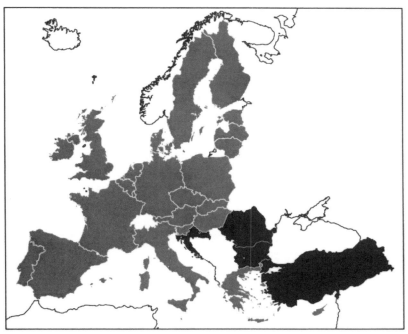

On 1 January 2007, candidate countries Bulgaria and Romania will become member states of the European Union. Membership dates for candidate countries Croatia and Turkey will be set at the conclusion of their accession negotiations.

Chronology

1946 19 September: Winston Churchill gives his "United States of Europe" speech at the University of Zurich.

1947 14 May: Based on ideas and support from Winston Churchill, the United Europe Movement is created. **5 June:** The United States (U.S.) government announces the launch of the Marshall Plan to assist Europe with its postwar economic recovery.

1948 1 January: The Benelux Customs Union enters into force. **17 March:** The Brussels Treaty on Economic, Social, and Cultural Collaboration and Collective Self-Defense is signed by Belgium, France, Luxembourg, the Netherlands, and the United Kingdom (UK), creating the Western European Union (WEU). **16 April:** The Organization for European Economic Cooperation (OEEC) is created to coordinate the funding available from the U.S.-sponsored Marshall Plan for European economic recovery. **7–11 May:** The Congress of Europe, chaired by Winston Churchill, meets in The Hague, giving impetus to the creation of the Council of Europe.

1949 4 April: Belgium, Canada, Denmark, France, Iceland, Italy, Luxembourg, the Netherlands, Norway, Portugal, the UK, and the United States sign the North Atlantic Treaty, establishing the North Atlantic Treaty Organization (NATO). **5 May:** The Council of Europe is founded through the signing of the Treaty of London. **3 August:** The Treaty of London establishing the Council of Europe enters into force.

1950 9 May: Robert Schuman proposes the pooling of the French and German coal and steel resources under a high authority in the Schuman Declaration. **4 November:** The Council of Europe signs and adopts the European Convention for the Protection of Human Rights and Fundamental Freedoms in Rome.

1951   18 April: Belgium, France, Germany, Italy, Luxembourg, and the Netherlands sign the Treaty of Paris, creating the European Coal and Steel Community (ECSC).

1952   27 May: The treaty establishing the European Defence Community (EDC) is signed in Paris by Belgium, France, Germany, Italy, Luxembourg, and the Netherlands. **23 July:** The Treaty of Paris enters into force. **10 August:** The ECSC High Authority begins operations under the presidency of Jean Monnet. **10 September:** The Common Assembly of the ECSC meets for the first time under the presidency of Paul-Henri Spaak.

1953   3 September: The European Convention for the Protection of Human Rights and Fundamental Freedoms enters into force.

1954   11 May: Alcide de Gasperi is elected president of the Common Assembly of the ECSC. **30 August:** The French parliament rejects the EDC Treaty. **23 October:** The Paris Agreements are signed, amending the Brussels Treaty and reestablishing the WEU with the added membership of Italy and West Germany. **10 November:** Jean Monnet resigns as president of the ECSC's High Authority. **21 December:** The European Court of Justice (ECJ) renders its first judgment.

1955   1–2 June: The foreign ministers of the ECSC member states meet in Messina, Italy, to discuss the future of European integration. **3 June:** René Mayer assumes the presidency of the ECSC High Authority.

1956   6 May: The Spaak Report on the creation of the European Economic Community (EEC) and the European Atomic Energy Community (EURATOM) is presented to the ECSC. **26 June:** The intergovernmental conference (IGC) that drafted the Treaties of Rome creating the EEC and ERUATOM begins. **27 November:** Hans Furler is elected president of the Common Assembly of the ECSC.

1957   25 March: The Treaties of Rome are signed by the six founding members, creating the EEC and EURATOM.

1958   1 January: The Treaties of Rome enter into force. **7 January:** Walter Hallstein is elected first president of the EEC Commission. Louis Armand is elected president of the EURATOM Commission. Paul Finet is elected president of the ECSC High Authority. **26 January:** The

Committee of Permanent Representatives (COREPER) is created by the six founding members, to aid in the preparation of the work of the Councils. **19 March:** The European Parliamentary Assembly is established, replacing the Common Assembly of the ECSC. Robert Schuman is elected president of the European Parliamentary Assembly. **19 May:** The European Economic and Social Committee (EESC) begins operations.

1959 2 February: Etienne Hirsch is elected president of the EURATOM Commission. **10–11 September:** Piero Malvestiti is elected president of the ECSC High Authority. **18 September** The European Court of Human Rights is established in Strasbourg, France.

1960 4 January: The Stockholm Convention is signed, establishing the European Free Trade Association (EFTA). **28 March:** Hans Furler assumes the presidency of the European Parliamentary Assembly. **3 May:** The EFTA comes into force.

1961 31 July: Ireland formally submits its application for membership in the European Community (EC). **9 August:** The UK applies for membership in the EC. **10 August:** Denmark applies for membership in the EC.

1962 10 January: Pierre Chatanet is elected president of the EURATOM Commission. **27–30 March:** Gaetano Martino is elected president of the European Parliamentary Assembly. The European Parliamentary Assembly changes its name to the European Parliament (EP). **30 April:** Norway formally submits its application for membership in the EC. **30 July:** The Common Agricultural Policy (CAP) is adopted by the European Council, establishing a single market for agricultural products. **1 November:** The association agreement between the EEC and Greece enters into force.

1963 14 January: French President Charles de Gaulle vetoes the UK's first application for membership in the EC. **22 January:** French President Charles de Gaulle and German Chancellor Konrad Adenauer sign the Treaty of the Elysée. **5 February:** The ECJ makes its ruling in the *Van Gend en Loos* case, establishing the direct effect of EC law in the member states. **20 July:** The members of the EC and 18 associated African states and Madagascar hold the first Yaoundé Convention. **8 October:** Dino Del Bo is elected president of the ECSC High Authority.

1964   21 March: Jean-Pierre Duvieusart is elected president of the EP. **1 June:** The Yaoundé Convention enters into force. **15 July:** The ECJ makes its *Costa/ENEL* ruling, establishing the supremacy of EC law over national legislation. **1 December:** The association agreement between the EEC and Turkey enters into force.

1965   2 March: Victor Leemans is elected president of the EP. **8 April:** The Merger Treaty is signed by the six founding members, merging the institutions of the three European Communities. **1 July:** The Empty Chair Crisis begins with the French government's recall of its representatives to the EC institutions.

1966   28–29 January: Agreement is reached on the Luxembourg Compromise, resolving the Empty Chair Crisis. **7 March:** Alain Pohler is elected president of the EP.

1967   11 May: The UK submits its second application for membership in the European Community (EC). **1 July:** The Merger Treaty, combining the Commissions of the EEC and EURATOM with the ECSC's High Authority enters into force. **6 July:** The European Commission under the presidency of Jean Rey takes office.

1968   1 July: The common external tariff is established and the EC customs union begins operation.

1969   11 March: Mario Scelba assumes the presidency of the EP. **29 July:** The second Yaoundé Convention is signed. **1–2 December:** A Summit is held in The Hague where EC leaders advocate for increased political coordination between the EC member states.

1970   2 July: The European Commission under the presidency of Franco Maria Malfatti takes office. **27 October:** The heads of state of the EC member states adopt the Davignon Report, which establishes the foundations of European Political Cooperation.

1971   1 January: The second Yaoundé Convention enters into force. **9 March:** Walter Behrendt assumes the presidency of the EP. **22 March:** The Council adopts the Werner Plan for economic and monetary union. **1 April:** An association agreement between the EC and Malta enters into force.

1972   21 March: European Commission President Franco Maria Malfatti resigns. **22 March:** Sicco Mansholt replaces Franco Maria Malfatti as president of the European Commission. **23 April:** A referendum is held in which the French people vote in favor of Britain's membership in the EC. **10 May:** A referendum is held in Ireland and the people vote in favor of Irish EC membership. **24–25 September:** A public referendum is held in which the Norwegian people vote against EC membership. **2 October:** Denmark holds a referendum in which the majority vote in favor of Danish EC membership.

1973   1 January: Denmark, Ireland, and the United Kingdom become EC member states. **6 January:** François Xavier Ortoli assumes the office of the presidency of the European Commission. **13 March:** Cornelis Berkhouwer is elected president of the EP. **1 June:** An association agreement between the EC and Cyprus enters into force. **3–7 July:** The opening session of the Conference on Security and Cooperation in Europe (CSCE) is held in Helsinki, Finland.

1974   9–10 December: The EC Heads of State and Government establish the European Council at the Paris Summit.

1975   28 February: The EC and 46 African–Caribbean–Pacific (ACP) states sign the first Lomé Convention in Lomé, Togo. **10–11 March:** The first meeting of the European Council is held in Dublin, Ireland. **11 March:** Georges Spénale is elected president of the EP. **5 June:** Nearly two-and-a-half years after joining the EC, a referendum is held in the UK during the premiership of Harold Wilson in which the British people vote in favor of Britain's continued EC membership. **1 August:** The CSCE process is founded by the Helsinki Final Act. **12 July:** Greece submits its application for membership in the EC.

1976   1 April: The first Lomé Convention enters into force.

1977   6 January: The European Commission under the presidency of Roy Jenkins takes office. **28 March:** Portugal officially submits its application for membership in the EC. **28 July:** Spain submits its application for membership in the EC. **25 October:** The Court of Auditors begins operating in Luxembourg.

1979   20 February: The ECJ rules in the *Cassis de Dijon* case, reinforcing mutual recognition, which becomes an underlying principle of the single market. **13 March:** The European Monetary System (EMS) enters into force. **7–10 June:** The first direct elections for members of the European Parliament (EP) take place in the EC member states.

17 July: Simone Veil is elected president of the first directly elected EP. **31 October:** The second Lomé Convention (Lomé II) is signed between the EC and ACP countries.

1981   1 January: Greece becomes an EC member state. **20 January:** The European Commission under the presidency of Gaston Thorn takes office. **7 November:** The Genscher–Colombo Plan, or Draft European Act, is introduced to increase EC institutional authority in the area of foreign policy.

1982   19 January: Piet Dankert is elected president of the EP.

1983   25 January: The Council adopts the Common Fisheries Policy (CFP). **14 September:** The Draft Treaty establishing the European Union is introduced in the EP by Altiero Spinelli.

1984   14 February: The Draft Treaty establishing the European Union proposed by the Institutional Affairs Committee of the EP is overwhelmingly passed by the EP (but ultimately rejected by the member states). **14 & 17 June:** The second direct elections to the EP are held in the EC member states. **25–26 June:** Agreement is reached on the British budgetary rebate at the Fountainebleau European Council meeting. **24 July:** Pierre Pflimlin is elected president of the EP. **8 December:** The third Lomé Convention is signed by the EC member states and the ACP countries.

1985   7 January: The European Commission under the presidency of Jacques Delors comes into office. **29–30 March:** Agreement is reached on the Integrated Mediterranean Programmes (IMP) at the Brussels European Council meeting. **29–30 March:** The Dooge Report on institutional reform is presented to the European Council. **28–29 June:** The European Commission presents a White Paper on "Completing the Internal Market" to the European Council. **9 September:** The IGC on the single market begins.

1986   1 January: Portugal and Spain become EC member states. **17 & 28 February:** The Single European Act (SEA) is signed by the 12 EC member states. **1 May:** The third Lomé Convention enters into force.

1987   20 January: Lord Henry Plumb is elected president of the EP. **14 April:** The Turkish government officially submits an application to join the EC. **1 July:** The SEA enters into force.

1988   27–28 June: During its meeting in Hanover, Germany, the European Council appoints Commission President Jacques Delors to head a committee charged with drafting a report on economic and monetary union.

1989   12 April: The Delors Committee submits its report on economic and monetary union. **15–18 June:** The third direct elections to the EP are held. **27 June:** The EC imposes an arms embargo on China following the human rights abuses and killings of the Tiananmen Square protests. **17 July:** Austria submits its application for membership in the EC. **25 July:** Enrique Barón Crespo is elected president of the EP. **1 September:** The Court of First Instance of the European Communities is created. **9 November:** The Berlin Wall begins to be torn down. **8–9 December:** The Charter of the Fundamental Social Rights of Workers is adopted by 11 of the 12 EC member states (all except the UK). **15 December:** The fourth Lomé Convention between the EC and ACP countries is signed. **21 December:** The EC adopts the 1989 merger regulation.

1990   19 April: French President François Mitterrand and German Chancellor Helmut Kohl co-author a letter to the president of the European Council in support of increased European efforts toward constructing a European Political Union. **3 July:** Cyprus submits its application for membership in the EC. **16 July:** Malta submits its original application for membership in the EC. **3 October:** The reunification of east and west Germany is complete with the election of Helmut Kohl as the first chancellor of the reunified Federal Republic of Germany. **8 October:** The UK joins the exchange rate mechanism (ERM) of the EMS. **14–15 December:** The IGC on economic and monetary union and the IGC on political union begin.

1991   14 April: The European Bank for Reconstruction and Development begins operations. **1 July:** Sweden formally submits its application for membership in the EC. **1 September:** The fourth Lomé Convention enters into force. **9–10 December:** A European Council meeting is held in Maastricht during which they approve the Treaty on European Union (TEU). **16 December:** Europe Agreements are signed by the EU, Czechoslovakia, Hungary, and Poland.

1992   14 January: Egon Klepsch is elected president of the EP. **7 February:** The TEU is signed in Maastricht, the Netherlands. **18**

March: Finland submits its application for membership in the EC. **20 May:** The Swiss government applies for membership in the EC. **21 May:** The Council agrees to the MacSharry reforms to the CAP. **2 June:** In a national referendum, Danish voters reject the TEU. **18 June:** Irish citizens vote to approve ratification of the TEU in a national referendum. **19 June:** The Council of Ministers of the WEU adopts the Petersberg Declaration, outlining the tasks in which they would become militarily involved. **16 September:** Known as "Black Wednesday," Italy and the UK are forced to withdraw from the ERM. **20 September:** A national referendum is held in France in which the citizens vote in favor of ratifying the TEU. **25 November:** Norway submits its official application for membership in the EC. **6 December:** Swiss citizens reject ratification of the European Economic Area (EEA) agreement in a national referendum.

1993   1 January: The EC's single market becomes fully operational. **1 January:** The Czechoslovak Federation is dissolved and replaced by the sovereign independent Czech and Slovak Republics. **2 May:** The EEA agreement is signed. **18 May:** After negotiating opt-outs in several issue areas, in a second national referendum held on the subject, the Danes approve of the TEU. **21–22 June:** The Copenhagen European Council agrees that all Central and Eastern European countries (CEECs) that so desire shall become members of the European Union (EU), subject to fulfillment of the Copenhagen criteria. **1 November:** The TEU enters into force.

1994   1 January: The second stage of Economic and Monetary Union (EMU) begins, including the creation of the European Monetary Institute (EMI). **1 January:** The EEA agreement enters into force. **9–10 March:** The Committee of the Regions begins operations. **29 March:** The foreign ministers of the EU agree to the Ioannina Compromise on qualified majority voting following the 1995 enlargement. **31 March:** Hungary is the first former Soviet bloc country to apply for membership in the EU. **5 April:** Poland submits its application for membership in the EU. **19 April:** The Council agrees to a Common Foreign and Security Policy (CFSP) Joint Action in support of the Middle East Peace Process. **9–12 June:** The fourth direct elections to the EP are held. **12 June:** The citizens of Austria vote in favor of EU membership in a national referendum. **14 June:** A Partnership and Cooperation Agreement (PCA) is signed between the EU and Ukraine. **19 July:** Klaus Hänsch is elected president of the EP. **16 October:** In a national referendum, Finnish citizens vote in favor of joining the EU. **13 November:** The Swedish government holds a national referendum in which the majority of the voting citizens approve of membership in the EU. **28 November:** Moldova and the EU sign a PCA. **28 November:** Norwegian voters reject EU membership in a public referendum. **9–10 December:** The Essen European Council agrees to the pre-accession strategy for the CEECs.

1995   1 January: Austria, Finland, and Sweden become EU member states. **1 January:** The World Trade Organization (WTO) is established. **24 January:** The European Commission under the presidency of Jacques Santer takes office. **26 March:** The Schengen Agreement between Belgium, France, Germany, Luxembourg, the Netherlands, Portugal, and Spain enters into force. **12 June:** Europe Agreements are signed by the EU and Estonia, Latvia, and Lithuania. **22 June:** Romania submits its application for membership in the EU. **27 June:** Slovakia submits its application for membership in the EU. **26 July:** The EUROPOL Convention is signed by the EU member states. **13 October:** Latvia submits its application for membership in the EU. **24 November:** Estonia submits its application for membership in the EU. **27–28 November:** The Barcelona Declaration is adopted at a conference between the EU and Mediterranean foreign ministers, launching the Euro–Mediterranean Partnership. **30 November:** The Eurocorps becomes operational. **3 December:** The New Transatlantic Agenda is signed at the EU–U.S. Summit in Madrid. **8 December:** Lithuania submits its application for membership in the EU. **14 December:** The Dayton peace accords for cease fire and the stipulation of the boundaries and political system of Bosnia-Herzegovina are signed. **14 December:** Bulgaria submits its application for membership in the EU.

1996   17 January: The Czech Republic submits its application for membership in the EU. **1–2 March:** The first EU–Asia Summit is held in Bangkok, Thailand. **26 March:** The EU imposes a ban on British beef in an effort to prevent the spread of mad cow disease. **29 March:** The IGC begins to discuss reforms to the TEU. **22 April:** PCAs are signed by the EU and Armenia, Azerbaijan, and Georgia. **10 June:** Slovenia submits an application for membership in the EU.

1997   14 January: José María Gil-Robles is elected president of the EP. **15–16 April:** The second Euro–Mediterranean Conference is held in Malta. **2 October:** The Treaty of Amsterdam is signed by the Ministers of Foreign Affairs of the 15 EU member states. **11 December:** The Kyoto Protocol to the United Nations Framework Convention on Climate Change (UNFCCC) is adopted.

1998   1 February: Europe Agreements between the EU and Estonia, Latvia, and Lithuania enters into force. **1 March:** The PCA between the EU and Ukraine enters into force. **3–4 April:** The second EU–Asia Summit is held in London. **1 June:** The European Central Bank (ECB) is established and replaces the EMI to manage the euro and the common monetary policy. Wim Duisenberg takes office as the first president of the ECB. **1 July:** The PCA between the EU and Moldova enters into force. **17 July:** The Rome Statute creating the International Criminal Court (ICC) is adopted. **4 December:** The Saint-Malo Declaration by French President Jacques Chirac and British Prime Minister Tony Blair calls for an autonomous EU defense force for crisis management.

1999   1 January: Stage III of EMU begins; the euro is introduced as the common currency for 11 of the EU member states. **1 January:** The ERM II becomes operational. **15 March:** The Santer Commission resigns en masse after the publication of the negative report by the EP's Committee of Independent Experts. **24–25 March:** The European Council reaches agreement on Agenda 2000. **15–16 April:** The third Euro–Mediterranean Conference is held in Stuttgart, Germany. **23 April:** The Council adopts a common position banning the sale of petroleum and petroleum products to the Former Yugoslavia. **26 April:** The Council adopts a joint action to support refugees and displaced persons in the Western Balkan countries. **1 May:** The Treaty of Amsterdam enters into force. **1 June:** The European Anti-Fraud Office (OLAF) begins operations. **3–4 June:** A European Council meeting is held in Cologne, Germany, during which agreement is reached on a common EU defense strategy, based on the development of a European Security and Defence Policy. Javier Solana is designated as the first High Representative of the CFSP. **10 June:** The EU becomes responsible for the reconstruction and economic pillar of the United Nations Interim Administration in Kosovo (UNMIK). **10–13 June:** EP elections are held in the EU member states. **21–22 June:** Agenda 2000 is adopted by the Council. **28–29 June:** The first EU–Latin America–Caribbean Summit takes place in Rio de Janeiro, Brazil. **20 July:** Nicole Fontaine is elected president of the EP. **15 September:** The European Commission under the presidency of Romano Prodi takes office. **10–11 December:** The Helsinki European Council officially recognizes Turkey as a candidate country.

2000   4 February: The ascent of a coalition government in Austria including the far-right Freedom Party led by Jörg Haider results in the other 14 EU member states imposing diplomatic sanctions on Austria. **14 February:** The IGC to discuss treaty and institutional reforms begins. **23–34 March:** The Lisbon Strategy is adopted by the European Council. **23 June:** Representatives of the EU member states and the ACP countries sign the new ACP-EU (Cotonou) Agreement. **28 September:** A referendum is held in Denmark in which voters reject the adoption of the euro as their national currency. **20–21 October:** The third EU–Asia Summit is held in Seoul, South Korea. **15–16 November:** The fourth Euro–Mediterranean Conference is held in Marseilles, France. **7–9 December:** At a European Council meeting, the heads of state and government reach agreement on the Treaty of Nice.

2001   1 January: Greece joins Stage III of EMU. **1 January:** The European Commission inaugurates the EuropeAid Cooperation Office. **26 February:** The Treaty of Nice is signed. **9 April:** The EU and the Former Yugoslav Republic of Macedonia (FYROM) sign a Stabilization and Association Agreement. **7 June:** Irish voters reject ratification of the Treaty of Nice in a public referendum. **20 July:** The European Union Satellite Centre is created. **20 July:** The European Union Institute for Security Studies is created. **29 October:** Croatia and the EU sign a stabilization and cooperation agreement. **11 December:** China becomes a member of the WTO. **14–15 December:** European Council held in Laeken, Belgium, adopts a declaration on the future of the EU, and opens way for the preparation of a European constitutional treaty.

2002   1 January: Euro notes and coins are introduced into circulation in the euro zone. **15 January:** Pat Cox is elected president of the EP. **28 February:** The European Convention is inaugurated to debate the future of Europe. **1 March:** The euro completely replaces national currencies and becomes the only legal tender of the euro zone. **26 March:** The Galileo satellite radio navigation system project is launched. **7 April:** Eurojust becomes operational. **17–18 May:** The second

EU–Latin America–Caribbean Summit is held in Madrid, Spain. **31 May:** The Kyoto Protocol is ratified by the EU. **22 June:** The EU establishes its position with regard to the settlement of the Israeli–Palestinian conflict in its Seville Declaration. **1 July:** The Rome Statute creating the ICC goes into effect. **23 July:** The 1951 Treaty of Paris creating the ECSC expires. **19 October:** Irish voters approve the Treaty of Nice in a second referendum on this issue. **12–13 December:** Accession negotiations are concluded with Cyprus, the Czech Republic, Estonia, Hungary, Latvia, Lithuania, Malta, Poland, Slovakia, and Slovenia, and the Copenhagen European Council welcomes them to join the EU on 1 May 2004.

2003 1 January: A new CFP is adopted. **15 January:** The first EU Police Mission begins in Bosnia-Herzegovina. **1 February:** The Treaty of Nice enters into force. **21 February:** Croatia submits its application for membership in the EU. **8 March:** The citizens of Malta vote in favor of EU accession in a public referendum. **17 March:** Berlin Plus is adopted and enters into force. **23 March:** The Slovenian government holds a national referendum in which the citizens vote in favor of joining the EU. **1 April:** The Cotonou Agreement enters into force. **12 April:** In a national referendum Hungarian citizens vote in favor of EU accession. **10–11 May:** A national referendum is held on EU membership in Lithuania and the citizens vote in favor of joining the Union. **16–17 May:** The Slovakian government holds a national referendum on joining the EU and the citizens vote in favor of membership. **7–8 June:** The citizens of Poland vote in favor of EU accession in a public referendum. **13–14 June:** The government of the Czech Republic holds a referendum on joining the EU and the citizens vote in favor of membership. **16 June:** The Council adopts a common position on the ICC. **19–20 June:** The European Convention submits a draft Treaty Establishing a Constitution for Europe to the European Council in Thessaloniki, Greece. **20 June:** The European Council agrees to the potential future membership of the Western Balkan countries on condition of economic, political, and judicial reforms. **14 September:** Voters reject the adoption of the euro in a referendum held in Sweden. **14 September:** Estonian citizens vote in favor of EU membership in a national referendum. **20 September:** Latvian citizens vote in favor of EU membership in a national referendum. **4 October:** The ICG on the draft constitutional treaty begins in Rome. **1 November:** Jean-Claude

Trichet succeeds Wim Duisenberg as the president of the ECB. **12 December:** The European Council adopts the European Security Strategy.

2004 1 January: The European Arrest Warrant enters into force. **11 March:** Al-Qaeda attacks Madrid, killing hundreds and wounding thousands. **22 March:** The FYROM applies for membership in the EU. **25 March:** Gijs de Vries is appointed as the first counter-terrorism coordinator of the EU by the European Council. **16 April:** The Treaties of Accession are signed by the EU and Cyprus, Czech Republic, Estonia, Hungary, Latvia, Lithuania, Malta, Poland, Slovakia, and Slovenia. **24 April:** Referendums are held on the UN reunification plan for Cyprus. **1 May:** Cyprus, Czech Republic, Estonia, Hungary, Latvia, Lithuania, Malta, Poland, Slovakia, and Slovenia become member states of the EU in the largest enlargement in EU history. **28–29 May:** The third EU–Latin American–Caribbean Summit is held in Guadalajara, Mexico. **10–13 June:** EP elections are held for the first time for an EU of 25 member states. **18 June:** Croatia is granted official candidacy status at the European Council meeting. **29 June:** The European Council reappoints Javier Solana as the High Representative of the CFSP. **12 July:** The European Council adopts a Joint Action to establish a European Defense Agency. **20 July:** Josep Borrell Fontelles is elected president of the EP. **11 October:** The EU and Tajikistan sign a PCA. **26 October:** President-elect of the European Commission, José Manuel Barroso, withdraws his proposal for the College of Commissioners scheduled to take office on 1 November 2004. **29 October:** The Treaty Establishing a Constitution for Europe is signed in Rome, Italy. **11 November:** The Lithuanian Parliament approves the Treaty establishing a Constitution for Europe. **22 November:** The Barroso Commission assumes office. **2 December:** The EU replaces NATO as the primary peacekeeping force in Bosnia-Herzegovina. **16–17 December:** The European Council agrees to begin accession negotiations with Turkey in 2005. **20 December:** The Hungarian Parliament approves the Treaty establishing a Constitution for Europe.

2005 25 January: The Italian Congress approves the Treaty establishing a Constitution for Europe. **1 February:** An association agreement between the EU and Croatia enters into force. **1 February:** The Slovenian Parliament approves the Treaty establishing a Constitution for Europe. **16 February:** The Kyoto Protocol to the UNFCCC enters into force. **20 February:** Spain is the first member state to hold a national referendum on the Treaty establishing a Constitution for Europe and the Spanish citizens vote in favor of adopting the treaty. **17 March:** Accession negotiations between the EU and Croatia scheduled to begin on this date are postponed due to the perception that Croatia was not fully cooperating with the United Nations International Criminal Tribunal for the former Yugoslavia. **6 April:** The Italian Senate approves the Treaty establishing a Constitution for Europe. **12 April:** The European Commission announces that Serbia and Montenegro have made enough progress to begin negotiations for a Stabilization and Association Agreement. **19 April:** The Greek Parliament approves the Treaty establishing a Constitution for Europe. **28 April:** The Spanish Congress approves the Treaty establishing a Constitution for Europe. **11 May:** The Slovakian Parliament approves the Treaty establishing a Constitution for Europe. **11 May:** The Austrian Nationalrat approves the Treaty establishing a Constitution for Europe. **12 May:** The German Bundestag approves the Treaty establishing a Constitution for Europe. **28 April:** The Belgian Senate approves the Treaty establishing a Constitution for Europe. **18 May:** The Spanish Senate approves the Treaty establishing a Constitution for Europe. **19 May:** The Belgian Chamber approves the Treaty establishing a Constitution for Europe. **25 May:** The Austrian Bundesrat approves the Treaty establishing a Constitution for Europe. **27 May:** The German Bundesrat approves the Treaty establishing a Constitution for Europe. **29 May:** In a national referendum French citizens reject the Treaty establishing a Constitution for Europe. **1 June:** In a national referendum Dutch citizens vote against the Treaty establishing a Constitution for Europe. **2 June:** The Latvian Parliament approves the Treaty establishing a Constitution for Europe. **28 June:** The Parliament of Luxembourg approves the Treaty establishing a Constitution for Europe. **30 June:** The Cypriot Parliament approves the Treaty establishing a Constitution for Europe. **6 July:** The Maltese Parliament approves the Treaty establishing a Constitution for Europe. **10 July:** In a referendum the people of Luxembourg vote in favor of the Treaty establishing a Constitution for Europe.

Introduction

PEOPLE, INSTITUTIONS, LAWS

People, whether ordinary citizens or leaders, may soon be forgotten after their lifetimes. Institutions, on the other hand, the irreplaceable backbone of the state, remain for as long as they are useful and well designed. Laws are necessary to foster the proper relationship between people and institutions. Unfortunately for Europeans, typical international organizations could not effectively prevent conflict during the first half of the 20th century. This serious shortcoming would eventually have to be addressed and corrected.

*   *   *

Jean Monnet was the heir of a cognac-making family and a seasoned businessman dealing in world trade. He skillfully planned and implemented commercial and development enterprises on three continents, not only designing the programs but convincing the appropriate leaders at the highest levels of the advantages of the proposed actions. Having achieved much success in these endeavors, Monnet was sent by British Prime Minister Winston Churchill to negotiate the United States (U.S.) contributions to the war effort with U.S. President Franklin Delano Roosevelt. According to economist J. M. Keynes, the launch of the negotiated plan (known as the Victory Program) shortened World War II by one year.

Monnet had a favorite bedtime reading: an anthology of philosophers and poets.[1] Some lines of the Swiss philosopher Henri-Frédéric Amiel[2] attracted his attention and influenced his proposals regarding the uniting of Europe and the foundation of the original European Coal and Steel Community (ECSC). Biographers, friends, and colleagues seem to agree that central to Monnet's strategic thinking was this annotation in Amiel's diary: "Each man's experience starts again from the beginning. Only institutions grow wiser; they accumulate collective experience; and owing to this experience and this wisdom, men subject to the same rules will not see their own nature changing, but their behavior gradually transformed. . . . Institutions govern relationships between people. They are the real pillars of civilization."[3]

Following the end of World War II, Monnet designed the French reconstruction plan, and inspired French Minister of Foreign Affairs Robert Schuman's historic Declaration that provided the impetus for the birth of today's European Union (EU). In Monnet's vision, institutions were the mechanism to correct the mistakes of Europe's past: "Europeans had gradually lost the ability to live together and combine their creative strength. There seems to be decline in their contribution to progress and to the civilization, which they themselves had created— doubtless because in a changing world they no longer had institutions capable of leading them ahead. National institutions had proved that they were ill adapted to this task. The new Community institutions, it seems to me, were the only vehicle through which Europeans could once more deploy the exceptional qualities they had displayed in times past."[4] Unmatched in his conviction, Monnet declared: "Nothing is possible without men: nothing is lasting without institutions."[5] As a consequence, the ECSC was born out of the Treaty of Paris with the idea of having common and supranational institutions.

Monnet prophetically set the record straight regarding the aims of the new European Community: "We can never sufficiently emphasize that the six Community countries are the forerunners of a broader united Europe, whose bounds are set only by those who have not yet joined. Our Community is not a coal and steel producers' association: it is the beginning of Europe. . . . The beginning of Europe was a political conception; but even more, it was a moral idea."[6] The primary objective of the European Community (EC) was political, as the Schuman Declaration explicitly states: "A united Europe was not achieved and we had war."[7] In light of this failure and its tragic consequences, "the pooling of coal and steel production should immediately provide for the setting up of common foundations for economic development as a first step in the federation of Europe, and will change the destinies of those regions which have long been devoted to the manufacture of munitions of war, of which they have been the most constant victims."[8] In sum, "the solidarity in production thus established will make it plain that any war between France and Germany becomes not merely unthinkable, but materially impossible."[9] The state, in fact, was created in war; the EU was born in peace to guarantee a lasting peace.[10] This foundational raison d'etre is often forgotten by new generations of Europeans.

Practical as he was, Monnet not only proposed the original idea of pooling the steel and coal resources and designed the original institutions to administer the resulting shared sovereignty, but also supervised the process. He was named president of the High Authority, the executive body intended to manage the integration of the coal and steel industries.

* * *

The EU's founding fathers, and certain of its subsequent leaders, sincerely shared Monnet's fundamental ideas. They took advantage of an environment conducive to integration and constructed a peaceful Europe based on institutions, laws, symbols, and people, all of which are irreplaceable. In this context, Monnet's words have not been forgotten, especially in terms of the importance of lasting institutions.

PECULIAR INSTITUTIONS

As a metaphorical aid, the structure of the EU has been presented as a sort of Greek–Roman temple, sustained by three pillars.[11] This symbolism was enshrined in the 1992 Treaty on European Union (TEU).

In an allegory used by Enrique Barón, former president of the European Parliament (EP), the EU is like a medieval cathedral under construction.[12] The first and most integrated pillar is the EC, composed of all areas in which the EU has competence, generally subject to qualified majority voting (QMV), rendering decision-making free from the threat of a single national veto. The second pillar is the Common Foreign and Security Policy (CFSP), and the third is Justice and Home Affairs (JHA).

The spirit of pooled sovereignty, a trademark of the EU,[13] has dominated the first pillar in which the member states have renounced their traditional autonomy. In contrast, the sensitive issues of the second and third pillars, even though they belong to the overall framework of the EU, are only shared in a regime of intergovernmental cooperation. While some competences of the third pillar have been gradually shifted to the first, the member states have been very reluctant to share control over issues encompassed by the second pillar, and, in fact, in some instances, have tried to regain competences located in the first Community pillar.

Since the dawn of the EC, the member states have delegated portions of their sovereignty to institutions that simultaneously represent the national, Community, and citizens' interests.[14] They are political entities run by officers, but that have accumulated their own powers over time, derived from the *acquis communautaire*, the EU treaties, laws, and regulations. These institutions have a unique mission: to manage the "interdependence" and integration of the EU member states. This is in essence what the EU does.

Of the major EU institutions, the European Commission has been recognized as entirely unique, unmatched in other organizations. It is the successor of the High Authority, the body that supervised the management of the two strategic products of the ECSC. It is the guardian of the treaties, which represent the "constitutional" documents of the EU. While the national governments are represented in the Council of the EU, previously known as the Council of Ministers, the citizens exert their influence when directly electing the members of the EP (MEPs).

The Commission promotes and defends the general interests of the Union.[15] The president and the members of the Commission are nominated by the member state governments, appointed by the European Council, and approved by the EP for a period of five years. The Commission is the engine of the EU institutional framework as it possesses the right of legislative initiative, proposing future laws to the EP and the Council. This right of initiative is shared with the Council in the second and third pillars. It functions as an executive (as the Council acts in the second and third pillar competences) when guaranteeing the execution of the laws (directives, regulations, and decisions), manages the budget, and supervises programs adopted by the EP and the Council. Among its responsibilities, the Commission represents the Community to the rest of the world and negotiates international agreements on trade and development aid.

Each member state has one commissioner. The Treaty of Nice rules, however, stipulate that after the EU has 27 members, the number of Commissioners will have to be lower than the number of member states, a rotating formula which would then be decided by the European Council.

The EP is composed of 732 members, to be augmented to 786 with the expected membership of Bulgaria and Romania in 2007. MEPs are elected for a period of five years by direct and universal suffrage, in democratic representation of the European citizens in 25 countries.[16] Ideologically, it houses the main political tendencies existing in the member states, represented by pan-European political formations (social democrats, Christian democrat-conservatives, liberals, former Communists, Greens, nationalists, etc.). The EP's main functions are legislative decision-making (along with the Council) and ultimately approving or rejecting the entire EU budget. The Commission is responsible to the EP, which must approve the appointment of the commissioners, may ask oral and written questions, and has the right to a vote of censure. The EP also appoints the European Ombudsman who receives complaints from citizens, residents, and representatives of registered companies in the EU regarding maladministration in the activities of the EU institutions.

The Council of the EU is the main decision-making body of the EU. The interests of the member state governments are represented in this institution.[17] Depending on the issue to be decided, the Council meets in nine different formations: Economic and Financial Affairs; JHA; Employment, Social Policy, Health and Consumer Affairs; Competitiveness; Transport, Telecommunications and Energy; Agriculture and Fisheries; Environment; and Education, Youth and Culture. The Council shares most legislative power with the EP. It adopts decisions in the areas of the CFSP and JHA.

Two institutions share the label of "Court," but one has strictly judicial functions, while the other deals with the control of expenses. The Court of Justice of the European Communities guarantees the uniform interpretation and respect of Community law, which has direct effect and supremacy over national laws.[18] The Court hears cases submitted by member states, the EU institutions, companies, and citizens. The Court of Auditors oversees the legality and accuracy of the financial management of the EU's budget.[19]

The European Investment Bank is the financial institution responsible for investment projects designed to promote development inside and outside the EU. The European Central Bank is the primary financial institution for the management of the euro, responsible for establishing and implementing the European monetary policy, managing exchange operations, and guaranteeing the efficacy of the payment systems.

A CLOSER LOOK

Since its creation the EU has suffered from a sort of chronic identity crisis. In part, this is self-inflicted and results from its ever-changing official name: European Economic Community, European Communities, European Community, and European Union. Therefore, it is difficult for the rest of the world to understand its personality.

In scope and means, aims and objectives, structure and spirit, the EU is a unique entity. Consequently, precisely identifying it in the realm of standard political entities is continuously a topic of scholarly debate. Misunderstandings are numerous amongst the general public.

Even experienced scholars often fell into the temptation of labeling the EU with subjective and metaphorical illustrations, such as the "dizzying complexity" of the framework and the "inimitable and mystifying" EU institutions.[20] Unable to arrive at an explanation, it is no wonder that Jacques Delors, a former president of the Commission, one day offered the apparent perfect definition: the EU is a UPO, an Unidentified Political Object.[21] It is not surprising, therefore, that the EU also seems incomprehensible to outsiders. Former U.S. Secretary of State Madeleine Albright, weary of dealing with the different EU high-level officials responding to varied interests, once allegedly exploded in frustration: "to understand the European Union you must be French or very intelligent . . . or both."

On a practical level, for millions of citizens in Europe, the EU is simply seen as a development bank that provides grants and loans. Many still talk about the Common Market as a territorial entity. For others, "Brussels" is a distant, wasteful bureaucracy. For thousands of well-educated and well-trained government officials and recent university graduates, the EU is the place to obtain a highly paid job, with generous benefits, long vacations, and a secure retirement. For idealists, the

EU is a worthy political project that guarantees peaceful coexistence. For many Third World leaders it is the culprit of agrarian protectionism. For many anonymous downtrodden in developing countries it is the source of aid that alleviates hunger and poverty. For economic competitors and political allies the EU is a fortress, an obstacle, a partner.

One of the EU's supplemental benefits can be described as a recovery of power.[22] Following the end of World War II (if not earlier), states began to experience a decrease in national control. On the one hand, power was "lost" upwards through regional and international economic integration. On the other hand, "devolution" on the domestic level produced a "loss" of power to lower levels of government. Paradoxically, the end of the Cold War generated an environment in which the world powers and the only remaining superpower now enjoy relatively less influence than when the world was governed by some unwritten rules of mutual deterrence. In this apparently confusing panorama, the EU appears to be a mechanism for the recovery of long lost European influence and power.[23]

Although a somewhat theoretical and still imperfectly defined entity, the EU has a distinct character and structure, composed of institutions, agencies, representatives, and offices. Not a typical, impersonal international organization, chats and briefings in any of the EU institutions have a flair that is completely absent from the United Nations (UN) headquarters in New York and Geneva. Famous for their internal culture of intrigue (United Nations Educational, Scientific, and Cultural Organization [UNESCO]), or plagued by intra-regional clashes among staff and government representatives (Organization of American States [OAS], World Bank, International Monetary Fund [IMF]), most international organizations share an atmosphere of coldness and a lack of common purpose. In Brussels, with a myriad of think tanks, business lobbies, non-governmental organizations, and government representations, there is a feeling of distinction. There is a sense of community, of belonging to a special mission, transcending state borders but not resembling the typical profile of other international and regional organizations.

The existence of this sort of "culture," difficult to prove with an empirical methodology, is rather easy to detect in comparative terms when visiting or attending briefings in the other major organization based in Brussels, the North Atlantic Treaty Organization (NATO). In fact,

NATO officials refer to the EU as "them." This shocks and intrigues the observer particularly because most NATO signatories are also members of the EU. European states behave differently in the EU setting than they do in the NATO environment, or for that matter in any other international organization. In the daily exchanges within the EU, any minister of a given member state knows that a decision made one day, a vote cast in a peculiar manner, or a veto will have strategic consequences. The pooling of sovereignty combined with the exclusive and shared competences of the EU and the member states makes the EU unique, and consequently, inherently different than NATO. Hence, the awkward use of "they" and "us" in Brussels by governments that share the most common values.

The Commission (the most clearly executive branch of the EU) is sometimes referred to by insiders as "this place." The extended family, the framework of EU institutions, demonstrates that the EU has a dynamic of its own.

INTERPRETING UNIQUENESS

The aims of the EU, created since birth to guarantee a lasting peace on the continent, set it apart from other members of a generally broad species. The plan was to accomplish this mission not by the traditional methods of interstate cooperation, but through (for lack of a better term) "supranationalism." This quality is contrasted with its nemesis, "intergovernmentalism." "Supranational" is generally defined as a method of decision and policy making whereby the individual member states pool their sovereignty under a higher authority. It is an innate ingredient in the political DNA of the EU. Taken as in a photograph, the EU seems to show this quality as a "set of laws or institutions that are above the state. The power and authority they exercise is not confined to one state but to many. Thus, supranationalism refers to decision-making bodies which supercede or override the sovereign authority of individual states who are constituent members of the organization involved."[24] As in a motion picture film, supranationalism appears as "a process in which the EU institutions enjoy political autonomy and authority."[25]

The clearest example of supranational institutions in the EU are those that have "a common political structure authorized to make decisions within the prescribed areas for Member States."[26] Many observers consider the Commission to be the most supranational of the EU institutions, with its executive-style responsibilities and monopoly on legislative proposals associated with the Community competences. The European Court of Justice (ECJ) can also be considered highly supranational as this independent institution uniformly interprets and applies Community law and makes decisions that are binding in all member states. The Council of the EU can be considered either more supranational or more intergovernmental, depending on the topic at hand. Here we have two basic decision-making methods: unanimity and QMV. When the Council is making a decision based on a competence in the first pillar, by QMV, the Council can be considered more supranational because binding decisions can be made without the approval of all of the member states. In contrast, when the Council makes a decision based on a competence in one of the other two pillars, by unanimous vote, the Council can be considered more intergovernmental because no decisions can be made without the consent of all involved.

This supranationality, however, does not eliminate the existence, influence, and power of the EU's member states. This dual notion is explicitly illustrated through the EU's official declarations, released by "The European Union and its Member States."

This hybridism has forced scholars to oscillate between different poles of comparative points of reference.[27] On the one hand, common sense indicates that the EU is more than a standard intergovernmental organization, but on the other (despite the efforts of the most ardent integrationists) it is not a typical federation.[28] Some label the EU as a confederation. Most resist comparing it to a nation-state, although some scholars have skillfully pointed out that the state and the EU are similar in the sense that they are a means to an end, not a finished product.[29]

In the EU there is multilevel governance, characterized by a web of interconnected institutions, policy-making processes and decision-making procedures. There is also a principle of subsidiarity, present in any federal structure, that intends to ensure decisions are made at the closest possible level to the citizen.[30] From a theoretical point of view, this combination supports the aims of the European federalists and lobbyists pressuring for a "closer Union" and deeper integration in the EU. However, the term "federation" (the "F" word, as Margaret Thatcher used to refer to it) and its spirit are vigorously opposed by intergovernmental-ists who explicitly insist on banning it from the EU treaties.

In sum, there is no accepted consensus on the nature of the EU. A practical and easy solution is to refer to the spirit and the letter of the treaties. What exists in essence is the EU and its member states. The problem lies in the fact that in practice "the European Community," also known as the first pillar, has competences for which the Commission is basically in control and defends the collective interests, whereas the member states maintain complete sovereign control over most other is-sues and decisions. The EU is an experiment in which the national in-terests are embedded in the European entity, and the European ethos is inserted in the national state.[31] For this reason, energetic Europeanists have been pressuring for a single personality for the EU, as a legal ac-tor and a juridical entity.[32]

In any event, from whatever angle one may look at the EU, observers and researchers have four basic options for classifying the entity as a form of political cooperation. Rejecting erroneous or risky comparisons with state entities and typical international organizations, there remain two reasonable alternatives.

One choice is simply to accept the EU as a mixture of a state and an intergovernmental international organization. The other is the bold proposition that the EU is a new polity species, the only one of its kind today, although several modest imitations have been experimented with at least on a partial scale. In this line of thought, the EU is proposed as a "regional state, a union of nation-states in which the creative tension between the Union and its member-states ensures both ever-increasing regional integration and ever-continuing national differentiation."[33] The uniqueness of the EU as such a regional state is that its sovereignty is "shared with its constituent members . . . dependent upon internal ac-ceptance by EU member-states as well as on external recognition by other nation-states, policy area by policy area. On these bases, the EU has already been accepted and recognized as a sovereign region in in-ternational trade and competition and competition policy but certainly not in defense and security policy."[34]

Regardless of the federalists who have been enthusiastically pushing for this solution, the fact remains that the EU in many ways parallels the state *and* international organizations. Hence, a solution has been gain-ing ground in the scholarly literature and in the sophisticated EU jargon:

intergovernmental federalism. Magic words, a sort of talisman, they compose in principle an oxymoron, an attempt to square the circle.

In the EU there is not one institution that monopolizes customary functions of governance and decision-making, as is the goal of modern democracy based on the sacrosanct division of power in the Montesquieu tradition.[35] Several bodies share real and legal power, to an intriguing extent, while the EP, which in principle should have a first choice and voice, plays only a secondary role. The Council of the EU, composed of representatives of the member state governments, plays the role of a legislature in the decision-making process of the equivalent of EU federal laws. The Council has no political responsibility to the EP. Meanwhile, the directly elected representatives of the peoples of Europe, MEPs, have the least amount of power when acting independently. The EU is supervised by periodic gatherings of heads of state or government who make crucial decisions (general guidelines and strategies) for the collective body of European citizens, yet they do not respond to any court for their actions. The ECJ has jurisdiction only on matters of Community competence, but does not act as an appeals court above the national courts.

This raises questions from the constitutional and strictly legal point of view about the apparently absurd hypothesis: If the EU applied for EU membership, it would be rejected based on the democratic criteria. Part of the so-called democratic deficit is based on this assumption. However, there is no political or scholarly consensus on this issue, with bands as far apart as federalists and intergovernmentalists. While many scholars claim that the more supranational the EU becomes, the less democratic and the more distanced from the people it becomes, others do not see this as a problem provided the citizens receive the benefits of a deeper pooled sovereignty,[36] while some innovative views point out that in the EU, "democracy is more fragmented than that of any nation-state. Instead of having a central government *by*, *of*, and *for* the people—through political participation, electoral representation, and governing effectiveness—as well as . . . government *with* the people—through interest consultation—the EU level emphasizes governance *for* and *with* the people while leaving to national level government *by* and *of* the people."[37]

National ministers sitting in the Council have been responsible to their national parliaments. When most of the decisions were taken by unanimity, members of national parliaments could always question ministers regarding their positions in the Council. Since the increased use of QMV following the adoption of the Single European Act, members of the Council can hide behind the majority. They can, for example, argue that they were actually against a decision but that they were out-voted.

Perceptions of a democratic deficit and a lack of legitimacy have emerged in the context of the EU and its institutional framework. These problems are also associated with the idea that the European citizens are distanced from the EU. The responsibility of these alleged shortcomings also lies, however, in the hands of national leaders, who have been unable (or unwilling) to explain this complex, multifaceted organization.

Domestic pressures and/or ambitions have resulted in postponements and failures to reach crucial agreements, such as in the case of the European Defense Community in the 1950s, the completion of Economic and Monetary Union by 1980 as proposed in the 1971 Werner Plan, and the delay in approving, and after the negative results in the Dutch and French referendums, ultimately the ratification of the constitutional treaty. Although not the only case, a recent illustration was the role of Spain in the Convention and the intergovernmental conference (IGC) on the Treaty establishing a Constitution for Europe. Unable to weaken the solid coalition formed by Germany and France, the Spanish government in conjunction with Poland opposed the new distribution of votes in the QMV system, insisting on the continuation of the advantageous framework negotiated in the Treaty of Nice. (The result was a continuation of the IGC into the first semester 2004 during which time agreement was reached.) While this type of political behavior may be interpreted as an aggressive defense of national interest, citizens often get a reinforced image of an EU beyond their control, in constant flux, and far from becoming a consolidated entity.[38]

REMODELING A MODERN CATHEDRAL

As in one rare cosmic coincidence, 2002 encompassed two crucial events: the completion of the original term of the ECSC and the 150th anniversary of the birth of architect Antoni Gaudí. The Holy Family temple, the most emblematic work of this Catalan architect, is best-known for its perennial state of construction. Since the beginning of the 20th century, it has been tenaciously rising, stone by stone, tower after tower, over the city of Barcelona. While with some disdain, critics would dismiss Gaudí's temple as the last of the medieval cathedrals, others would respond that it is the first of the 21st century. In a way, it shares its destiny with the EU. Both are fascinating, enigmatic, and unfinished. Apparently, they are both incomparable and inimitable. As others of Gaudí's works that have puzzled architectural experts, the EU has challenged the definitions of political scientists.

There is no doubt that the present panorama of the European process of integration can be judged by the popular question: Is the glass half full or half empty? According to the optimists, the balance of the EU, after more than half a century, is impressive. From a chronological perspective, it is certain that the EU has never taken a dangerous step backwards. Qualitatively, in terms of competences transferred from the states to the Community, the volume of the common legacy has always expanded. The number of members continues to increase. Even in the persistent stage of uncertainty while the enlargements proceed on schedule, it does not seem that this will change. Its attractiveness is irresistible. As the late Minister of Foreign Affairs of Spain, Francisco Fernández Ordóñez ingeniously detected: "Outside of the EU it's very cold."

It is true that the EU has suffered periods of stagnation. However, shared sovereignty and geographical size have never been reduced. When compared politically and economically with other regional integration experiments, the EU is by far the most ambitious experiment in state cooperation. Nonetheless, European integration still has a long way to go to complete its architectural structure.

Architectural similes have been constant in the history of the EU. When it was resolved to convert the Community into a Union in the TEU, the text explicitly inserted the description of the new framework with the metaphor of the three pillars.

GROWING PAINS AND CHALLENGES

The most formidable challenge to a building under constant construction has been the EU's decision to enlarge its membership.[39] The cathedral was designed in 1950 for two faithful members (France and Germany), accompanied by another four (Belgium, Italy, Luxembourg, and The Netherlands) committed to ending European wars. This Community of Six was gradually joined by nine more European countries, creating the EU-15 by 1995. The fall of the Berlin Wall in 1989 and rapid transitions to democracy and open market economies in the Central and Eastern European countries (CEECs) created a new European dynamic and greatly increased the number of possible future EU member states. Although the EU was at first reluctant, it opted, once again, for unity rather than division, declaring that those CEECs that met the requirements of the Copenhagen Criteria would be welcome to join the EU.

With this daunting backdrop, a European Convention was established to engage in a discussion and design of reforms for the EU institutions and procedures to accommodate the growing number in its ranks. This European Convention was composed of a Praesidium, representatives of the governments of the member states and the candidate countries, representatives of the national parliaments of the member states and candidate countries, and representatives of the European Commission and the EP. It was inaugurated on 28 February 2002, and worked in three phases during the span of three Council presidencies. The leading members of the European Convention justified the need for a thorough legal and institutional reform considering that the esthetically balanced image of the Greco–Roman temple did not reflect reality. The EU might be comparable to a cathedral in construction, but it was more like a baroque conglomerate, the result of the accumulation of elements according to timely circumstances, with no apparent effort to eliminate decorations or useful pieces of the past.[40] In the opinion of Giuliano Amato, former Italian Prime Minister and co-vice-chairman of the Convention, cathedrals of other eras are beautiful to see, but Europe demands to function through a complete simplification of its structure.[41] In this context, the European Convention submitted a draft Treaty establishing a Constitution for Europe to the European Council during its meeting of 19–20 June 2003 in Thessaloniki, Greece.

The draft constitutional treaty was then discussed, as with all previous treaties, during an IGC that began during the Italian presidency in October 2003 and came to a conclusion during the Irish presidency of the first semester 2004. In June 2004 the European Council approved the draft constitutional treaty, and on 29 October 2004 its representatives signed the Treaty establishing a Constitution for Europe in Rome, Italy, opening the door for the treaty ratification process to begin. All treaties must be ratified by every EU member state in order for them to enter into force. This ratification process may take place in the parliaments of the member states only, or a public referendum may also be held, depending on the individual country.

At the time this publication is going to press, a total of 14 countries have ratified this constitutional treaty (12 through parliamentary procedures and two through consultative referendum and parliamentary approval). This process has been postponed, however, due to negative outcomes in referendums held in France and The Netherlands, in May and June 2005, respectively. The results of these referendums are troublesome, not only because they create a possibly insurmountable obstacle to the ratification process but also because they emanate from two of the founding members of the EU, and because France, along with Germany, have been traditionally considered as the motor of European integration. Nevertheless, it cannot be forgotten that the EU has experienced prior ratification crises (Denmark with the Treaty of Maastricht and Ireland with the Treaty of Nice) that were eventually overcome. The EU and its member states are currently engaged in a period of reflection and discussion regarding the Treaty establishing a Constitution for Europe, and while its future remains unclear, this project which has been in the making for four years, has not been abandoned.

In the meantime, the EU's institutional structure will remain solidly anchored in a legal framework, agreed upon democratically.[42] It is a series of treaties that includes the Treaty of Paris, the Treaties of Rome,[43] the Single European Act,[44] Maastricht, and Amsterdam,[45] and the Treaty of Nice of 2000.[46] They form, in the absence of another text that reforms, frames, or replaces them,[47] the existing European "Constitution" that governs this Community of law.[48]

The long road toward "an ever closer union" reveals one of the crucial innate characteristics of the EU. In the words of Jacques Delors, a Tour de France fan, it is like cycling—if one stops, one falls. As a consequence, the proper procedure to observe its anatomy is not by photographing it, like in a sort of juridical exercise in static scholarship. There is also a need to record it like in a film, by applying the more dynamic tools of international relations.

A GLIMPSE OF THE FUTURE

In the very near future, the EU will have become a really unique creature and cease to be a hybrid. From a traditional federal perspective, observers could say that the language continues to be hypocritical and prudent, always avoiding constitutional expressions that may indicate the limit of states' sovereignty in "hard" competences.

Only time will tell the future of the EU, and we will all have to wait approximately until the moment in which the temple of Gaudí is finished. Even if in 2022 it has not met the planned schedule and the EU is still in construction, both dreams would be faithful to their essence. Both projects deal with architecture, artistic (in the case of Gaudí) and political (with respect to the EU). In any event, it would be advisable not to base all speculations on the future of the EU on the format of its architectural framework, but on the essence of its political ambition. Perhaps a commentary attributed to the impeccable diplomat, and current High Representative of the CFSP, Javier Solana, will serve to clarify the point: when he was asked about the substance and modifications needed for the architecture of the EU, he opined rather modestly: "I am not an architect, just a physicist."

NOTES

1. Robert Seymour Bridget, *The Spirit of Man: An Anthology in English & French from the Philosophers & Poets* (New York: Green & Co., 1916).

2. Henri-Frédéric Amiel, *Amiel's Journal: Le Journal Intime de Henri-Frédéric Amiel* (London: Macmillan, 1889).

3. Jean Monnet, *Memoirs*, 393.

4. Ibid.

5. Monnet, *Memoirs* (London: Collins, 1978), 304–5.

6. Ibid, 304.

7. Robert Schuman, "The Schuman Declaration," 9 May 1950.

8. Ibid.

9. Ibid.

10. Gary Marks, "A Third Lens: Comparing European Integration and State Building," *European Integration in Social and Historical Perspective* (Lanham, Md.: Rowman & Littlefield, 1997).

11. Lawrence Gormley, "Reflections on the Architecture of the European Union after the Treaty of Amsterdam," *Legal Issues of the Amsterdam Treaty* (Portland, Ore.: Oxford, 1999), 57; Cebada Romero, "La naturaleza jurídica de la Unión Europea: Una Contribución al Debate sobre su Personalidad Jurídica a la Luz de los Trabajos de la Convención Sobre el Futuro de Europa," *Revista de Derecho Comunitario Europeo* (14, 2003), 281–304; Niels Blokker, "The European Union: Historical Origins and Institutional Changes," *The European Union after Amsterdam: A Legal Analysis* (London: Kluwer Law International, 1998), 21; B. De Witte, "The Pillar Structure and the Nature of the European Union: Greek Temple or French Gothic Cathedral?" *The European Union after Amsterdam: A Legal Analysis* (London: Kluwer Law International, 1998), 64; Renaud Dehousse, "'We the States': Why the Anti-Federalists Have Won," *EUSA Review* (16/4, 2003), 5–7; Guy Isaac, "Le pilier communautaire de l'Union Européenne, un pilier pas comme les autres," *Cahiers de Droit Européen* (2001), 1–2, 49, 89.

12. Enrique Barón. *Europa en el alba del milenio* (Madrid: Acento Editorial, 2000).

13. Robert Keohane, "Ironies of Sovereignty: The European Union and the United States," *Journal of Common Market Studies* (40/4, 2002), 743–65.

14. Marks, "A Third Lens"; Eleanor Zeff, *The European Union and the Member States: Cooperation, Coordination, and Compromise* (Boulder, Colo.: Lynne Rienner, 2001).

15. Michelle Cini, *The European Commission* (Manchester: University of Manchester, 1997); Kieran Bradley, "The European Court of Justice," *The Institutions of the European Union* (New York: Oxford University Press, 2002), 118–138; Neil Nugent, *At the Heart of the Union: Studies of the European Commission* (New York: Palgrave Macmillan, 2000).

16. Francis Jacobs, *The European Parliament* (London: Longman, 1992); Caroline Bradley, "European Court of Justice," 118–38.

17. Fiona Hayes-Renshaw and Helen Wallace, *The Council of Ministers* (New York: St. Martin's Press, 1997).

18. Caroline Bradley, "European Court of Justice", 118–38.

19. Brigid Laffan, "Financial Control: The Court of Auditors and OLAF," *The Institutions of the European Union* (New York: Oxford University Press, 2002), 233–53.

20. John Peterson, "The College of Commissioners," *The Institutions of the European Union* (New York: Oxford University Press, 2002), 71–94.

21. Helen Drake, *Delors, Perspectives on a European Leader* (London: Routledge, 2000); Joaquín Roy, "La Unión Europea: Historia, Instituciones, Políticas," *Europa en Transformación: Procesos Económicos, Políticos y Sociales* (México: UNAM, 2000), 133–60; Phillipe Schmitter, "Examining the

Present Euro-Polity with the Help of Past Theories," *Governance in the European Union* (London: Sage, 1996).

22. Andrés Ortega, *La Razón de Europa* (Madrid: Aguilar-El País, 1994).

23. Richard Whitman, *From Civilian Power to Superpower? The International Identity of the European Union* (New York: St. Martin's Press, 1998); Andrew Moravcsik, "Europe without Illusions," Third Spaak Foundation Presentation: Harvard University Conference (Brussels, 2002), 3.

24. Graham Evans and Jeffrey Newnham, *The Dictionary of World Politics* (Hertfordshire, UK: Harvester-Wheatsheaf, 1990), 382.

25. Helen Wallace and William Wallace, *Policy-Making in the European Union* (Oxford: Oxford University Press, 2000), 6.

26. Evans & Newsham, *Dictionary*, 382.

27. Bradley, "European Court of Justice," 2.

28. William Wallace, "Less than a Federation, More than a Regime: The Community as a Political System," *Policy-Making in the European Community* (John Wiley & Sons, 1983).

29. Marks, "A Third Lens," 23–43.

30. Gary Marks, "An Actor-Centered Approach to Multilevel Governance," *Regional & Federal Studies* (6/2, 1996), 21–36.

31. Brigid Laffan, Rory O'Donnell, and Michael Smith, *Europe's Experimental Union: Rethinking Integration* (London: Routledge, 2000).

32. Natividad Fernández Sola, "La Subjetividad Internacional de la Unión Europea," *Revista de Derecho Comunitario Europeo* (11, 2002), 85–112.

33. Vivien Schmidt, "Democratic Challenges for the EU as 'Regional State,'" *EUSA Review* (17/1, Winter 2004), 4.

34. Ibid.

35. Araceli Martín Mangas, "La Unión Europea y su futuro: el debate competencial," *Noticias de la Unión Europea* (218, 2003), 79–93.

36. Phillipe Schmitter, "The European Union Is Not Democratic—So What?" *EUSA Review* (17/1, Winter 2004), 3–4.

37. Schmidt, "Democratic Challenges."

38. Josep Borrell, Carlos Carnero, and Diego López Garrido, *Construyendo la Constitución Europea : Crónica política de la Convención* (Madrid: Real Instituto Elcano, 2003); Carlos Closa, "El fracaso del Consejo Europeo de Bruselas y el futuro de la Constitución," Real Instituto Elcano (18/1, 2004).

39. Santiago Gómez-Reino, "La Actualidad del Pensamiento de Robert Schuman en el Contexto de la Convención Sobre el Futuro de Europa," Working Paper, European Union Center, University of Miami, 2002.

40. Paul Magnette, "Coping with Constitutional Incompatibilities: Bargains and Rhetoric in the Convention on the Future of Europe," *Jean Monnet Papers* (New York: New York University, 2003),14.

41. Ibid.

42. Joaquín Roy, "La Unión Europea: De la arquitectura a la alquimia," *Retos e interrelaciones de la Integración Regional: Europa y América* (México: Plaza y Valdés, 2003), 53–77.

43. Action Jean Monnet, *Europe 2004: De Grand Debat* (Brussels: European Commission, 2002).

44. Jean De Ruyt, *L'Acte Unique Européen* (Brussels: Editions de l'Université de Bruxelles, 1987).

45. Mario Telo and Paul Magnette, *De Maastricht a Amsterdam: L'Europe et son nouveau tracté* (Brussels: Université de Bruxelles, 2002); Andreu Olesti Rayo, *Las incertidumbres de la Unión Europea después del Tratado de Ámsterdam* (Barcelona: J. M. Bosch, 2000).

46. Blanca Vilà Costa, *El horizonte institucional de la UE tras la Conferencia Intergubernamental (de Biarritz a Niza)* (Barcelona: Institut Universitari d'Estudis Europeus, 2001); José Ignacio Torreblanca, "El marco institucional y político en la Europa ampliada: más allá de Niza," *Papeles de Economía Española* (91, 2002), 228–38; Kiernan Bradley, "Institutional Design in the Treaty of Nice," *Common Market Law Review* (38, 2001), 1095–1124.

47. Mariola Urrea Corres, "El dilema de la Convención: La búsqueda de una solución alternativa al modelo clásico de reforma de los Tratados," *Revista de Derecho Comunitario Europeo* (14, 2003), 265–80; Jo Shaw, "Flexibility in a 'Reorganized' and 'Simplified' Treaty," *Common Market Law Review* (2, 2003), 279–311.

48. Albert Galinsoga Jordà, "El 'modelo europeo' en un mundo globalizado: un caracterización de la Unión Europea en el nuevo siglo," *Las Relaciones Exteriores de la Unión Europea* (México: Universidad Nacional Autónoma de México, 2001), 45–66.

The Dictionary

– A –

ACQUIS COMMUNAUTAIRE. Consisting of **European Community (EC) law** and all other obligations of the member states of the **European Union** (EU), including but not limited to those set forth in the treaties, **regulations**, **directives**, common agreements made under **Common Foreign and Security Policy** and **Justice and Home Affairs**, and international agreements and commitments, the acquis communautaire must be fully implemented (except in rare and exceptional cases) by all EU member states. All candidate countries must adopt the acquis communautaire and incorporate it into their national legislations, and demonstrate the ability to continuously implement it in order to accede to the EU.

ADENAUER, KONRAD (1876–1967). Mayor of Cologne from 1917 to 1933 when he was imprisoned for his opposition to the Nazis. Following the end of World War II, Konrad Adenauer became the first chancellor of the Federal Republic of **Germany** in 1949. He served in this position until 1963, and led the country through its "economic miracle." Adenauer was among the founders of the Christian Democratic Union, one of the most influential and powerful political parties in Germany.

Konrad Adenauer, one of the founding fathers of European integration, accepted **Robert Schuman**'s proposal of 9 May 1950, to pool the French and German coal and steel industries under a **High Authority** as he believed Germany's inclusion in this project would facilitate its economic recovery and the restoration of its respect in the international community. He also supported Franco–German reconciliation as a necessary element for stable and peaceful European relations. In this context, in January 1963 he signed, along with French President **Charles de Gaulle**, the **Elysée Treaty** on Franco–German friendship and reconciliation. Konrad Adenauer is remembered by many as one of Germany's greatest statesman.

ADVOCATES-GENERAL. The advocates-general of the **European Court of Justice** (ECJ) are eight highly qualified legal professionals who impartially and independently assist the judges with the ECJ's rapidly increasing caseload. They comprehensively consider cases and provide opinions based on applicable **laws** to the judges of the ECJ. Although the judges have no legal obligation to accept the opinions of the advocates-general, the opinions are used as a reference when making the final decisions on each case, and in most instances are favorably received.

These legal advisers are appointed, based on professional merit, by consensus of the member state governments for a six-year renewable term. Since there are only eight advocates-general, there is obviously a significant number of member states (though these generally do not include the "large" member states) without one in the ECJ at any given time.

AFRICAN–CARIBBEAN–PACIFIC (ACP) COUNTRIES. From Antigua to Palau to Zimbabwe, the ACP countries are a group of 78 states, most of which are ex-colonies of the **European Union** (EU) member states. The EU maintains a special partnership with these countries through an institutionalized EU-ACP framework, although two of the countries, Cuba and South Africa, do not formally take part in all of its agreements and actions. The predecessor of this official association between the **European Community** (EC) and the former European colonies is the **Yaoundé Agreement**, signed by the 17 francophone countries of the Associated African States and by Madagascar.

When the EC enlarged its membership in 1973 to include **Denmark**, **Ireland**, and the **United Kingdom**, the predecessor of the ACP group was simultaneously expanded to incorporate former British dependencies, spanning from the Caribbean to islands in the Pacific. This group of countries, dependencies, and ex-colonies would come to be known as the ACP countries. Their relations with the EC were originally administered under the **Lomé Conventions**, which emphasized cooperation among the European and ACP countries in addition to the distribution of unilateral aid and the recognition of trade preferences established by the EU. Currently governed by the **Cotonou Agreement**, which was signed on 23 June 2000, this partnership includes political dialogue and references to the respect for **human rights**. *See also* DEVELOPMENT POLICY.

AGENCIES OF THE EUROPEAN COMMUNITY. Created through acts of secondary legislation, **European Community** (EC) agencies assist with the management of specific policies, and depending on the agency and the policy, at times contribute to the policy-making process itself. There are basically four types of agencies: regulatory; monitoring; executing, particularly for policies requiring highly scientific and/or technical expertise; and those that promote cooperation and dialogue at the European level. Currently, there are 16 EC agencies: **European Centre for the Development of Vocational Training** (CEDEFOP), **European Foundation for the Improvement of Living and Working Conditions**, **European Environment Agency** (EEA), **European Training Foundation** (ETF), **European Monitoring Centre for Drugs and Drug Addiction** (EMCDDA), **European Medicines Agency** (EMEA), **Office for Harmonization in the Internal Market** (trademarks and designs) (OHIM), **European Agency for Safety and Health at Work**; **Community Plant Variety Office** (CPVO), **Translation Centre for the Bodies of the European Union**; **European Monitoring Centre on Racism and Xenophobia** (EUMC), **European Agency for Reconstruction**, **European Food Safety Authority** (EFSA), **European Maritime Safety Agency** (EMSA), **European Aviation Safety Agency** (EASA), and **European Network and Information Security Agency** (ENISA).

AGENDA 2000. Within the context of the 1 May 2004 and future **enlargements**, Agenda 2000 is a comprehensive program designed for change in the new millennium by way of strengthening Community policies and adopting a new financial framework for the **European Union** for the period 2000–2006. Agenda 2000 addresses reforms of the **Common Agricultural Policy** and the **cohesion policy**, and contains recommendations on how to face the challenges of enlargement. It also proposes a reinforced **pre-accession strategy**, including the extended participation of the applicant countries in Community programs and the mechanisms for applying the **acquis communautaire**.

These priorities were integrated into strengthening legislative proposals submitted by the **European Commission** in 1998. The Berlin **European Council** reached an overall political agreement on the legislative package in 1999, and the measures were adopted that same year.

AGRICULTURAL POLICY. The development of an agricultural policy became an overriding goal early in the European integration process. In response to the perceived benefits highly industrialized **Germany** would reap as a result of the creation of the **European Economic Community** through the **Treaty of Rome** (1957), **France** advocated a counterbalancing **Common Agricultural Policy** (CAP) which was proposed by the **European Commission** in 1960. The CAP evolved into one of the most controversial policies of the **European Union** (EU), representing the most expensive item on the EU's **budget**, and currently undergoing a much needed, yet sensitive reform process.

Following the food shortages experienced in Europe during World War II, there was a general consensus between the **European Community** (EC) countries that one of the primary objectives of the CAP would be to increase agricultural productivity, guaranteeing sustained supplies of food products. In an effort to balance the effects of the CAP, additional objectives include ensuring fair standards of living for agricultural workers and ensuring fair consumer prices for agricultural products. The principles upon which the CAP was created include a **common market** for EC agricultural products; giving EC agricultural products preference over those from other parts of the world; and giving the EC, rather than the member states, financial responsibility for this policy. In order to meet the CAP's established objectives, and maintain its principles, this policy is highly interventionist in terms of subsidies and price controls. Although the CAP enabled modernization and increased efficiency in the agricultural sector in a relatively short period of time, it became progressively more costly and European prices were much higher in comparison to world market prices. A series of reforms known as the **MacSharry reforms** addressed this situation in 1992 by cutting guaranteed farm prices.

The British budgetary rebate negotiated by Prime Minister **Margaret Thatcher** in 1984, and still valid today is indicative of some of the inequalities associated with the CAP. Due to the **United Kingdom**'s relatively small farming industry coupled with its relatively high gross national product, the British government contributed more to the EC budget (the majority of which funded the CAP) than it received in benefits.

The impetus for the recent reforms to the CAP stem from a variety of sources, the most pressing amongst them being the 1 May 2004 **enlargement** and the **Uruguay Round** negotiations on trade in agriculture. The May 2004 enlargement, incorporating into the EU several **Central and Eastern European countries** with large agricultural sectors in need of modernization, made the CAP subsidies unsustainable. Proposed reforms for 2000–2006, part of **Agenda 2000**, include a greater emphasis on the stabilization of agriculture expenditure, rural development, **environmental** protection, and **food safety** regulations.

There is continuous controversy between the EU and third world countries over the EU's intervention in its agricultural markets. Many of these disputes are addressed in the **World Trade Organization** (WTO) where especially the **United States** and the Cairns Group of 17 agricultural exporting countries have put pressure on the EU. *See also* FOOD SAFETY; GENETICALLY MODIFIED ORGANISMS (GMOS).

ALBANIA. Since its first free elections following the ongoing transition from Communism in 1991, Albania has experienced economic and political turmoil. Political unrest and economic crisis in the mid-1990s led to internal conflict. Order was restored with the presence of an international peacekeeping mission.

Albania receives funding from the **European Union** (EU) in the form of humanitarian assistance and from the **Community Assistance for Reconstruction, Development, and Stability** (CARDS) program. As with many of the Western Balkan countries, EU aid is directed toward strengthening **justice and home affairs**, police, rebuilding and developing new infrastructure, cross-border cooperation, education, democracy, and **human rights**, among other important issue areas that receive EU attention and support. Considered a possible future EU member state, negotiations for a **Stabilization and Association Agreement** between the EU and Albania began on 31 January 2003.

AMATO, GIULIANO (1938–). A reform-minded politician, formerly of **Italy**'s Socialist Party, Giuliano Amato served as the government's prime minister from 1992 to 1993 and from 2000 to 2001. During his first administration, in September 1992, the Italian lira was forced out of the **European Union**'s **exchange rate mechanism**, prompting Amato to implement economic reforms to reduce the budget deficit and prepare the Italian economy for meeting the **convergence criteria** and adopting the **euro**.

In December 2001, Giuliano Amato was appointed by the Laeken **European Council** as one of two vice-chairmen of the **European Convention**. Along with Vice-Chair **Jean-Luc Dehaene**, he assisted the Convention's Chair, **Valéry Giscard d'Estaing** from February 2002 to June 2003 during which time the future of Europe was debated and the **Treaty establishing a Constitution for Europe** was drafted.

In addition to twice serving as head of the Italian government and vice-chair of the European Convention, Giuliano Amato was a member of Italy's Parliament from 1983 to 1994, and he served as a member of the Italian Government in various functions from 1987 to 1989 and from 1998 to 2000. Amato was elected to Italy's Senate in 2001, where he continues to serve as a member of the mixed parliamentary group.

ANTHEM. The European anthem is the final movement of Ludwig Van Beethoven's Ninth Symphony, set to the words of "Ode to Joy," which was written by the **German** poet Friedrich von Schiller. It has been the anthem of the **Council of Europe** since 1972 and was adopted by the **European Council** as the **European Union**'s official anthem in 1985.

AREA OF FREEDOM, SECURITY, AND JUSTICE. The **Justice and Home Affairs** pillar of European integration, established in the **Treaty on European Union**, was reformed in the **Treaty of Amsterdam**. The main objective behind the changes was to establish an Area of Freedom, Security, and Justice, an area in which there is complete free movement of people within the internal borders of the **European Union** (EU) and increased security and guarantees of equal justice within a common external border. In order to accomplish this goal several policies (i.e., asylum, immigration, visas) were moved from the intergovernmental third pillar to the first pillar of the EU. Furthermore, the **Schengen Agreement** was annexed to the treaties, and a framework for facilitated cooperation between police and judicial authorities was developed.

ARMAND, LOUIS. Refer to appendix B.

ASIA. The **European Union**'s (EU) relations with Asia cover more than 30 countries in the wider Asian and Asian–Pacific region, including Australia and New Zealand. The three main pillars of these relations are economic and commercial; global and regional security dialogue; and cooperation programs and **humanitarian aid**. The six objectives of the EU's strategy toward Asia are to contribute to peace and security in the region; to strengthen trade and investment; to promote development; to encourage the respect for **human rights**, democracy, good **governance**, and the rule of law; to build global partnerships and alliances; and to promote understanding of the EU in Asia. The relations between the EU and Asia are sustained by the **Asia–Europe Meeting (ASEM)** process of which Asia–Europe Summits are the most important element, and ministerial dialogues between the EU and the countries of the Association of Southeast Asian Nations (ASEAN).

The EU also maintains bilateral relations with each of the Asian countries individually. While relations with all of these countries are institutionalized and play an important role in the overall regional strategy and partnership, given China's market and Japan's economy, the EU has given special attention to strengthening its relations with these countries.

Diplomatic relations between the **European Community** and China were established in 1975, suspended in June 1989 following the violent repression of the student demonstrations in Tiananmen Square, but were subsequently normalized and are intensifying in the beginning of the 21st century particularly as a result of China's growing international economic capacity. After years of difficult negotiations, the EU and China finally reached agreements acceptable to the EU to approve China's accession to the **World Trade Organization** (WTO), of which it officially became a member on 11 December 2001. China is one of the EU's largest non-European trading partners, second only to the **United States**, and EU companies continue to make considerable investments in China. One of the EU's main objectives in economic terms is to attempt to reduce its more than €50 billion trade deficit with China.

Although trade relations are a key component, the EU's relations with China are comprehensive. EU–China Summits of Heads of Government were institutionalized on an annual basis in 1998; the seventh summit took place on 8 December 2004 in The Hague during which several agreements were reached including those related to tourism and cooperation in science and technology. The **European Commission**'s cooperation program provides development funding to China in an effort to combat poverty and support its economic and social reforms. Continued concern regarding China's human rights record prompted the initiation of an EU–China human rights dialogue in 1996 and it is in this context that issues such as individual freedoms and the situation in Tibet are addressed.

Following the 1989 incident in Tiananmen Square, the **European Council** imposed an arms embargo on China. One controversial element of EU–China relations leading into 2005 has international implications: the Chinese government's continued campaign to have this embargo lifted.

In 1991 the EU and Japan adopted a Political Declaration outlining common principles on political, economic, sectoral, and cultural cooperation within a framework of annual summits between the Presidents of the European Council and the European Commission and the Prime Minister of Japan. The 13th EU–Japan Summit took place in Tokyo on 22 June 2004, coinciding with the inauguration of the first EU Institute in Japan.

An Action Plan for Japan–EU Cooperation was adopted in December 2001 to strengthen bilateral relations over a period of 10 years. The main objectives of this plan are reinforcing economic and trade relations, developing stronger links between people and cultures, promoting peace and security, and dealing with global challenges. One of the initiatives of the Action Plan is policy cooperation between the EU and Japan in the WTO.

The EU–Japanese economic partnership is growing both in terms of trade and investment, and there are several initiatives underway to support market and business access. Since 1994, the EU and Japan have engaged in a Regulatory Reform Dialogue through which they present deregulation requests to each other. Through the EXPROM program, the European Commission encourages and financially supports EU export and business ventures in Japan.

ASIA–EUROPE MEETING (ASEM). Recognizing the need and value in strengthening the relations between **Asia** and Europe, in 1994, Singapore and **France** proposed holding an EU–Asia Summit. As a result, the first ASEM, an informal process of dialogue and cooperation, was held in Bangkok, Thailand, in March 1996, and one has taken place every two years since, alternating meeting locations between Asian and European cities. Until 2004, the participants in ASEM were the heads of state and government of the EU(15), the heads of state and government of Brunei, **China**, Indonesia, **Japan**, South Korea, Malaysia, the Philippines, Singapore, Thailand, and Vietnam. Today ASEM has incorporated the 10 member states that joined the EU on 1 May 2004, as well as Cambodia, Laos, and Burma/Myanmar.

One of the principle aspects of ASEM is its informal nature in facilitating dialogue, policy-making, and managing more comprehensive relations between these two regional partners. There is emphasis placed on the idea that cooperation will take place complementarily but not redundant to bilateral and other multilateral frameworks for Asia–Europe cooperation. The three main issue areas for cooperation are political, economic, and cultural. In addition to the summit meetings, ministerial level meetings are held between all ASEM partners on an annual basis, and there has been an increasing interest in the process from civil society organizations. ASEM has produced several tangible outcomes: the Asia–Europe Foundation (ASEF), located in Singapore and dedicated to promoting intellectual, cultural and social exchanges between Asia and Europe; the Trans-Eurasian Information Network (TEIN) Project to increase direct research and education co-operation between Asia and Europe; the ASEM Trust Fund, which is managed by the World Bank and provides technical assistance for specific actions in the financial and social sectors for the Asian countries trying to recover from financial crisis.

ASSENT PROCEDURE. The assent procedure is one of the mechanisms by which the **European Parliament** (EP), in conjunction with the **Council of the European Union** (EU), participates in the EU's **decision-making** process. Proposals that fit into specific and explicitly outlined categories in the treaties such as certain international agreements, **enlargements**, and the framework for the **structural funds**, must be approved by both the EP and the Council through the assent procedure. The implementation of this procedure only allows for the EP to simply approve or reject a measure, but not to amend it.

AUDIO-VISUAL POLICY. Designed to support the European audio-visual industry in its development and competitiveness as well as bringing it in line with the **single market**, the audio-visual policy has established broad framework guidelines to meet these objectives. Much of the audio-visual policy is based on television broadcasting. **Directives** have been passed with regard to the different means of broadcasting, including cable, satellite and high-definition television. The cornerstone legislation of the audio-visual policy is the Television without Frontiers Directive, which was adopted in 1989 and modified in 1997. This directive provides for the free movement of audio-visual productions through the internal borders of the **European Union** (EU), and the coordination of member states' national legislation in the areas of advertising and the protection of minors. Television without Frontiers also stipulates that whenever possible television channels reserve at lest half of their air time for European productions.

The MEDIA program financially supports the development of the European audio-visual industry and its productions. There have thus far been three MEDIA programs, 1990–1995, 1996–2000, and

2001–2006. In addition to supporting production and distribution, the current MEDIA program also provides funding to support training in the audio-visual industry.

AUSTRIA. The post–World War II Allied occupation of Austria ended in 1955 when it was granted independence on the condition that it maintained a policy of neutrality. Relatively isolated from the West during the remaining years of the Cold War, the Republic of Austria submitted its application for membership in the **European Community** on 17 July 1989. Similar to **Sweden**, one of Austria's accession partners, inclusion in the **European Union** (EU) despite founding membership in the **European Free Trade Association**, was controversial and pitted domestic political actors and parties against one another. Issues such as Austria's policy of neutrality, high **environmental** standards, and advanced social welfare system were key factors in the debate. Economic and trade concerns, however, outweighed all others and Austria became a member state of the EU on 1 January 1995.

Five years later in early 2000, the ascent of a coalition government including the far-right Freedom Party led by **Jörg Haider** provoked a short-lived but significant political crisis between Austria and the EU and its member states. Under Haider's leadership, the Freedom Party demonstrated xenophobic and racist characteristics, causing alarm within the EU. Not only did the party's intolerant policies clash with the EU's strong democratic principles, but its anti-immigration stance and opposition to the Central and Eastern European **enlargement** were also contrary to some of the EU's then pending objectives. In protest, the other 14 EU member states unprecedentedly imposed diplomatic sanctions on Austria in February 2000. While the sanctions were lifted later that same year, they demonstrated that the EU would not tolerate deviations toward extremism and away from the values on which the European integration project has been based since its foundation following the end of World War II. Refer to appendix A.

AZNAR, JOSE MARIA (1953–). Former leader of **Spain**'s center-right Popular Party, José María Aznar became prime minister of the Spanish government on 5 May 1996, replacing veteran socialist premier **Felipe González**. Aznar remained in office for two terms, the first with a relative majority and a coalition government, and the second, beginning in 2000, with an absolute majority. Aznar declared that he would not be a candidate for the March 2004 elections, yet his party under the leadership of Mariano Rajoy was considered a front-runner. Three days prior to the 14 March 2004 elections, Madrid was the subject of a deadly Al-Qaeda attack and Aznar's management of the situation, specifically with regard to the dissemination of information, was highly criticized. The Spanish Socialist Workers Party won the elections, and its leader, **José Luis Rodríguez Zapatero**, became the new Spanish Head of Government, replacing Aznar on 17 April 2004.

Aznar consistently emphasized the need to fight **terrorism**. He unwaveringly supported **United States** President George W. Bush and the 2003 intervention in Iraq (despite 90 percent of the Spanish population opposing this policy).

During the negotiations on the **Treaty establishing a Constitution for Europe**, Aznar's position was firm in that Spain should maintain the same relative influence and weighted votes (only two less than the member states with the most votes: **France**, **Germany**, **Italy**, and the **United Kingdom**) in the **Council of the European Union** as had been agreed upon and included in the **Treaty of Nice**. Aznar's uncompromising stance partly contributed to a delay in the negotiation process.

– B –

BALLADUR PLAN. *See* STABILITY PACT FOR SOUTHEASTERN EUROPE.

BARCELONA PROCESS. *See* EURO–MEDITERRANEAN PARTNERSHIP.

BARON CRESPO, ENRIQUE (1944–). A member of the Socialist Group in the 2004–2009 **European Parliament** (EP), Enrique Barón Crespo is the chairman of the Committee on International Trade and a member of the Delegation for relations with the **United States**. He has been a member of the EP since 1986, serving as the EP's vice-president from 1987 to 1989 and as its president from 1989 to 1992. Barón Crespo is from **Spain** where he graduated with a law degree from the University of Madrid and was a member of the Spanish Congress of Deputies from 1977 to 1986, and a member of the Spanish government as Minister for Transport, Tourism and Communications from 1982 to 1985. Refer to appendix D.

BARROSO, JOSE MANUEL (1956–). On 22 November 2004, José Manuel Barroso officially assumed the office of president of the first enlarged 25-member **European Commission**. He accepted the nomination to this position in June 2004, at which time he resigned from his post as prime minister of **Portugal** (April 2002 to June 2004) in order to prepare for this leadership transition. After a speech emphasizing the Commission's future role in building a "Partnership for Europe," a "partnership for prosperity, solidarity and security" to meet Europe's modern challenges, the **European Parliament** approved his candidacy in July 2004.

Although Barroso was neither the expected nor the first-choice candidate, he was the one who raised the least objections, and in addition, his past political experience and qualifications are indisputable. A longtime politician, he served as Portuguese secretary of state for foreign affairs during which time he demonstrated his diplomatic skills as a leader in the negotiations for a temporary ceasefire (1990) in the civil war in Angola, a former Portuguese colony. As the Portuguese prime minister, he was instrumental in reversing the government's excessive deficit in order to comply with the **Stability and Growth Pact**, despite opposition to the policies implemented to meet this goal.

One of the challenges facing the Barroso Commission is to bring the **European Union** and its institutions, including the Commission, closer to the citizens, particularly important during the ratification process for the **Treaty establishing a Constitution for Europe**. Barroso has already made it clear that a strong, independent Commission is what is needed to meet the challenges of the future of Europe. It is suspected that he will champion the interests of the small states, coming from a small, peripheral, **enlargement** country himself. Refer to appendix B.

BEHRENDT, WALTER. Refer to appendix B.

BELARUS. Following its independence from the Union of Soviet Socialist Republics in 1991, Belarus and the **European Union** (EU) began to develop economic and political relations. The election of President Alexander Lukashenko in 1994, and his disregard for democratic elections and implementation of authoritarian measures caused a rupture between the EU and Belarus. Representative of the EU's insistence on the respect for democracy and **human rights** in the countries with which it maintains institutionalized **external relations**, the Partnership and Association Agreement between the EU and Belarus has not entered into force and funding for Belarus from the **Technical Assistance for the Commonwealth of Independent States** (TACIS) has been suspended (except for humanitarian assistance). Furthermore, a **common position** adopted by the Council in December 2004 places visa restrictions on all people from Belarus who were in any way associated with the fraudulent elections and referendum in October 2004 and on all people responsible for the violation of human rights in the country. The EU encourages fundamental political and economic reforms in Belarus as minimal requirements for the strengthening of relations, of particular interest to the EU considering Belarus borders three EU member states— **Latvia, Lithuania**, and **Poland**.

BELGIUM. Belgium is one of the six founding members of the **European Union** (EU) as a signatory to the 1951 **Treaty of Paris**, which created the **European Coal and Steel Community**. Not a novice to European cooperation, Belgium had become a member of the **Benelux Customs Union** in 1948 and a member of the **North Atlantic Treaty Organization** (NATO) and the **Council of Europe** in 1949.

Despite a regional divide within Belgium between Dutch Flanders and French Wallonia, and perhaps as a result of it, Belgium has always been a strong supporter of European integration and is considered to be a generally Euro-federalist member state. Belgium's capital, **Brussels**, is the unequivocal center of EU politics and has come to be known as the unofficial capital of the EU. Brussels is host to several of the main EU institutions such as the **European Parliament** (Brussels headquarters), the **European Commission**, and the **Council of the EU**. Based on an agreement made at the Nice **Euro-**

pean Council of 2000, all required European Council meetings take place in Brussels. Establishing Brussels as the permanent location for these summits has been phased in over the past several years.

Belgium has taken part in all aspects of EU integration including the adoption of the **euro**. The Belgian **presidency of the EU** of the second semester 2001 successfully promoted the acceptance of the **European Convention** which was agreed to at the **Laeken** Summit in Belgium on 14–15 December 2001. Refer to appendix A.

BENELUX CUSTOMS UNION. Prompted by the impending economic recovery and the need to augment their security after being occupied by **Germany** during World War II, **Belgium**, **The Netherlands**, and **Luxembourg**, small neighboring European countries, agreed to pursue economic cooperation as a means of reaching their postwar goals. In 1948, these three countries formed the Benelux Customs Union, a **free trade area** with a **common external tariff**. Thus, at the time of the **Schuman Declaration** on 9 May 1950, the Benelux countries had already implemented a form of advanced economic cooperation and were therefore prepared to accept the proposal to join the **European Coal and Steel Community**.

BERKHOUWER, CORNELIS. Refer to appendix D.

BERLIN PLUS. The Berlin Plus agreements provide the **European Union** (EU) with access to **North Atlantic Treaty Organization** (NATO) planning and command capabilities and assets in cases when NATO itself is not officially and wholly involved in crisis management operations. Berlin Plus is known as such because the conclusions of the agreements at the April 1999 NATO Summit in Washington, D.C., were developed within the scope of the first mutual understanding between the EU and NATO in Berlin in 1996. Berlin Plus was adopted and went into effect on 17 March 2003, and since then was implemented with the EU-led Operation Concordia in the **former Yugoslav Republic of Macedonia** in March 2003 and in **Bosnia-Herzegovina** at the end of 2004.

BERLIN WALL. After decades of Cold War tensions and divisions, economic crisis and popular protest combined to delegitimize the

Soviet Union and Soviet satellite communist governments and eventually led to their collapse. The fall of the Berlin Wall on 9 November 1989 symbolized the possible reunification of western and eastern Europe. The independence of the former Soviet bloc countries as well as former Soviet republics created new economic, political, and security implications for the **European Community** (EC), and would be followed by a **deepening** and **widening** of European integration in scope and dimensions never previously experienced by the EC.

By 3 October 1990, German reunification was complete and the former German Democratic Republic de facto became a member of the EC. Thereafter, the Federal Republic of **Germany** became the largest member state in terms of population, and its five eastern states became eligible to receive EC **structural funding**. Notwithstanding the perceived political and social benefits, low levels of development and the transition to an open market economy in the east made German reunification an expensive process for both the EC and the German government.

Strategic concerns regarding the EC's new borders, as well as historic opportunity and a declared desire on the part of the **Central and Eastern European countries** compelled the EC and its member states to accept the future membership of these countries. After lengthy negotiations and despite the economic costs it entails, on 1 May 2004, five former Soviet bloc countries and three former Soviet republics (along with **Cyprus** and **Malta**) joined the **European Union** in the largest accession in its history.

BERLUSCONI, SILVIO (1936–). The founder and leader of the *Forza Italia* political party, Prime Minister Silvio Berlusconi is a billionaire businessman who owns several media outlets amongst other high profile investments. Elected into office in 2001, Berlusconi has presided over **Italy**'s longest lasting government since the end of World War II. As of mid-2005 he heads the center-right House of Freedom coalition which includes *Forza Italia*, the National Alliance, and the Northern League, along with several other political parties. Berlusconi had previously been Italy's prime minister in 1994, a brief political exercise that lasted less than one year due to a break from the coalition government by the Northern League.

Berlusconi's government has at times been criticized for assuming a **Euro-skeptic** stance. In 2002, Foreign Minister Renato Ruggiero resigned in protest of the attitudes of some fellow cabinet members, particularly toward the launch of the **euro** and the seemingly nonchalant response it received from the Italian government.

In July 2003, Italy, under Berlusconi's leadership, assumed the **presidency of the European Union** (EU). Correspondingly, Italy also chaired the start of the **intergovernmental conference** (IGC) on the **Treaty establishing a Constitution for Europe**. Given the prior uncertainties in terms of the Berlusconi government and the EU, anxieties were naturally high. Nevertheless, although the IGC was extended into the Irish presidency, the delay in the negotiations was not directly related to the Italian government and the 2003 Italian presidency of the EU took place without any major incidents. On 29 October 2004, Prime Minister Berlusconi hosted the signing of the constitutional treaty in Rome.

BLAIR, TONY (1953–). After 18 consecutive years of Conservative-run government in the **United Kingdom** (UK), Tony Blair, leader of the Labour Party, became the British prime minister on 2 May 1997. He began a second term in office after Labour's victory in the 2001 general elections, and a third after winning the general elections held in May 2005.

Blair, while generally maintaining the traditional **Euro-skeptic** British attitude and emphasis on **intergovernmentalism**, has taken a more positive approach toward some of the policies that had been rejected by his predecessors. For example, he reversed the UK's position on the **Social Charter** and allowed for its full inclusion in the **Treaty of Amsterdam**, effectively making Britain subject to all of its provisions. Blair is also more receptive to the idea of Britain's adoption of the **euro** as its national currency. However, given the controversy over this topic and the possible political implications, a decision on such action has been indefinitely postponed.

Prime Minister Blair has also indicated a propensity for a more proactive role in developing and implementing an EU **defense policy**. To this end, in a December 1998 Summit with French President **Jacques Chirac**, Blair and his French counterpart called for an autonomous EU defense force for crisis management in what came to be known as the **Saint Malo Declaration**. On the other hand, Blair also has been careful to clearly express that such a force would not conflict in any way with the **North Atlantic Treaty Organization** and Britain's relations with the **United States**. Prime Minister Blair's administration has been the strongest military ally of the United States in the 2003 intervention in Iraq.

Following the **budget** crisis begun in the June 2005 **European Council**, and in response to calls for reducing or eliminating the British budgetary rebate, Blair called for a modernization of the EU and its policies, particularly the **Common Agricultural Policy**.

BO, DINO DEL. Refer to appendix B.

BORRELL FONTELLES, JOSEP (1947–). Elected president of the **European Parliament** (EP) in 2004 (following an agreement between the **Socialist Group in the European Parliament** [PES] and the **Group of the European Peoples' Party [Christian Democrats] and European Democrats** [EPP-ED] that the EPP-ED group president would take over the EP presidency mid-term) and a member of the PES, Josep Borrell Fontelles is also the chairman of the temporary committee on policy challenges and budgetary means of the enlarged Union 2007–2013 and chairman of the delegation to the Euro–Mediterranean Parliamentary Assembly. Borrell Fontelles is from **Spain** where he was a member of the Congress of Deputies from 1986–2004, serving as a member of the Spanish government as secretary of state for finance from 1984 to 1991 and minister for public works, transport, the environment and telecommunications from 1991 to 1996. He also served from 2002 to 2003 as a member of the **European Convention**, which drafted the **Treaty establishing a Constitution for Europe**. Refer to appendix D.

BOSNIA-HERZEGOVINA. Ethnically diverse Bosnia-Herzegovina declared its independence from the **former Yugoslavia** in 1992. The Serb minority in the country developed its own national entity and engaged in an exercise of ethnic cleansing supported by Serbia. Despite several attempts at peace negotiations and meetings organized in part by the **European Union** (EU), it was not until **North Atlantic Treaty Organization** (NATO) bombings of Serb targets in 1995 followed by the 1995 Dayton Accords that an agreement was reached on the territorial boundaries and administrative government of Bosnia-Herzegovina. This peace agreement was first enforced by a NATO peacekeeping mission and was replaced by Operation EUFOR-Althea, launched on 2 December 2004. Almost one year previously, in January 2003, the first European Union Police Mission (EUPM) was initiated in Bosnia-Herzegovina.

Bosnia-Herzegovina receives **humanitarian aid** from the EU and also benefits from the **Community Assistance for Reconstruction, Development, and Stability** (CARDS) program. The main objectives of the EU in Bosnia-Herzegovina are the reconstruction of infrastructure, the return of refugees and displaced persons, democratization, institution building, and economic regeneration.

BRANDT, WILLY (1913–1992). Chairman of the Social Democratic Party from 1964 to 1987, mayor of West Berlin from 1957 to 1966, foreign minister and vice chancellor during the grand coalition Christian Democratic–Social Democratic government from 1966 to 1969, Willy Brandt became the chancellor of the Federal Republic of **Germany** in October 1969, and remained in that position until May 1974. One of Brandt's most noteworthy policies was his *Ostpolitik*; political, economic, and cultural relations with the German Democratic Republic as well as with the Soviet Union and many **Central and Eastern European countries**. Not without controversy, and even highly questioned by members of his own party, Brandt sought to pursue this policy as a country with a firm foundation in the **European Community**. Despite the original criticisms, in 1971, Brandt received the Nobel Peace Prize for his efforts toward détente and reconciliation between East and West.

In 1974, Willy Brandt, engulfed in a scandal regarding one of his personal assistants being a spy for East Germany, resigned as the West German chancellor. Brandt, however, continued to play an active role in German and European politics. He remained chairman of the Social Democratic Party until 1987, and Honorary Chairman from 1987 until 1992. He was also a member of the **European Parliament** from 1979 to 1983. Willy Brandt, mayor of West Berlin during the construction of the **Berlin Wall**, witnessed its destruction and the reunification of Germany, before he died in 1992.

BROAD ECONOMIC POLICY GUIDELINES (BEPG). Based on a recommendation from the **European Commission** and conclusions from the **European Council**, the **Council of the European Union** adopts by method of **qualified majority voting** a recommendation establishing the BEPG. This process takes place on a yearly basis. The adopted BEPG are used as a basis for coordinating the economic policies of the **European Union** and the member states.

BRUSSELS. The capital of **Belgium**, Brussels, has become the unofficial capital of the **European Union** (EU), and is undoubtedly the EU's political center. The **European Commission**, the **Council of the EU** and the **European Parliament** (Brussels headquarters) all have their seats in Brussels. Brussels has also become the permanent site for all required meetings of the **European Council**. A great deal of the EU's policy-making and **decision-making** processes take place in Brussels.

In addition to many of the EU institutions, the headquarters of the **North Atlantic Treaty Organization** (NATO) is also located in Brussels.

BUDGET. Funded through multiple sources known as "own resources," the budget of the **European Union** (EU) is proposed by the **European Commission** and decided on by the **Council of the EU** and the **European Parliament** (EP). The budget is categorized into specific areas of expenditure and broadly divided between compulsory and noncompulsory spending. Amendments to the budget may be proposed by both the Council and the Parliament, but when disagreements arise, the Council has the ultimate authority over compulsory spending and the Parliament over noncompulsory spending. The EP alone has the power to reject the overall budget with a two-thirds vote.

Since the late 1980s, a multi-year budget framework is negotiated approximately every seven years. The current financial perspective is for 2007–2013, during which time the EU will have access to €826.4 billion for spending on its internal and external policies. The total EU budget for 2006 was €121.2 billion. The largest EU budget expenditures are in the areas of **agriculture** and **structural funds**, together representing approximately 65 percent of the total budget. The rest of the monies are spent on other internal policies, external actions, and administration. Regardless of how the EU budget is allocated, it must always be balanced.

The EU's "own resources" consist of customs duties, agricultural levies, a percentage of the value-added tax collected in each member state, and an automatic contribution from each member state based on its gross national product (GNP). The member state contributions began in 1988, in large part to offset the declining income from the duties and levies.

The budget often has caused controversy amongst the EU member states. Commission proposals to revise the financing for the Common Agricultural Policy and to grant more budgetary authority to the EP (amongst others) led to the **Empty Chair Crisis** in 1965. British Prime Minister **Margaret Thatcher**'s concerns regarding her country's budgetary contribution consistently remained on the agenda until the matter was resolved through the British budgetary rebate in 1984, still a subject of contention in the EU. In the negotiations for the 2007–2013 financial perspective, one of the sticking points was the budgetary ceiling in terms of the budget as a percentage of the EU's total GNP. *See also* TAXATION; UNITED KINGDOM.

BULGARIA. On 14 December 1995, Bulgaria officially submitted its application for membership in the **European Union** (EU). Despite its official candidacy and ongoing negotiations, Bulgaria was not included in the group of 10 candidate states deemed to have successfully completed their accession negotiations and to be prepared for membership in 2004. Along with **Romania**, Bulgaria's 1 January 2007 accession negotiations were completed in December 2004, and it signed its accession treaty in April 2005.

The decision to postpone Bulgaria's EU membership was made at the Copenhagen **European Council** in December 2002. The **European Commission** considered that Bulgaria needed to make additional efforts in the areas of **human rights**, business regulations, and education. Furthermore, Bulgaria needed to make significant improvements to its administrative and judicial capacity. Refer to appendix A.

BUREAUCRACY. *See* CIVIL SERVICE.

– C –

CASSIS DE DIJON. A landmark case for the **European Community** (EC), *Cassis de Dijon*, was decided by the **European Court of Justice** (ECJ) in 1979 and established the principle of mutual recognition.

The dispute arose when German authorities ruled that the French liquor, Cassis de Dijon, could not be sold in **Germany** as such because it did not meet the minimum alcohol content requirements as established by German law. The ECJ ruled that preventing the import of this product was contrary to the EC's **common market** and that as long as goods met comparable health and safety standards, their importation could not be restricted by any other EC member state. This principle of mutual recognition became one of the foundations of the **single market** program in the 1980s.

CECCHINI REPORT. Officially known as *The Economics of 1992*, the Cecchini Report was the result of a **European Commission**–funded group of independent consultants led by former Commission official, Paolo Cecchini, in 1986 and 1987. The objective of this research project was to determine the costs of not adopting a **single market** for the **European Community** (EC). The results of the report showed a rise in GDP, lower deficits, and increased jobs if the single market were to be implemented. **Jacques Delors**, President of the European Commission from 1985 to 1995, relied on the findings of the Cecchini Report to promote support for his single market program.

CENTRAL AND EASTERN EUROPEAN COUNTRIES (CEECs). Although there is no precise definition, the CEECs are generally considered to consist of the Balkan countries, the Baltic countries, and those countries in between **Germany** and **Austria** to the west and **Russia** to the east. Eight of these countries (**Czech Republic**, **Estonia**, **Hungary**, **Latvia**, **Lithuania**, **Poland**, **Slovakia**, and **Slovenia**) became member states of the **European Union** (EU) on 1 May 2004; **Bulgaria** and **Romania** have successfully completed their accession negotiations and will join the EU on 1 January 2007; **Croatia** submitted an application for membership in February 2003 and was subsequently granted official candidacy status; and the **Former Yugoslav Republic of Macedonia** applied for membership on 22 March 2004.

All of the 1 May 2004 Central and Eastern European accession countries (except Slovenia) were former members of the Soviet bloc or former Soviet republics that quickly made transitions to democracy and open market economies following the collapse of the Soviet

Union. In an effort to support the reform processes in these countries, in December 1989, the **European Community** (EC) created the Poland and Hungary Assistance for the Reconstruction of the Economy (**PHARE**) programme, which would eventually be extended to all of the Central and Eastern European applicant countries. The EC subsequently negotiated association agreements with all of these countries, called **Europe Agreements** to indicate their uniqueness as compared to association agreements with other countries, as they were a means of preparation for eventual EU membership. In June 1993 the **European Council** agreed to accept these countries as future EU member states if they met the established **Copenhagen criteria**. Based on the recommendations of the **European Commission**, the first accession negotiations began with the Czech Republic, Estonia, Hungary, Poland, and Slovenia on 31 March 1998, and in 2000, with Bulgaria, Latvia, Lithuania, Romania, and Slovakia. (Although not CEECs, **Cyprus** and **Malta** also took part in these negotiations, Cyprus beginning in 1998 and Malta with the second group of countries in 2000.) Ten of these countries, all except Bulgaria and Romania, and including Cyprus and Malta, completed their accession negotiations by December 2002, and were invited to join the EU on 1 May 2004.

Although a historic and strategic opportunity to reunite eastern and western Europe, EU membership for the CEECs also presents certain difficulties. The inclusion of the CEECs in the EU required institutional reforms to accommodate the **enlargement** from 15 to 25 member states. This enlargement also necessitates substantial EU funding given the relatively low levels of development of the majority of the CEECs compared to the EU-15. *See also* PRE-ACCESSION STRATEGY.

CHARTER OF FUNDAMENTAL RIGHTS. For the first time in the history of the **European Union** (EU), the civil, political, economic, and social rights of all EU citizens and residents were elaborated in 2000 in a single text—the Charter of Fundamental Rights. This document includes the limitations and responsibilities of the EU government, as well as the freedoms of the EU citizens, divided into six main categories: dignity, freedoms, equality, solidarity, citizens' rights, and justice.

The **German** government proposed the Charter of Fundamental Rights during its **presidency of the EU** in 1999. With limited opposition, general agreement was reached by 2000 during a Convention responsible for drafting the Charter. (This was the first time the Convention method was used to debate future EU policy and would be borrowed from in order to design the **European Convention** on the future of Europe.)

The Charter of Fundamental Rights is not yet legally binding. Included in the **Treaty establishing a Constitution for Europe**, the Charter would only gain legal recognition after the treaty's ratification and its subsequent entry into force and is thus presently in limbo.

CHATENET, PIERRE. Refer to appendix B.

CHINA. *See* ASIA.

CHIRAC, JACQUES (1932–). Prime Minister of the French Government from 1974 to 1976 and from 1986 to 1988, founder of the Gaullist Rally for the Republic political party in 1976, and Mayor of Paris from 1977 to 1995, Jacques Chirac became the president of **France** on 17 May 1995, replacing socialist **François Mitterrand** who had previously defeated Chirac in the presidential elections of 1981 and 1988. A miscalculated early call for elections resulted in a period of cohabitation from 1997 to 2002 during which Chirac had to govern in collaboration with socialist Prime Minister **Lionel Jospin**. Chirac was reelected in 2002, and is currently a member of the conservative political party, Union for a Popular Movement (UMP), which was founded in 2002 through the merging of Rally for the Republic with the Liberal Democrats and part of the Union for French Democracy.

Although the Gaullist tendencies of his political party assume a cautious approach toward European integration, President Chirac became a strong supporter of **Economic and Monetary Union**. In December 1998, together with British Prime Minister **Tony Blair**, Chirac also called for an autonomous **European Union** defense force for crisis management in what came to be known as the **Saint-Malo Declaration**. Going against the majority of the members of his own party (UMP), in December 2004 Chirac approved beginning EU accession negotiations with **Turkey**, claiming that the candidate country should eventually be granted membership if it fulfills all of the requirements.

Chirac adamantly opposed the 2003 **United States** invasion of Iraq. He became disconcerted with member states and then candidate countries that did not follow the traditional Franco–German motor of European integration in this **foreign policy** matter. At the beginning of his second administration, Chirac had placed a high priority on reinforcing Franco–German relations. Although he strongly supported approval of the **Treaty establishing a Constitution for Europe**, in a May referendum, it was rejected by a majority of the French voters.

CHURCHILL, WINSTON (1874–1965). British prime minister during World War II (1940–1945) and during the critical postwar period (1951–1955), Winston Churchill has not only come to be known as one of the greatest European statesmen but also as one of the first supporters of some form of European unity. Churchill gave his now famous "United States of Europe" speech at the University of Zurich in 1946 and he founded the **European Movement** in May 1947. His promotion and leadership of this venture resulted in the **Congress of Europe** in The Hague in 1948, during which an agreement was reached on the creation of the **Council of Europe**. While the Council of Europe is a distinct entity with a different approach to integration (loose, limited, and intergovernmental) than that which would evolve into the **European Union**, Churchill's contributions to the advancement of the idea of a united Europe were fundamental.

CITIZENSHIP. The idea of European citizenship was introduced in the Treaty of Rome, and today citizens of all EU member states are also citizens of the EU. Some of the benefits provided by EU citizenship include: the right to vote and run in local or **European Parliament** elections anywhere in the EU; the right to receive consular protection from any EU member state when in a third country in which a person's country of citizenship does not have a consular office; and the right to file a complaint with the European **Ombudsman**. European citizenship and the rights and responsibilities associated with it fall under the jurisdiction of the **European Court of Justice** (ECJ). The **Charter of Fundamental Rights** included in the

Treaty Establishing a Constitution for Europe outlines specific rights in the areas of dignity, freedom, equality, solidarity, citizenship, and justice that should be guaranteed to all EU citizens.

CIVIL SERVICE. The approximately 25,000 civil servants that work for the **European Union** (EU) are selected through a highly competitive process that includes oral and written evaluation. The **European Commission** staff work in different areas of the Commission administration including translation and interpretation, research, and policy-making in the Commission's directorates-general and associate programs. EU civil servants are extremely well paid and receive excellent benefits, making a position in the EU's bureaucracy an attractive option for many university graduates.

There are, however, negative aspects associated with a job in the EU's civil service. The Commission staff has different administrative grades and high level positions are even more limited and competitive and are subject to a balance amongst all of the EU member states, not to mention the political aspects often associated with appointment to one of these high level positions. Mobility is thus not always related to ability and performance, a fact that has brought significant criticism and moves for reform, thus far without much success. The civil service has at the same time been criticized for its inefficiency and its size, though it is smaller per capita than most national bureaucracies.

CO-DECISION PROCEDURE. In an effort to give more real legislative powers to the **European Parliament** (EP), the only directly elected institution of the **European Union** (EU), the co-decision procedure was introduced in the **Treaty of Maastricht**. This procedure theoretically allows the EP to participate as an equal co-legislator with the **Council of the EU** in the adoption of proposed legislation that falls under issue areas specifically identified in the treaties. Co-decision was considered to be too complex a process as established in the Treaty of Maastricht and, therefore, it was simplified in the **Treaty of Amsterdam**. In the Treaty of Amsterdam, additional issue areas were also added to co-decision and the EP was given significantly increased powers, truly equaling those of the Council of the EU. With each treaty reform, co-decision has become the legislative process for additional issue areas. Most, but not all, decisions that can be made by **qualified majority voting** (QMV) in the Council of the EU are also subject to the co-decision procedure.

In general, co-decision can be a one-, two-, or three-stage process. If after the first reading of a legislative proposal by both the EP and the Council, there is agreement in both institutions, the proposal can be passed. This one-stage process was part of the attempt at simplification in the Treaty of Amsterdam as previously proposals were required to have at least two readings. If there is no agreement after the first reading, the Council adopts a **common position** after receiving the EP's opinion on the proposed legislation. If the EP rejects the Council's common position by an absolute majority after the second reading, the proposal fails. If the EP amends the common position by an absolute majority after the second reading and the Council does not agree on the amendments, the third stage of the co-decision procedure ensues. The third stage involves the convening of a **conciliation committee** composed of an equal number of representatives from both the Council and the EP. If agreement is reached in the conciliation committee, the proposal goes back to the Council and the EP for final adoption. If agreement cannot be reached in the conciliation committee, the proposal fails. As co-decision was established in the Treaty of Maastricht, if agreement was not reached in the conciliation committee, the proposal could still be adopted by the Council approving its common position through QMV. This possibility was eliminated in the Treaty of Amsterdam, hence the failure of the proposal if agreement is not reached and the increased legislative powers of the EP.

COCKFIELD, FRANCIS ARTHUR (1916–). Baron Cockfield is a member of the British Conservative Party. He served under Prime Minister **Margaret Thatcher** as secretary of state for trade from 1982 to 1983 and as chancellor of the Duchy of Lancaster from 1983 to 1984. Cockfield was subsequently appointed by Thatcher to the 1985–1990 **European Commission** where he was responsible for the internal market as well as vice president of the Commission.

Commissioner Cockfield was responsible for drafting the 1985 White Paper on "Completing the Internal Market" by the end of 1992 in which he outlined over 300 Commission proposals that still had to be decided by the **Council of Ministers** in order to complete the **single market** within the suggested time frame. This White Paper was an influential document in the elaboration of the **Single European Act**, which indeed included the goal of completing the single market by the end of 1992. Adopting more of a pro-European integration attitude during his tenure in the European Commission, Prime Minister Thatcher did not reappoint Cockfield for a second term. Baron Cockfield currently sits as a life peer in the House of Lords, a position he has held since 1978.

COHESION POLICY. Unique to European-style integration, the cohesion policy is designed to encourage more balanced levels of development throughout the **European Union** (EU). Cohesion became particularly prominent during the **single market** negotiations in the 1980s. In order to meet the single market requirements, each member state would have to implement economic liberalization measures, putting more stress on the weaker EU economies. As a means of ensuring that the strongest economies would not benefit at the expense of the weakest, leaders such as **Jacques Delors**, former president of the **European Commission**, and **Felipe González**, former prime minister of **Spain**, lobbied for the institutionalization of the cohesion policy and the **budgeting** of the **structural funds** needed to support it.

Prior to the May 2004 **enlargement**, Spain, **Portugal**, **Ireland**, and **Greece** were the four net beneficiaries of the structural funds. Basically these funds are transferred through the EU institutions from the contributor member states (most economically developed) to the least economically developed countries and regions. Thus, the structural funds are not only distributed to countries but also to specific regions within countries in need of development assistance.

The May 2004 enlargement significantly alters the development dynamic within the EU, considering the relatively lower levels of development of the enlargement countries compared to the pre-May 2004 EU-15. Not only does the enlargement require revisiting the cohesion policy in order to accommodate the new EU member states while not putting the others at a disadvantage, it also provides the opportunity to evaluate existing methods of implementation and to make any necessary changes. As the territory of the EU expands, territorial cohesion becomes a more difficult yet increasingly important objective to meet.

COLOMBO, EMILIO. Refer to appendix D.

COMITOLOGY. The Community legislation adopted by the **Council of the European Union** (EU) and the **European Parliament** contains specific rules regarding how the legislation is to be implemented, known as implementing measures or implementing acts. Although the **European Commission** as representative of the executive body of the EU is responsible for the implementation of legislation, in many cases the Commission must consult with committees composed of member state representatives and chaired by the Commission in order to adopt these implementing measures. This committee process and the hundreds of committees involved in it are referred to as comitology.

The committees involved in this process are normally divided into three categories: advisory committees, managerial committees, and regulatory committees. All committee opinions must be taken into account but only disagreements between the Commission and the managerial or regulatory committees are forwarded to the Council for further review.

COMMITTEE OF PERMANENT REPRESENTATIVES (COREPER). The COREPER is a **European Union** (EU) body, first recognized in the 1957 **Treaty of Rome**, and is responsible for assisting the **Council of the EU**. The COREPER is composed of the ambassadors (better known as permanent representatives) of each of the member states to the EU. Meeting in **Brussels** on a regular basis and in continuous contact with the **European Commission**, this body is instrumental in completing the preparations and establishing the agenda for the meetings of the Council (except those of the Agriculture Council). Its ability to shape the agenda and in effect its influence over the Council makes COREPER a powerful element in the EU's legislative and **decision-making** processes.

COMMITTEE OF THE REGIONS. The Committee of the Regions, one of the consultative bodies of the **European Union** (EU), was created through the **Treaty on European Union** and began operations in 1994. Not only was this body considered a means of meeting the EU objective of bringing the EU closer to its people, but also as a way in which to provide an institutionalized voice to those responsible for implementing the majority of EU legislation—the local and regional governments.

The Committee of the Regions serves as a liaison between the EU and local and regional authorities of the member states. The 317 members of this Committee are nominated by the governments of their respective member states and appointed by the **Council of the EU** to a four-year mandate. The **European Commission**, the Council of the EU and the **European Parliament** are required to consult the Committee of the Regions on issues directly related to the interests of local and regional governments as specified in the **Treaties** of **Maastricht** and **Amsterdam**. With its own internal administrative and political structure, the Committee of the Regions is responsible for providing responses to these institutions as well as initiating its own opinions on other issues considered by the Committee to be of particular interest to local and regional governments. While there is no obligation of the EU institutions to follow the Committee's recommendations, the Committee does provide a formal outlet in which local and regional authorities can be heard through direct access to the EU institutions and their policy and **decision-making** processes.

In the context of the 1 May 2004 and future **enlargements**, the **Treaty of Nice** and the **Treaty establishing a Constitution for Europe** stipulate 350 as the maximum number of members of the Committee of the Regions. In order to be eligible for Committee membership one must hold a regional or local authority electoral mandate, or be politically accountable to an elected assembly.

COMMON AGRICULTURAL POLICY (CAP). *See* AGRICULTURAL POLICY.

COMMON COMMERCIAL POLICY. *See* TRADE POLICY.

COMMON CUSTOMS TARIFF (CCT). *See* COMMON EXTERNAL TARIFF (CET).

COMMON EXTERNAL TARIFF (CET). The goal of completing the **common market** for the **European Community** (EC) was first incorporated in the 1957 **Treaty of Rome** establishing the **European Economic Community**. Although it would take several decades before actually achieving this objective, some of its elements and foundations were implemented in the earlier stages of the European integration process. The CET was established in 1968, creating one tariff for goods entering the EC regardless of which member state serves as the point of entry, and thus, completing the **customs union** for the EC. The CET is one of the main instruments of the EC's **common commercial policy**.

COMMON FOREIGN AND SECURITY POLICY (CFSP). Some form of European political integration has been the subject of community debate since the early 1950s. However, economic integration dominated the agenda of the first decades of the **European Community** (EC), and it was not until 1970 that the member states initiated **European Political Cooperation** (EPC), based on the **Davignon Report**. The objective of EPC was to better coordinate member states' **foreign policies**. Nevertheless, EPC remained fully **intergovernmental** and was not formally recognized until the **Single European Act** of 1986.

With the reorganization of integration into the **three-pillar** system of the **Treaty on European Union** (TEU), however, the institutionalization of political cooperation became a reality. The CFSP was developed into the second pillar, encouraging systematic cooperation between the member states in the field of foreign policy. The **decision-making** method was unanimity for the most part but member states could agree to cooperate within the scope of the **European Union** through **common positions** and **joint actions**.

Each treaty following the TEU has addressed the issue of enhancing the CFSP: the **High Representative for the CFSP** was created in the **Treaty of Amsterdam**; and **qualified majority voting** became the decision-making method for an increased but still limited number of issues related to CFSP in the **Treaty of Nice**. If the **Treaty establishing a Constitution for Europe** is ratified the executive position of Union Minister for Foreign Affairs will be created. In each of the reforms to the CFSP, the objectives are both to increase internal operations and improve the external visibility of CFSP. *See also* DEFENSE POLICY; EUROPEAN SECURITY AND DEFENCE POLICY; EXTERNAL RELATIONS.

COMMON MARKET. *See* SINGLE MARKET.

COMMON POSITION. There are two types of common positions in the **European Union** (EU); one is part of the **decision-making** process between the **Council of the EU** and the **European Parliament** (EP) and the other is one of the tools available in the second pillar of the EU, the **Common Foreign and Security Policy** (CFSP).

In the **cooperation** and **co-decision procedures**, the Council of the EU, taking into consideration the opinion and any proposed amendments of the EP, adopts a common position if agreement is not reached between the Council and the EP on proposed legislation after its first reading. When the co-decision procedure was first established in the **Treaty of Maastricht**, failure to reach agreement on a proposal still enabled the Council to adopt a proposal by passing the common position by a **qualified majority vote**. Although the Council still adopts a common position if the co-decision procedure goes beyond the first stage, the possibility of "overruling" the EP through the adoption of the common position was eliminated in the **Treaty of Amsterdam**, giving the EP more legislative powers.

In terms of the CFSP, a common position is adopted when all of the member states agree to act in a unified way on a particular issue falling within the second pillar of the EU. Most common positions are adopted by a unanimous vote. Once common positions are adopted, all member states are obligated to comply with their contents.

COMMON STRATEGY. A tool introduced in the **Treaty of Amsterdam**, the common strategy is used within the scope of the **Common Foreign and Security Policy** (CFSP). Common strategies are adopted by the **European Council** and establish guidelines regarding the objectives and timeframe for CFSP issues. These common strategies are implemented by the Council through the adoption of **joint actions** and **common positions**.

COMMONWEALTH OF INDEPENDENT STATES (CIS). The CIS is a group of countries composed of 12 sovereign former Soviet republics, Armenia, Azerbaijan, **Belarus**, Georgia, Kazakhstan, Kyrgyzstan, **Moldova**, **Russia**, Tajikistan, Turkmenistan, **Ukraine**, and Uzbekistan. The members of the CIS, according to its charter, are required to solve disputes peacefully, respect current borders, and allow for a unified control of nuclear weapons. Coordinating bodies of the CIS also facilitate economic cooperation between members that desire such agreements.

After the collapse of the Soviet Union in 1991, the **European Union** began to negotiate **Partnership and Cooperation Agreements** (PCAs) with the individual members of the CIS. These PCAs are framework agreements that include, among other issue areas encompassed by the EU's relations with these countries, **trade**, aid, and political dialogue. In 1991, the EU also initiated the **Technical Assistance for the Commonwealth of Independent States** (TACIS) program which has provided billions of **euros** in assistance to the CIS countries. The objectives of TACIS are helping to complete transitions to open market economies, to consolidate democratic institutions and processes, and to encourage respect for the rule of law.

COMMUNITY ASSISTANCE FOR RECONSTRUCTION, DEVELOPMENT, AND STABILITY (CARDS). Established in 2000 to provide assistance to the countries of the Western Balkans (**Albania**, **Bosnia-Herzegovina**, **Croatia**, **Serbia and Montenegro**, and the **Former Yugoslav Republic of Macedonia**), CARDS was designed to assist with reforms necessary for future membership in the **European Union** (EU). Considering the Western Balkan republics as potential future EU candidate countries, the EU developed the **Stability Pact for Southeastern Europe** and agreed to begin **Stabilization and Association Agreements** with these countries. CARDS, providing €4.6 billion to the Western Balkan countries between 2000 and 2006, is considered to be an instrument for reaching the objectives of the Stabilization and Association Process (SAP) including reconstruction, democratic stabilization, and the return of refugees; institutional and legislative development; sustainable economic and social development; and closer relations with the EU, other SAP countries, and other countries in the region.

COMMUNITY CHARTER OF THE FUNDAMENTAL SOCIAL RIGHTS OF WORKERS. *See* SOCIAL CHARTER.

COMMUNITY PLANT VARIETY OFFICE (CPVO). Established in 1994 and located in Angers, **France**, the CPVO is an **agency of the European Community**. It is responsible for registering plant variety rights. These rights provide their owners with rights valid in all of the member states of the Community.

COMPETITION POLICY. As with many related **European Community** (EC) policies, the competition policy, which was established with the 1957 **Treaty of Rome** creating the **European Economic Community**, was reborn with the **Single European Act** of 1986. With the rapid increase in mergers and acquisitions provoked by the imminent completion of the **single market**, there was a real need to ensure that the companies involved in these activities did not engage in unfair competition practices such as price fixing and production controls. Competition policy also aims to improve the welfare of consumers and the competitiveness of the European economy in international markets.

Due to the post–World War II Western European consensus that the state would have to play a significant role in the economic recovery process, there has been a tradition of state intervention in the economy and state support of so-called national champions that would lead the economic recovery and development forward. Therefore, the EC competition policy is designed to ensure fairness in both private and public business transactions.

The **European Commission** is largely responsible for monitoring and ensuring compliance with the competition policy, an exclusive EC competence. The Commission's main areas of action pertain to mergers, state aid, anti-trust, and liberalization. If advisories and warnings do not suffice, the European Commission can take questionable cases to the **European Court of Justice**.

The 2004 merger regulation gives the European Commission the right to analyze the possible impacts of mergers that would have an effect on the European market, and requires the Commission's authorization prior to the finalization of the merger. (This authority has existed since the 1989 merger regulation which was recently replaced and revised by the 2004 regulation.) The merger regulation applies to all companies that conduct business in the **European Union** (EU), regardless of their country of origin, which has caused controversy between the EU and third countries, most notably the **United States**.

CONCILIATION COMMITTEE. If no agreement is reached between the **Council of the European Union** (EU) and the **European Parliament** (EP) after the second stage of the **co-decision procedure**, a third stage ensues which entails the convening of a conciliation committee composed of an equal number of representatives from both the Council and the EP who are assisted by members of the **European Commission**. If an agreement on the proposal is reached in the form of a joint text in the conciliation committee, the proposal goes back to the Council and the EP for final adoption within a six-week time period. If agreement cannot be reached in the conciliation committee, the proposal fails.

CONFEDERAL GROUP OF THE EUROPEAN UNITED LEFT-NORDIC GREEN LEFT (GUE/NGL). The GUE/NGL is the fifth-largest **political group in the European Parliament** with members from 16 political parties and 14 **European Union** member states, including four of the May 2004 **enlargement** countries. This group was first established in 1994 as the Confederal Group of the European United Left. With the association of the Scandinavian Green parties one year later, it evolved into the GUE/NGL.

The GUE/NGL represents the non-Socialist parties of the left and is considered to be the farthest left European parliamentary group. The interests of the GUE/NGL include unemployment, poverty, equal rights, and **environmental** protection.

CONGRESS OF EUROPE. Held in May 1948 in The Hague, the Congress of Europe was attended by hundreds of prominent Europeans from across the continent. The Congress was chaired by **Winston Churchill** who had made his famous "United States of Europe" speech two years earlier at the University of Zurich. Agreement was reached on the need to have a stronger unity between the European countries. The most visible result of the Congress of Europe was the creation of the **Council of Europe**, an intergovernmental organization designed primarily to encourage cooperation between the European countries and to promote **human rights**, democracy, and the rule of law.

CONSTITUTION. *See* TREATY ESTABLISHING A CONSTITUTION FOR EUROPE.

CONSTRUCTIVE ABSTENTION. Introduced in the **Treaty of Amsterdam**, constructive abstention is a procedure that attempts to facilitate the **decision-making** process on issues of **Common Foreign and Security Policy** (CFSP). Prior to the creation of this procedure, all CFSP decisions were made by unanimity. Constructive abstention, however, allows for decisions to be made with some member states (not representing more than one-third of the weighted votes in the **Council of the European Union**) abstaining from the decision and still allow the initiative to pass and be binding on the **European Union**, with the exception of the member states that abstained from the decision.

CONSULTATION PROCEDURE. In the **Treaty of Rome** the **European Parliament** (EP) was given the right to participate in the legislative **decision-making** process in the **European Union** (EU) through the consultation procedure. Consultation is a single reading process in which the EP has the right to provide a nonbinding opinion to the **Council of the EU** in specified issue areas. Although the EP's opinion may technically be disregarded according to the rules of this procedure, the Council must wait to receive the EP's opinion, which has no time limitations, before passing a piece of legislation into law. If the Council moves forward without receiving the EP's opinion, the **European Court of Justice** may rule the law invalid as occurred with the famous *Isuglocose* case in 1980.

Since the **Single European Act**, the EP has been gaining additional legislative powers through the **cooperation** and **co-decision procedures**. As a growing number of issue areas are covered by these procedures, the use of the consultation procedure has been steadily decreasing. Consultation is, however, still used for decisions regarding **agriculture** and issues of **justice and home affairs** that are included in the first pillar of the **Treaty of Maastricht**.

CONSUMER POLICY. Although the idea of consumer protection was included as an overall objective in the **Treaty of Rome**, the first program for consumer information and protection was not adopted until 1975. The completion of the **single market** has inspired a new generation of consumer policy with the belief that the freedoms of movement should be accompanied by common levels of consumer protection and safety standards throughout the **European Union** (EU).

A General Product Safety Directive was adopted in 1992, and revised in January 2004, to include new and stricter rules for defective product recalls as well as general safety rules for additional consumer products. Complementing this general Directive are individual product measures for articles such as toys and cosmetics, to name but a few. In 2002, a consumer policy strategy was adopted by the **European Commission** for the period 2002–2006 with three main objectives: a high level of consumer protection; effective enforcement of consumer protection rules, and proper involvement of consumer organizations in EU policies.

CONVERGENCE CRITERIA. The adoption of a common currency for the member states of the **European Union** was not a matter taken lightly on the national or Community levels. In order to encourage passage of the **Treaty on European Union** (TEU), a **euro opt-out** clause was included for the **United Kingdom** and **Denmark** following the Danes rejection of treaty ratification in the first public referendum. At the same time, **euro zone** membership for the other member states was not a guarantee. Given the magnitude and virtual irreversibility of the third stage of **Economic and Monetary Union**, the TEU includes convergence criteria that all countries must meet before adopting the euro as their national currency.

The convergence criteria were designed to promote the long-term strength, reliability, and sustainability of the euro not only as the internal legal tender of the euro zone countries but also as a competitive international currency. The main elements of the convergence criteria are price stability (an inflation rate within 1.5% of the average inflation rate of the three member states with the lowest levels of inflation); currency stability (adherence to the **exchange rate mechanism**); interest rate convergence (long-term interest rates within two percentage points of the average rates of the three best performing member states); and budgetary discipline (a deficit less than 3% GDP and public debt less than 60% GDP).

COOPERATION PROCEDURE. Granted to the **European Parliament** (EP) in the **Single European Act** (SEA), the cooperation procedure increased the EP's legislative powers. The cooperation procedure involves two readings of legislation proposed by the **European Commission**. The EP provides its opinion and suggested amendments of the proposal to the **Council of the European Union**. The Council then develops a **common position**, including reasons for omitting suggested changes from the EP. Following this first stage, the EP has the opportunity to reject or amend the Council's common position through an absolute majority vote. In order for the Council to overturn the EP's decision after the second reading, the vote in the Council must be unanimous.

In the SEA 10 issue areas were covered by the cooperation procedure. The number of areas was extended to 14 in the **Treaty of Maastricht**. Rather than increasing this number once again in the **Treaty of Amsterdam**, the EP was given real co-decision power with the Council and the number of issues covered by the **co-decision procedure** was extended. Currently the cooperation procedure is used exclusively to make decisions regarding **Economic and Monetary Union**.

COPENHAGEN CRITERIA. The fall of the **Berlin Wall** and the collapse of the Soviet Union sparked a new dynamic in European and international relations, one that would eventually drastically alter the composition and scope of the **European Union** (EU). Following the difficult passage of the **Treaty on European Union**, attention finally turned to what became the inevitable **enlargement** to Central and Eastern Europe. At the **European Council** of Copenhagen in June 1993, the EU formally declared that those **Central and Eastern European countries** that wished to join the EU would have the opportunity to do so, conditional upon the fulfillment of certain criteria. The EU established several conditions these countries would have to meet before being considered for membership. Known as the Copenhagen criteria, these requirements are: democratic institutions and processes; respect for **human rights** including minority rights; functioning open market economies; and the ability to adopt the **acquis communautaire** into national legislation, all of which are non-negotiable in terms of EU accession.

COPPE, ALBERT. Refer to appendix B.

COSTA V. ENEL. Through several of its key judgments, the **European Court of Justice** (ECJ) has played a significant role in the institutionalization of **European Community (EC) law**. *Costa v. ENEL* was first introduced in **Italy**'s national court system. ENEL, an Italian electricity company had been nationalized by the Italian government and Costa, a shareholder in the company, refused to pay his electricity bill on the basis that the nationalization of the company was illegal according to EC law. The Italian court sent the case to the ECJ for a preliminary ruling and the ECJ passed a judgment in 1964 reinforcing the fact that by creating the European Communities, the member states had restricted some of their sovereign rights in certain fields, and that in so doing, they allowed a body of law to be created at the European level which would be binding on all member states and their residents. Thus, the ECJ established the autonomy of EC law as well as its **supremacy** over the national laws of the EC's member states.

COTONOU AGREEMENT. On 23 June 2000, representatives of the **European Union** (EU) member states and the **African–Caribbean–Pacific (ACP) countries** signed the new ACP-EU Agreement, commonly known as the Cotonou Agreement, in Cotonou, Benin. This agreement, revised every five years, is based on the experience of 25 years (1975–2000) of successive **Lomé Conventions** that had previously governed ACP-EU relations, and establishes a 20-year framework for the future of institutionalized relations between these two groups of countries. The agreement entered into force on 1 April 2003 and represents a major component of the EU's **external**

relations and particularly of its **development cooperation policy**. In this respect, the Cotonou Agreement includes but goes beyond the traditional preferential trade agreements and economic aid. In fact, mixed results from the Lomé Conventions, notably on the effect of EU measures on poverty reduction in the ACP countries, coupled with new domestic and international challenges provoked a reassessment of this partnership, leading to post-Lomé negotiations beginning in September 1998 and resulting in the Cotonou Agreement.

In order to address some of the underlying problems in the less developed and developing countries, political and institutional concerns would also have to be addressed. In response, the Cotonou Agreement is based on five pillars of partnership: a comprehensive political dimension including **human rights** and good **governance**; participatory approaches; a strengthened focus on poverty reduction; a new framework for economic and trade cooperation; and a reform of financial cooperation. This enhanced partnership agreement has a **budget** of €13.5 billion for the first five years and is designed to provide additional benefits to a greater number of people in the ACP countries.

COUNCIL OF EUROPE. The most visible result of the **Congress of Europe** held in The Hague in 1948 and attended by hundreds of prominent Europeans was the Council of Europe: an **intergovernmental** organization designed primarily to encourage cooperation and increased unity between the European countries and to promote **human rights**, democracy, and the rule of law. Founded in 1949 by its 10 original members (**Belgium**, **Denmark**, **France**, **Ireland**, **Italy**, **Luxembourg**, **Netherlands**, **Norway**, **Portugal**, and the **United Kingdom**), there are now 46 countries in the Council of Europe. Headquartered in Strasbourg, France, the loose institutional framework of the Council of Europe consists of the Committee of Ministers, the Parliamentary Assembly, the Congress of Local and Regional Authorities, and a General Secretariat.

One of the greatest achievements of the Council of Europe has been its work to promote, monitor, and assist with the protection of human rights throughout Europe. The **European Convention for the Protection of Human Rights and Fundamental Freedoms**, which includes the establishment of the European Court of Human Rights, was adopted by the Council of Europe in 1950. Human rights in the

European Union (EU) are based on this Convention, which all of the EU member states have ratified. Since the beginning of the political transitions in the **Central and Eastern European countries** in 1989, much of the Council of Europe's general attention and work in the area of human rights has focused on these countries.

COUNCIL OF MINISTERS. *See* COUNCIL OF THE EUROPEAN UNION.

COUNCIL OF THE EUROPEAN UNION. Known as the Council of Ministers prior to the **Treaty on European Union**, and commonly referred to as simply the Council, the Council of the European Union (EU) is the main **decision-making** body of the EU and was created through its founding treaties. This institution represents the interests of the member states and is composed of their national ministers who have the power and responsibility to make binding decisions and commitments on behalf of their respective member state governments. While the Council of the EU is considered one institution, its configuration changes depending on the particular issue to be decided. In other words, finance ministers of each member state meet in the **Economic and Finance Council** (ECOFIN) to discuss issues related to economic and financial affairs while **environment** ministers meet in the "Environment Council" to discuss environmental issues. There are a total of nine different Council configurations: General Affairs and External Relations; Economic and Financial Affairs; **Justice and Home Affairs**; **Employment**, **Social Policy**, Health and Consumer Affairs; Competitiveness; **Transport**, Telecommunications and **Energy**; **Agriculture** and **Fisheries**; **Environment**; and Education, Youth, and Culture.

The presidency of the Council is held by each one of the member states for six months on a rotating basis. The minister from the country holding the presidency during this semester chairs the Council meetings, takes charge of the agenda, and facilitates negotiations for the legislative and decision-making processes.

Based on proposals of the **European Commission**, the Council negotiates and makes decisions on the future direction of EU policy, effectively deciding (at times in cooperation with the **European Parliament**) those proposals that will become **European Community**

(EC) **law**. There are two ways in which decisions are made in the Council, depending on the issue being decided. In most issue areas, especially those related to the **single market**, decisions are made by **qualified majority voting**. Decisions dealing with issues considered highly sensitive such as many of those within the **Common Foreign and Security Policy** must be made unanimously, effectively granting veto power to every EU member state.

While the members of the Council are regularly occupied with domestic and/or international issues and responsibilities as ministers of their national governments, the **Committee of Permanent Representatives** (COREPER), composed of the ambassadors of each of the member states to the EU, administratively assists the Council. This Committee meets in **Brussels** on a weekly basis and prepares a great deal of the Council's work and agenda.

Other committees and working groups help prepare the work of both the Council and COREPER. Council Committees generally cover issues similar to those in the main formations of the Council, such as energy, **competition**, political and security, economic and financial, and are usually composed of high level officials from the corresponding ministries of the member states. Working groups normally deal with specific and/or technical issues within pieces of proposed legislation.

The Council is headquartered in the Justus Lipsius building in Brussels.

COURT OF AUDITORS. Established in 1977 with the mandate to examine the financial transactions of all **European Union** (EU) institutions and member state governments responsible for EU budgetary incomes and/or expenditures, the Court of Auditors was recognized as a major institution in the **Treaty on European Union**. As the EU along with its **budget** continued to enlarge, coupled with allegations of fraud and mismanagement, the Court of Auditors was entrusted to detect and report financial irregularities.

This independent EU institution located in **Luxembourg** has 25 members, one from each of the member states. Justices are nominated by their member state governments and appointed by the **European Council** after non-binding consultations with the **European**

Parliament. They serve six-year renewable terms, and each one is responsible for auditing a specific section of the EU's yearly budget.

The **European Commission** is responsible for the implementation of the EU budget. However, for the majority of EU expenditure, represented by the **Common Agricultural Policy** and the **cohesion policy**, the management and control of funds is undertaken in cooperation with member states. Over the years the Court of Auditors has discovered that member state governments have occasionally been the source of financial inconsistencies.

COURT OF FIRST INSTANCE (CFI) OF THE EUROPEAN COMMUNITIES. Created in 1989 after the **Single European Act** provided the basis for the establishment of a new judicial body and the **Council of the European Union** agreed to a proposal submitted by the **European Court of Justice** (ECJ), the CFI was intended to ease the burden of the ECJ's increasing workload. The CFI has 25 judges, one from each of the member states of the **European Union**. The judges are appointed for six-year renewable terms. Although the CFI has no permanent **advocates-general**, any one of the judges can serve as such for a case in which they are not part of the deciding chamber. Most cases of the CFI are decided in chambers of between three and five judges. In certain specific circumstances in which a question arises regarding the points of law in a particular case decided by the CFI, the case may be appealed to the ECJ.

The jurisdiction of the CFI has steadily increased since its creation. When it first began operation in 1989, the CFI could decide cases regarding **competition policy**, the **European Coal and Steel Community**, and staff cases. With the **Treaty of Maastricht** the CFI became responsible for all cases brought by individuals and companies with the exception of antidumping cases. The CFI's authority was extended even further in the **Treaty of Nice** to include most **direct actions** and a limited number of specifically outlined **preliminary rulings**.

COURT OF JUSTICE OF THE EUROPEAN COMMUNITIES. *See* EUROPEAN COURT OF JUSTICE (ECJ).

COX, PAT (1952–). An Irish politician, formerly a member of the Irish Progressive Democrats Party, Pat Cox was a member of the

European Parliament (EP) from 1989 to 2004. From 1998 to 2002 he was the president of the European Liberal, Democratic, and Reformist Party, which since 14 July 2004 has been a part of the **Group of the Alliance of Liberals and Democrats for Europe**, the third-largest political group in the EP. Cox resigned from this position when he became President of the EP on 15 January 2002. Refer to appendix D.

CRESSON, EDITH (1934–). A member of the Socialist Party, Edith Cresson became **France**'s first female Fifth Republic prime minister under the presidency of **François Mitterrand** in 1991. As a result of her high levels of public disapproval, she was replaced one year later in June 1992.

From 1995 to 1999 Edith Cresson was a member of the **European Commission**, responsible for Research, Science, and Technology. The Committee of Independent Experts that was formed by the **European Parliament** to investigate the conduct of the **Santer** Commission found that Cresson had engaged in favoritism in the issuance of contracts under her responsibility. Despite the accusations and evidence uncovered in the report, Cresson refused to resign from her post in the Commission. The result was the en masse resignation of the Santer Commission in 1999, avoiding an EP vote of censure and the forced resignation of the **European Union**'s executive body.

CROATIA. Although the Republic of Croatia declared its independence from the **former Yugoslavia** in 1991 and received international diplomatic recognition from **Germany** by December of that year, it was not until 1995 that the intermittent fighting with the Serbs and the war had come to an end. Nevertheless, since 1991, the **European Community** has been providing Croatia with financial and **humanitarian aid**. In 2001, Croatia signed a **Stabilization and Association Agreement** with the **European Union** (EU) and began receiving funding from the **Community Assistance for Reconstruction, Development, and Stability in the Balkans** (CARDS), designed to assist with reforms necessary for future integration in the EU. On 21 February 2003, Croatia submitted its application for membership in the EU, and on 18 June 2004, it was granted official candidacy status. Accession negotiations were postponed in March 2005 due to an EU perception that Croatia was not fully cooperating with the United Nations International War Crimes Tribunal for the **Former Yugoslavia** (UNICTY). Refer to appendix A.

CROCODILE CLUB. Originally meeting in the Crocodile Restaurant in Strasbourg, **France**, where the **European Parliament** (EP) holds its plenary sessions, the Crocodile Club was organized in 1980 by **Altiero Spinelli**, one of the most avid supporters of European integration. Participants in the club whose membership significantly increased over the years agreed to the importance of reforming and stimulating the process of European integration. By 1981, many of Spinelli's Crocodile Club colleagues formed the Institutional Affairs Committee in the EP, proposing and drafting reforms that resulted by the end of 1983 in the Draft Treaty establishing the European Union. The treaty was passed overwhelmingly in the EP, and although it was not accepted by the member states, it did serve as an impetus for the resurgence of European integration, evidenced by the **Single European Act** followed by the **Treaty on European Union**.

CULTURAL COOPERATION. First formally and legally recognized in the **Treaty on European Union**, cultural cooperation is intended to heighten awareness of the individual member states' cultural diversity while concurrently promoting Europe's common cultural heritage. Following several pilot projects and the implementation of three cultural programs between 1996 and 1999, the **European Union** (EU) launched Culture 2000 which lasts until 2006 and has a **budget** of €236 million. This is the principle cultural program of the EU and its objectives include contributing to the establishment of a European cultural area; developing artistic and literary creation; promoting knowledge of European history and culture; developing heritage sites and cultural collections of European importance; and stimulating intercultural dialogue and social integration. The **European Commission** has proposed renewing the program for another seven years, from 2007 to 2013.

The EU's Capitals of Culture program was actually started in 1985, and currently receives funding from the Culture 2000 budget to finance cultural events and exhibitions in the one or two cities designated as cultural capitals of Europe each year. The 2004 European capitals of culture were Lille, **France**, and Genoa, **Italy**. Cork, **Ireland**, is the European cultural capital for 2005; Patras, **Greece** has been designated for 2006; and **Luxembourg** and Sibiu, **Romania**, for 2007.

As an EU competence, cultural cooperation includes the EU providing economic support to cultural industries to help them compete in international markets. Furthermore, cultural elements have been included in other EU issue areas such as **audio-visual** and **education policies**.

CUSTOMS UNION. A stage beyond a **free trade area** in terms of **regional integration**, a customs union represents the removal of all internal **trade** barriers between members as well as a **common external tariff** (CET) on all goods entering the area regardless of their point of entry. The **European Community** (EC) became a customs union in 1968 when the CET was set and all internal barriers on industrial trade were eliminated. The customs union is a significant element of the completed **common market**, a goal that was achieved by the EC by 1 January 1993.

CYPRUS. A former British colony, Cyprus gained its independence on 16 August 1960. This East Mediterranean island has been divided since 1974, when **Turkey** invaded and occupied the northern third in response to a **Greek** military coup against the Cypriot government. Since 1983, Turkey is the only country in the world to recognize the self-proclaimed independence of the Turkish Republic of Northern Cyprus.

In November 2002, United Nations (UN) Secretary General Kofi Annan presented a comprehensive resolution for the reunification of Cyprus, envisioning a two-part federation presided over by a rotating presidency. One month later at the **European Council** in Copenhagen, a reunited Cyprus was invited to join the **European Union** (EU) in 2004, contingent upon the acceptance of the UN peace plan without which only the Greek–Cypriot–led portion of the island would be granted EU membership. Negotiations for the settlement plan were long and strenuous; time and again, deals were brokered and subsequently rejected. On 24 April 2004, in an eleventh-hour attempt to achieve a united EU entry, dual referendums were held on the UN reunification plan. Although Turkish Cypriots approved the plan, the Greek majority overwhelmingly rejected it, and on 1 May 2004, only the Greek–Cypriot–governed Republic of Cyprus became an EU member state.

Given its strategic location, one of Cyprus' objectives within the EU is productive participation in the **Euro–Mediterranean Partnership** of which it has been a member since 1995. Strengthening economic and diplomatic ties with its regional neighbors is expected to be mutually beneficial for Cyprus and the EU. *See also* CENTRAL AND EASTERN EUROPEAN COUNTRIES (CEECs). Refer to appendix A.

CZECH REPUBLIC. On 1 January 1993, the former Czechoslovak Federation was dissolved and replaced with separate and independent Czech and **Slovak Republics**, the result of a diplomatic and peaceful agreement. The Czech Republic's formal application for **European Union** (EU) membership was submitted on 17 January 1996, and the country quickly emerged as a frontrunner among the candidate states from Central and Eastern Europe. In July 1997, it was one of five countries chosen to begin "fast track" accession negotiations.

On 1 May 2004, the Czech Republic became an EU member state. In a national referendum held in June 2003, the Czechs had demonstrated their overwhelming support for EU membership. Public support and interest has subsequently waned as evidenced in the low voter turnout (28 percent) in the **European Parliament** elections of June 2004.

Of particular significance to the Czech Republic's EU membership is its comparatively long geographic border with **Germany** as well as relations between these two countries. Political and legal concerns dating back to the Nazi regime and controversy over the Sudetenland loom over the German–Czech relationship. Not wanting the past to pose an obstacle to future progress, however, both countries have committed to strengthening their political ties and increasing cooperation. Welcomed as a sign of improved understanding by the EU, the Czech–German Declaration on Mutual Relations and their Future Development was signed on 21 January 1997. Bilateral economic exchanges between Germany and the Czech Republic are already quite solid and continue to intensify. Refer to appendix A.

– D –

DANKERT, PIET (1934–2003). A member of the social democratic Labour Party in **The Netherlands**, Piet Dankert was elected to the lower house of the Dutch parliament in 1968. In 1979 he became a member of the **European Parliament** (EP) to which he was elected president and served in this post from 1982 to 1984.

Under the 1989–1994 premiership of Ruud Lubbers, Dankert served as the secretary of state for European matters, a particularly critical role when the Dutch held the presidency of the Council and the chairmanship of the **intergovernmental conference** that would lead to the **Treaty on European Union** in the second semester of 1991. A supporter of deeper European integration, Dankert proposed to change the draft treaty in a way that would eliminate the **three pillar** system and create a unitary structure. His proposal was overwhelmingly rejected by the member states. Dankert served a second term in the 1995–1999 EP. Refer to appendix D.

DAVIGNON, ETIENNE (1932–). Etienne Davignon was, as **Belgian** foreign minister, largely responsible for the "Report on the Problems of Political Unification," known as the **Luxembourg** or **Davignon Report**. On 27 October 1970, in a meeting in Luxembourg, the foreign ministers of the **European Community** (EC) member states adopted this report which is considered to be the foundation of **European Political Cooperation**.

Davignon was also a key figure in garnering support for the completion of the **single market** and in attempting to increase the EC's competitive advantage in the 1980s. He was the commissioner responsible for industrial affairs and vice president of the **European Commission** from 1981 to 1985. Davignon was successful in convincing CEOs of major European manufacturing companies of the benefits of the **single market** and European cooperation in key areas. Largely as a result of Davignon's efforts, a research program was initiated, the **European Strategic Programme for Research** and **Development in Information and Technology** (ESPRIT), including manufacturers, small firms, and universities throughout the **European Union**.

DAVIGNON REPORT. On 27 October 1970, in a meeting in **Luxembourg**, the foreign ministers of the **European Community** member states adopted the "Report on the Problems of Political Unification," known as the Luxembourg or Davignon Report. **Etienne Davignon**, the **Belgian** foreign minister at the time was the chief architect and compiler of this report, which is considered to be the foundation of **European Political Cooperation**.

While the institutional structure established in the Davignon Report was weak, it represented the creation of an environment in which common diplomatic and **foreign policy** perceptions and objectives could eventually be developed. Coordination of member state foreign policies would be supported through regular exchanges of information during the required biannual meetings of the foreign ministers and more frequent lower level official meetings.

DECISION-MAKING. The two main decision-making bodies of the **European Union** (EU) are the **Council of the EU** and the **European Parliament** (EP), while the **European Commission** holds the power of legislative initiative in the first pillar and presents the members of these two institutions with proposals for legislation. Upon receipt of these proposals, there are three main procedures through which the Council and the EP share decision-making processes and responsibilities: consultation, assent, and co-decision.

The **consultation procedure** requires the Council to obtain the EP's opinion on proposed legislation before the Council can enact it into **law**. There are no stipulated time limits associated with this phase of the procedure, and therefore, the EP is able to exert its legislative influence through the power of delay. During this time, the EP can also encourage the European Commission to make amendments to the proposed legislation which would then have to be considered by the Council as well. Although the Council must wait to receive the EP's opinion, it is not bound to accept it or incorporate it in the final decision. Some of the policies decided through the consultation procedure are **agriculture**; visas, asylum and immigration; **competition** rules; and **enhanced cooperation**.

The **assent procedure** is one in which the EP has shared legislative powers, albeit restricted. It has the authority to reject or accept a Commission proposal in its entirety but cannot amend or delay the legislation. Policies that are decided through this procedure include **structural funds** and amending statutes of the **European Central Bank**. In addition to these legislative measures, the EP's assent is required in order to proceed with **enlargement** processes and association agreements.

Today, the most common decision-making procedure between the EP and the Council is **co-decision**, a process of readings, amendments, and possible conciliation between the two institutions in the event they have not reached an agreement. In the **Treaty on European Union**, the EP was given co-decision powers over most issues in the first pillar, however, this was an extremely complicated process and the Council maintained the prerogative to pass legislation in the form existent prior to the **conciliation committee** without the EP's consent. In the **Treaty of Amsterdam**, co-decision was reformed to increase the number of competences to be decided through this procedure; to give the EP real shared legislative powers with the Council (i.e., both institutions must agree on the final version of the proposed legislation, or it is rejected); and, to make this procedure easier and more efficient, though it remains complex. *See also* VOTING.

DECISIONS. A type of **European Union** (EU) law, decisions do not have general applicability but are binding on the member state, entity, or individual to which it is directed. Decisions may be made by the **European Commission** and are usually more specific such as a final evaluation regarding a merger in a competition case, or they may be made by the **Council of the EU** and the **European Parliament** through the **co-decision procedure** in which case they tend to be more general, for example, in the area of **justice and home affairs**.

DEEPENING. Including additional competences in the process of European integration is referred to as deepening. This means that an increased number of issue areas are encompassed within the treaties of the **European Union** (EU), and **decision-making** with regard to these policies is facilitated. There has been an ongoing debate as to whether deepening is complementary or contradictory to **widening**, or **enlarging** the EU.

DEFENSE POLICY. There has long been a consensus amongst the **European Union** (EU) member states on developing a stronger defense policy, but progress has been plagued by constant disagreement regarding its scope and mechanisms. The **Common Foreign and Security Policy** (CFSP) was incorporated into the **Treaty on European Union** (TEU) to complement the EU's economic integration and influence in the international community, yet this second pillar of TEU has remained the most **intergovernmental** and least integrated.

Specific national defense interests of each of the member states have complicated the creation of a common defense policy. For example, while some of the European countries maintain neutrality, others are committed to their Atlantic partners, and still others focus on the east, a situation not conducive to integration in this sensitive issue area. Nevertheless, the inability of the EU to successfully contain the outbreak of violence on its own borders in the **former Yugoslavia** demonstrated the continued need to enhance European defense capabilities.

At the Cologne Summit on 3 June 1999, an agreement was reached on a common defense strategy which was based on the development of a **European Security and Defence Policy** (ESDP) as a part of the CFSP. The ESDP is intended to encourage deeper European defense integration. *See also* FOREIGN AND SECURITY POLICY.

DEHAENE, JEAN-LUC (1940–). A Christian Democratic politician from **Belgium**, Jean-Luc Dehaene was minister of social affairs and institutional reform from 1981 until 1988 when he became Belgium's deputy prime minister. Dehaene served two terms as prime minister, from 1992 to 1995 and from 1995 to 1999. During his first administration he was considered the leading candidate to replace **Jacques Delors** as the president of the 1995–1999 **European Commission**. **John Major** vetoed Dehaene's nomination, considering him too federalist for the post. A compromise was reached and **Jacques Santer** of **Luxembourg** was appointed president.

After his last administration as Belgian prime minister, Dehaene remained active in Belgian and European politics. In 1999, he chaired a committee of "wise men" appointed by Commission President **Romano Prodi** to write a report on the institutional effects of the impending **enlargement** to the **Central and Eastern European countries**. Guy Verhofstadt, who became the Belgian prime minister following Dehaene's second administration as premier, nominated Dehaene to be vice-chairman of the **European Convention** responsible for drafting the **Treaty establishing a Constitution for Europe**, a position he would hold for the duration of the convention from February 2002 to June 2003. In 2004 Dehaene was elected to the **European Parliament** and is a member of the **Group of the European People's Party (Christian Democrats) and European Democrats**.

DELORS, JACQUES (1925–). Born in Paris, Jacques Delors is a veteran of **France**'s government in the economic, political, and banking sectors. Delors became a member of the French Socialist Party in 1974, was elected to the **European Parliament** in 1979, and was Chairman of the Economic and Monetary Committee until May 1981. In May 1981, Jacques Delors became the French minister of economics and finance, a post he held until July 1984. He was President of the **European Commission** from 1985 to 1995, and is considered one of the institution's most influential presidents.

During Delors' mandate, the **European Community** and its member states ratified the **Single European Act** and virtually completed the **single market**. **Economic and Monetary Union** was included in the **Treaty on European Union**, which was also ratified during his presidential administration of the Commission. Furthermore, following the fall of the **Berlin Wall** and the collapse of the Soviet Union, the **European Union** agreed to open its doors to the **Central and Eastern European countries** based on their fulfillment of the **Copenhagen criteria**.

In 1996, Jacques Delors founded the Groupement d'Études et de Recherches "Notre Europe," a prestigious think tank based in Paris. Refer to appendix B.

DELORS REPORT. In June 1988 the **European Council** established a committee, chaired by then President of the European Commission

Jacques Delors and consisting of top central bank officials from the then 12 member states as well as independent experts to develop and propose a plan for the construction of **Economic and Monetary Union** (EMU). Released in April 1989, the Report on Economic and Monetary Union, commonly referred to as the Delors Report, outlines the elements of Economic and Monetary Union and suggests that EMU would best be achieved through a three-stage process. The Delors Report, including the idea of the three-stage transition, provided the basis for EMU as incorporated in the **Treaty on European Union**.

DEMOCRATIC DEFICIT. The democratic deficit is a concept principally invoked in the argument that the **European Union** (EU) suffers from a lack of democracy, a low level of accountability, and seems inaccessible to the citizens because of its complex method of operations. Realizing how distanced the European government was from the citizens of the member states and as the European integration process progressed, there has been a concerted effort to bring the EU closer to the people through more openness, transparency, and accountability, as well as increased powers for the **European Parliament** (EP). Nevertheless, the EU's institutional and **decision-making** framework maintains significant elements of a democratic deficit.

The EU has only one directly elected institution, the EP, yet it is the least powerful when acting independently due to the EU's **decision-making** procedures. The **Council of the EU** is the EU's main decision-making body. Furthermore, once decisions regarding **single market** policies were made at the EU level by **qualified majority voting**, national parliaments of the EU member states lost substantial decision-making powers in these areas. **Intergovernmental conferences**, due to their nature of negotiating what are still considered to be international treaties, reserve the right to privately conduct their business of major EU treaty reforms.

Increasing democratic legitimacy and the transparency of the EU's institutions was given specific consideration in the 2001 **Laeken Declaration**, in which the **European Convention** was first proposed. This Convention was open and public, an attempt to bring the European people closer to the integration process, and make progress toward reducing the democratic deficit.

DENMARK. A member of the **European Free Trade Association** (EFTA) since 1960, the Kingdom of Denmark first applied for **European Community** (EC) membership in 1961 along with **Ireland**, **Norway**, and the **United Kingdom** (UK). Denmark's application, however, was effectively suspended in conjunction with French President **Charles de Gaulle**'s veto of the UK's EC accession. It was not until de Gaulle's resignation in 1969 that the French government lifted its objections under the leadership of **Georges Pompidou**. On 1 January 1973, Denmark officially became a member of the EC along with Ireland and the UK in the first of five **enlargements**.

Based on policies and attitudes regarding European integration since membership, the Danes have earned a reputation as "reluctant" Europeans. In a national referendum held on 2 June 1992, Danish voters rejected ratification of the **Treaty on European Union**. Later that year, in order to encourage a change in the **public opinion**, the government negotiated the Edinburgh Agreement in which Denmark was granted four **opt-outs** to European integration in the areas of **defense policy**, the third stage of **Economic and Monetary Union**, legal cooperation under the **Schengen Agreement**, and some **Justice and Home Affairs** cooperation. The Treaty finally took effect on 1 November 1993 following ratification by all member states, including Denmark. Today, Denmark is one of the three pre-2004 enlargement **European Union** (EU) member states that has not adopted the **euro** as its national currency, yet there is still hope for developing broad-based support for the common currency among the Danish citizens.

While Denmark may be perceived as passive, or even negative regarding these issues, it has taken a more active approach toward other EU-related policies. For example, the Danes energetically participate in the **Common Agricultural Policy** while trying to reform it, **social policy**, **employment policy**, and **environmental policy**. Denmark generally supported the enlargement to the **Central and Eastern European countries** and it was during the Danish **EU presidency** of the second semester 2002 that the accession negotiations with the candidate countries were concluded. Refer to appendix A.

DEVELOPMENT POLICY. The **European Union** (EU) and its member states provide the most official international development aid. The EU's development policy is predominantly carried out through **trade** and aid—lowering and in many cases eliminating barriers to trade with the EU for the developing countries, and providing direct technical and financial assistance to these countries. The overriding objectives of the EU's development policy are to support **sustainable development**; reduce poverty; help integrate the developing countries into the modern global economy; and promote democracy, **governance**, and respect for **human rights**.

Much of the EU's development assistance is directed toward the **African–Caribbean–Pacific** (ACP) countries, a group of 78 states, most of which are ex-colonies of the EU member states with which the EU sustains a special relationship. Institutionalized relations between the **European Community** (EC) and the less developed countries that would become part of the ACP began in 1963 with the **Yaoundé Conventions**, succeeded by a series of EC-ACP **Lomé Conventions** that began in 1975. The current framework for the EU-ACP relations is the **Cotonou Agreement**, which was signed in 2000 and went into force in 2003; it establishes a 20-year framework for the future relations between these two groups of countries. Financing for the Cotonou Agreement comes from the **European Development Fund**. Loans from the **European Investment Bank** are also available to help support all the developing countries and the objectives of the EU's development policy.

In addition to its relations with the ACP countries, the EU provides bilateral development assistance, including food, emergency, and humanitarian aid. The **European Community Humanitarian Aid Office**, created in 1992, is responsible for the administration of this aid.

The EU also has a Generalized System of Preferences by which developing countries obtain duty-free access to the EU's market for industrial and, more limitedly, agricultural goods. The Everything But Arms program was adopted in 2001, giving the world's least developed countries unlimited access (although some products are still going through a transition period) to the EU market, with the only exception being the importation of arms.

DIRECT ACTIONS. There are two ways to bring a case before the judicial institutions of the **European Union** (EU): **preliminary rulings** and direct actions. Direct actions involve an individual, company, member state, or EU institution claiming they have been treated unfairly. Prior to 1989, the **European Court of Justice** (ECJ) heard all preliminary ruling and direct action cases. In 1989, the **Court of First Instance (CFI) of the European Communities** was created to help ease the workload of the ECJ. Since its creation, the CFI has been given successive increases in its jurisdiction and the **Treaty of Nice** provides the CFI with the authority to hear most direct action cases.

DIRECT EFFECT. A fundamental principle of **European Community (EC) law** firmly established in the 1963 *Van Gend en Loos* case, direct effect means that the terms of the treaties (as well as most secondary legislation) apply directly to entities and individuals within the member states whether or not the member state has transposed the EC law into its national legislation.

DIRECTIVES. A type of **European Union** law, directives are binding on the member states to which they are directed. Directives do not specify but rather allow the member state governments to choose the method they deem appropriate to implement the directive in their particular country. Directives do, however, stipulate the final result and the date by which it must be achieved.

DOHA ROUND. In November 2001, the **World Trade Organization** ministerial meeting was held in Doha, Qatar. The main objectives of the meeting were to increase the liberalization of markets, negotiate agreements better suited to the developing countries, and start a new round of dialogue with the aim of reaching additional agreements.

The **European Union** (EU) has several of its own goals in the Doha Round including those related to **agriculture**, the **environment**, and labor standards. Although some compromises have been reached on agriculture and the environment (not always in favor of the EU's expectations), significant discussion on the issue of labor standards has been postponed.

DONNER, ANDREAS MATTHIAS. Refer to appendix F.

DOOGE REPORT. The Dooge Committee was established in 1984, based on a proposal by French President **François Mitterrand**, with a mandate to seek ways in which the institutions of the **European**

Community could be reformed in order to improve its efficiency both in the economic and political fields. Named after its chairman, former **Irish** foreign minister James Dooge, the Dooge Ad Hoc Committee on Institutional Reform presented its final report in 1985 arguing for facilitated **decision-making** processes, particularly for issues related to the **single market**, and an **intergovernmental conference** (IGC) for treaty reform. The Dooge Report was not unanimously accepted by the member states; however, it did provide impetus for a revitalization of the European integration process and the IGC that would lead to the **Single European Act**.

DRAFT EUROPEAN ACT. *See* GENSCHER–COLOMBO PLAN.

DRAFT TREATY ESTABLISHING THE EUROPEAN UNION. *See* CROCODILE CLUB.

DUBLIN GROUP. An informal group of officials responsible for the coordination of the external aspects of drug policies, the Dublin Group consists of representatives from all of the **European Union** (EU) member states, the **European Commission**, the **United States**, Canada, Australia, **Japan**, and **Norway**. The United Nations Office on Drugs and Crime also participates and the Secretariat of the Council of the EU acts as the secretary of the Group. The Group seeks to coordinate international action in the fight against the cultivation, production, trafficking and abuse of drugs. It was established in 1990 and meets on a semi-annual basis in **Brussels**.

DUE, OLE. Refer to appendix F.

DUISENBERG, WIM. *See* EUROPEAN CENTRAL BANK (ECB).

DUVIEUSART, JEAN-PIERRE. Refer to appendix D.

– E –

ECONOMIC AND FINANCE COUNCIL (ECOFIN). One of the nine configurations of the **Council of the European Union**,

ECOFIN is composed of the economics and/or finance ministers of each one of the member states. Along with the **General Affairs Council**, ECOFIN is one of the most influential of the Council formations. The completion of **Economic and Monetary Union** (EMU) improved and guaranteed ECOFIN's status. ECOFIN is a key element of EMU and as such assists in, among other associated obligations, establishing guidelines and coordinating macroeconomic policies. Since 2002, ECOFIN has also been responsible for the **European Union**'s **budget**.

ECONOMIC AND MONETARY UNION (EMU). The international economic crises of the early 1970s prompted European leaders to discuss the completion of EMU by 1980, a goal incorporated in the 1971 **Werner Report** but that was ultimately unattainable. It was not until several years after the signing of the **Single European Act** that the current EMU was proposed by **Jacques Delors** under the assumption that the **single market** would not be complete without a single currency.

President of the **European Commission** from 1985 to 1995, Jacques Delors was one of the most involved and influential actors in garnering acceptance for EMU. In the late 1980s, he headed a committee to determine the best approach to implementing this comprehensive policy. The conclusions emphasized that a gradual progression toward reaching the final goal would provide the best results and enable the member states to implement the necessary policies to meet the economic **convergence criteria**. Therefore, the **Delors Report** (1989) suggested a three-stage process for the completion of EMU. An **Intergovernmental Conference** on EMU and European Political Union was held in 1990, resulting in the inclusion of EMU as part of the first pillar of the **Treaty on European Union**.

Using the Delors Report as a guideline, EMU did proceed in three stages, similar but not identical to those proposed in the Report. In Stage I, the member states engaged in increased coordination of macroeconomic policies. Stage II, which began on 1 January 1994, included the creation of the **European Monetary Institute** (EMI) (a transitionary body that carried out preparatory work for the third stage of EMU), and intensified cooperation between the national central banks of the member states. On 1 June 1998, well into Stage

II and just prior to the commencement of Stage III, the **European Central Bank** (ECB) replaced the EMI as the independent EU institution that would perform the duties associated with the design and implementation of the common monetary policy. On 1 January 1999, Stage III began with the successful introduction of the **euro** as the single currency for 11 of the then 15 EU member states. **Greece** was a latecomer to Stage III, finally joining on 1 January 2001, after apparently fulfilling the convergence criteria. The 12 countries that did adopt the euro (**Austria, Belgium, Finland, France, Germany**, Greece, **Ireland, Italy, Luxembourg, The Netherlands, Portugal,** and **Spain**) comprise what is known as the **euro zone**. **Denmark, Sweden,** and the **United Kingdom** maintain the krone, krona, and pound, respectively.

Euros were introduced into circulation in the euro zone on 1 January 2002. By 1 March 2002, the national currencies of these 12 member states ceased to be legal tender, permanently replaced by the euro. The May 2004 **enlargement** and future enlargement countries will have to meet and maintain the same convergence criteria as those countries in the original euro zone in order to adopt and implement the euro as their national currencies.

Each member state had its own particular interests and role to play in the EMU process. France and Germany, the two countries traditionally representing the "motor" advancing and directing European integration, figured prominently as two of the strongest supporters of EMU, albeit for different reasons. While the French government desired greater influence in European economic **decision-making** and policy-making, which had traditionally been dominated by Germany, the German government was interested in increased political unity among the EU member states as a means of promoting its **foreign policy** interests in **Central and Eastern Europe** without risking the fears associated with Germany's World War II legacy and its central geographic location on the continent. In this measured exchange, Germany's insistence on modeling the ECB on the independence and price stability objectives of the Bundesbank became a reality.

As France and Germany advocated EMU, Spanish Prime Minister **Felipe González** led an insistent campaign to prevent a two-speed Europe, demanding EU funding for the poorer member states to assist them in meeting the economic requirements for membership in the euro zone. Thus, the **cohesion policy** was given higher priority in order for both the relatively rich and relatively poor member states (Greece, Ireland, Portugal, and Spain) to be able to not only participate in, but also benefit from EMU.

ECONOMIC PARTNERSHIP AGREEMENTS (EPAs). Negotiations for EPAs between the **European Union** (EU) and the **African–Caribbean–Pacific (ACP) countries** began in September 2002 and are scheduled to be completed in a time period not to exceed five years. The mandate for these negotiations is included in the **Cotonou Agreement**, and the results will eliminate the non-reciprocal system of trade preferences the ACP countries have had with the EU since the first **Lomé Conventions**. The waiver granted by the **World Trade Organization** for this type of preferential trade framework will end by 1 January 2008.

It is expected that the EPAs will most likely result in **free trade areas** between the EU and different ACP regions. Questions remain as to how the ACP countries can really benefit and not be further disadvantaged by these agreements, and how these agreements can help incorporate the ACP economies into the global economy and simultaneously address their development needs.

EDUCATION AND TRAINING. Educational and youth programs were formally recognized as a **European Union** (EU) competence in the **Treaty on European Union**. While the policy-making and management of the member states' national education systems remain the responsibility of the national governments, the EU-level programs are designed to complement member state initiatives; to increase experiences and opportunities related to studying, training, and working in different European countries; and to contribute to meeting the educational goals of the **Lisbon Strategy**.

The EU's main program for education is Socrates, which is divided into sub-programs addressing more specific objectives. For example, the Erasmus program provides funding for professor and student exchanges at the university level; and the Lingua program encourages the learning of European **languages**. The Leonardo da Vinci program is responsible for vocational training and lifelong learning, promoting exchanges, and improving the quality of training throughout the

EU. The **European Centre for the Development of Vocational Training** serves as an advisory body to EU institutions, member states and organizations involved in policy-making in this field.

In order to meet the education and training goals established in the Lisbon Strategy, a 10-year work program was designed to openly coordinate actions in the areas of education and training between the member states. Working groups have been established to focus on specific objectives and a standing group sets and monitors benchmarks to determine progress.

eEUROPE. First adopted as "eEurope—An **Information Society** for All," eEurope is an initiative of the **Lisbon Strategy** that intends to bring all European citizens, businesses, and governments online. In an effort to make digital Europe more efficient and productive, subsequent action plans were adopted for member states and candidate countries. The current action plan, eEurope 2005, was adopted at the Seville **European Council** in June 2002 and focuses on broadband access, secure services, and eGovernment. The objectives of eEurope 2005 are job creation and social cohesion, improving productivity and standards of living, modernizing public services, and ensuring that all European citizens have access to the information society.

ELYSEE TREATY. On 22 January 1963, French President **Charles de Gaulle** and Chancellor of the Federal Republic of **Germany Konrad Adenauer** signed the Elysée Treaty on Franco–German friendship and reconciliation. The rapprochement and gradual strengthening of relations between these former enemies provided the driving force behind European integration for most of the second half of the 20th century.

EMPLOYMENT AND SOCIAL POLICY. Since the early 1990s, average **European Union** (EU) sustained unemployment levels have been critically high, prompting officials to elevate the priority of this issue on the EU agenda. Given that many of the potential job opportunities that were assured to accompany the completion of the **single market** never materialized, an employment chapter was included in the **Treaty of Amsterdam**. Nevertheless, employment remains a national competence with each member state having its own social welfare system and policy and **decision-making** independence, which makes it extremely difficult for the EU to make progress in this area. Despite an EU framework established to coordinate economic, employment, and social policies, including guidelines to meet member state employment level goals, according to **Eurostat**, the Statistical Office of the European Communities, the overall EU unemployment rate in July 2005 was 8.6 percent.

In March 2000, the **European Council** adopted the **Lisbon Strategy**, a commitment to make the EU the most competitive and dynamic knowledge-based economy in the world by 2010. This comprehensive strategy includes recommendations, guidelines, and initiatives for many of the EU's policy areas, including **employment**. In order to achieve the goal of creating more and better jobs by the 2010 target date, several priorities have been set, including reducing the unemployment rate and encouraging **women** to enter the workforce.

EMPTY CHAIR CRISIS. In 1965, a transition period in the European **common market** came to an end, and the **European Commission** submitted proposals for increasing the issue areas to be decided by **qualified majority voting**, revising **Common Agricultural Policy** (CAP) financing, and granting more budgetary authority to the **European Parliament**. In protest against what he considered a move toward greater **supranationality**, a concentration of power in the institutions of the **European Community** (EC), and an unwelcome change to the CAP, a policy of high relevance for **France**, French President **Charles de Gaulle** ordered a boycott of the **Council of Ministers** and recalled France's permanent representative to the EC on 1 July 1965. This crisis paralyzed the EC for six months but was resolved in January 1966 with the **Luxembourg Compromise**.

ENERGY POLICY. The **European Union** (EU) member states' dependence on external sources of energy supply is increasing at a rate such that the **European Commission** estimates that by 2020, 70 percent of the EU's primary energy needs and 90 percent of its oil will have to be imported. The EU is currently funding research to find methods of guaranteeing a continuous supply of fairly priced energy; of ensuring **environmental** protection and **sustainable development** as related to the use of energy; and completing the single energy market. Securing the energy supply involves a two-pronged approach: developing institutionalized cooperation with external partners (such as **Russia**); and more efficient uses of energy internally, including heightened energy performance standards and the use of more renewable energy resources.

ENHANCED COOPERATION. The idea of flexibility, or enhanced cooperation, in the European integration process has been discussed for decades. It was institutionalized in the **Treaty of Amsterdam** and enables member states to pursue integration in certain fields, even if *all* of the member states have not decided to participate. Regardless, this integration takes place under the auspices of the **European Union** (EU) and is governed by EU institutions. Enhanced cooperation can only be implemented if it meets the following conditions: it covers an area that does not fall within the exclusive competence of the Community; it aims to further the objectives of the EU and respects the principles of the treaties; it is used only as a last resort; and it involves a minimum number of member states and allows for the gradual integration of other member states.

Enhanced cooperation under the Treaty of Amsterdam was a difficult procedure to implement given it could be effectively vetoed by any one member state and the issue areas in which it could be attempted were extremely limited. The constraints on enhanced cooperation, however, were eased in the **Treaty of Nice** in which the single member state veto was eliminated in the first and third **pillars**. Furthermore, the number of member states required to engage in enhanced cooperation was reduced by half, established at a set eight, irrespective of the total number of EU member states (not a majority as was previously the case). This modification has become particularly significant following the May 2004 **enlargement**.

Enhanced cooperation has thus far not become a trend in European integration, and in fact, attempts to make the integration process more "flexible" have often been blocked. Nevertheless, enhanced cooperation remains a viable **decision-making** and policy-making tool in the enlarged EU of 25 member states.

ENLARGEMENT. Each time additional member states are integrated into the **European Union** (EU), this process is referred to as enlargement. After the six founding members created the **European Community** (EC), there have been five enlargements bringing the total number of member states to 25 as of 2005. On 1 January 1973, **Denmark**, **Ireland**, and the **United Kingdom** joined the EC; on 1 January 1981, **Greece** became a member; and **Portugal** and **Spain** acceded on 1 January 1986. In the first enlargement of the EU, **Austria**, **Finland**, and **Sweden** became member states on 1 January 1995, and in the largest accession in the history of European integration, 10 new member states, eight of which were former Soviet bloc countries or former Soviet republics, joined the EU on 1 May 2004: **Cyprus**, **Czech Republic**, **Estonia**, **Hungary**, **Latvia**, **Lithuania**, **Malta**, **Poland**, **Slovakia**, and **Slovenia**. **Bulgaria** and **Romania** have been approved for the next enlargement process which is scheduled to take place on 1 January 2007, and **Croatia** and **Turkey** began their accession negotiations in October 2005.

In order for countries to become member states of the EU, they must meet economic, political, **human rights**, and legal requirements (as outlined in the **Copenhagen criteria** of 1993) in order for their applications to be accepted by the EU. The **European Commission** then makes a recommendation as to when the candidate states are ready to begin accession negotiations, and the **European Council** makes the final unanimous decision on this matter. Once all chapters of the membership negotiations are completed, the accession treaty must be approved by the **European Parliament** and the Council, then signed and ratified by the governments of all of the EU member states and the acceding country. This approval must be granted before the actual enlargement process takes place, by which the country officially joins the EU.

ENTERPRISE AND INDUSTRY. The industrial policy of the **European Community** has been strongly linked to the **single market** and **competition policy** since its broad guidelines were established in the **Treaty of Rome**, and increasingly so in the 1980s with the focus on completing the single market. Today industrial and enterprise policy are aiming to make the **European Union** (EU) more competitive in the global economy, to continue to modernize, to work toward sustainable growth, and to help meet the objectives of the **Lisbon Strategy**.

Enterprise policy remains a competence of the individual member states, and therefore, the role of the EU is to support and coordinate such policies and to encourage the integration of related policies (research, regional development, and **taxation** to name a few) in order to meet the EU's enterprise and industry objectives. The three main pillars of the enterprise policy are innovation, entrepreneurship, and competitiveness.

ENVIRONMENTAL POLICY. European Community (EC) environmental legislation first began to be introduced and adopted in the 1970s, but it was not until the **Single European Act** that it was included in the treaties. The environmental issue area has become more comprehensive in each of the subsequent treaties, and today environmental policy is one of the most developed in the **European Union** (EU).

The EU's environmental policy is concerned not only with protecting the environment but also with preventing future environmental degradation and other associated problems. The environmental policy is also based on the principles that the polluter should pay for all environmental damages, **sustainable development**, and the inclusion of environmental standards and additional EU policy areas. Since 1992, the Financial Instrument for the Environment has supported the EU's environmental policy.

Environmental Action Programs have served as the framework for EU environmental action since 1973. The current program, "Environment 2010: Our Future, Our Choice," covers the period 2001–2010, and according to the program itself focuses on making improvements in four main areas: climate change; nature and biodiversity; environment, **health**, and quality of life; and natural resources and waste.

The **European Environment Agency** (EEA) was established in Copenhagen and began work in 1994. The main responsibility of the EEA is to monitor the environment, provide coordinated assessments, and warn against potential future environmental hazards.

In addition to internal policies, the EU has been a leader in promoting international environmental standards. During the mid-1990s, the EU promoted legally binding limits on greenhouse emissions which became the basis of the **Kyoto Protocol**, adopted in 1997 and entered into force in 2005. Despite its intense negotiations and the leadership role it often assumed during them as well as the creation of an emissions trading system, the EU is currently having difficulties meeting its established reductions in greenhouse emissions.

ESTONIA. An annexed state of the former Soviet Union, the Republic of Estonia declared its renewed independence on 20 August 1991. On 24 November 1995, the country submitted its application for membership in the **European Union** (EU). Only two years later, at the **Luxembourg** Summit in 1997, Estonia was the sole Baltic state invited to begin the so-called fast track accession negotiations. Despite concerns to the contrary, Estonian EU membership was approved by 67 percent in a national referendum on 14 September 2003, and became a member state on 1 May 2004.

Estonia maintains strong economic, trade, and investment relations with its Nordic neighbors, particularly **Finland** and **Sweden**. In addition to strengthening and reaping increased benefits from these ties as a result of EU membership, the Estonian government places particular importance on the European issues of security and EU relations with **Russia**. Refer to appendix A.

EURO. The euro is the only legal tender of the 12 **euro zone** countries (**Austria**, **Belgium**, **Finland**, **France**, **Germany**, **Greece**, **Ireland**, **Italy**, **Luxembourg**, **The Netherlands**, **Portugal**, and **Spain**). The euro has also been adopted by several other European countries and overseas territories although they have no direct **decision-making** or policy-making powers in terms of its administration. The member states of the 1 May 2004 **enlargement** will join the euro zone upon sustained fulfillment of the **convergence criteria**.

The euro has existed in electronic form since 1999; it was introduced into circulation on 1 January 2002, and by 1 March 2002, replaced national currencies and became the only legal tender of the euro zone. With just over three years in circulation, the euro is one of the strongest currencies in the world. Since mid-2003, it has been valued higher than the **United States** dollar.

The **single market** was considered incomplete without a single common currency, and therefore, the implementation of the euro was the main objective of the third and final stage of **Economic and**

Monetary Union (EMU). The euro significantly reduces the transaction costs previously associated with the movement of people, goods, capital, and services. This currency is administered by an independent **European Union** (EU) institution, the **European Central Bank** (ECB).

Euro notes are issued and circulated by each participating member states' central bank subject to approval from the ECB. The notes have a common design in all countries and come in denominations of 500, 200, 100, 50, 20, 10, and 5. Euro coins, on the other hand, have one common side and one unique side depending on the country in which they are minted. The face of the coins of each member state were selected to represent artistic and cultural contributions, past and present national political leaders, monarchs, and national monuments among other designs. All euros, regardless of mint location, must be accepted in every euro zone member state. There are 100 cents in each euro, and coins come in the following denominations: 2 euros, 1 euro, 50 cents, 20 cents, 10 cents, 5 cents, 2 cents, and 1 cent. €is the international recognized symbol for the euro.

In addition to EMU, the euro has implications for European political integration as well. This currency is a tangible resource that citizens of all euro zone member states depend on and utilize on a daily basis for their monetary transactions, thereby more deeply uniting them physically and psychologically.

EURO–MEDITERRANEAN PARTNERSHIP. The increased membership of the **European Community** (EC) in the 1980s to include **Greece**, **Portugal**, and **Spain** significantly extended the EC's Mediterranean external border area, and arguably the importance of the overall region to the **European Union** (EU). In November 1995, at a meeting of the Ministers of Foreign Affairs of the EU and Mediterranean countries in Barcelona, the Euro–Mediterranean Partnership, also known as the Barcelona Process, was initiated. The Barcelona Declaration established a broad framework of cooperation for the Euro–Mediterranean Partnership, addressing political and security; economic and financial; and social, cultural, and human areas. The partnership is funded in large part through the MEDA program and to a lesser extent (but no less importantly) through loans from the **European Investment Bank**. One of its ambitious economic objectives is to establish a **free trade area** for all of the Euro–Mediterranean partners.

There are a total of 35 countries in the Euro–Mediterranean Partnership: the 25 EU member states and Algeria, Egypt, Israel, Jordan, Lebanon, Morocco, Palestinian Authority, Syria, Tunisia, and **Turkey**. Bilateral association agreements have been negotiated between the EU and each one of its Mediterranean partners, and relations are also institutionalized with the region as a whole.

EURO-SKEPTIC. Those who question the **European Union** (EU), particularly its **supranational** aspects and what they consider to be the concentration of power in **Brussels** (the unofficial capital of the EU), are often referred to as Euro-skeptics. Euro-skeptics generally prefer **widening** over **deepening** the European integration process. Traditionally the **United Kingdom** has been considered the most Euro-skeptic of the EU member states, however, groups of Euro-skeptics can be found in all of the EU countries.

EURO ZONE. The **European Union** member states that adopted the **euro** as their national currency constitute the euro zone. There are currently 12 countries that participate in this monetary initiative: **Austria**, **Belgium**, **Finland**, **France**, **Germany**, **Greece**, **Ireland**, **Italy**, **Luxembourg**, **The Netherlands**, **Portugal**, and **Spain**. Once additional member states meet the **convergence criteria** or decide to opt in to the third stage of **Economic and Monetary Union** (EMU), they will also become part of the euro zone.

EUROBAROMETER. *See* PUBLIC OPINION.

EUROCORPS. Established by **France** and **Germany** in 1992 and subsequently joined by **Belgium**, **Spain**, and **Luxembourg**, the Eurocorps became operational in November 1995. The Eurocorps is headquartered in Strasbourg, France, and is composed of a 60,000 soldier rapid reaction force principally for use in humanitarian and peacekeeping missions. It can be deployed at the behest of the **North Atlantic Treaty Organization** (NATO) or the **European Union**.

EUROGROUP. A key player in **Economic and Monetary Union**, the Eurogroup consists of the ministers of economics and finance of the twelve countries in the **euro zone**. The Eurogroup meets on a regular basis, usually directly prior to meetings of the **Economic and Finance Council**. The ministers as well as representatives of the **European Commission** and **European Central Bank** who are also invited to participate in these meetings, address issues related to the **euro**.

EUROJUST. Established as a means of improving security and advanced integration in **Justice and Home Affairs** particularly after the 11 September 2001 terrorist attacks on the **United States**, this relatively new **European Union** body began operations in 2002 and is located in The Hague. Its main objective is to coordinate cooperation between national prosecutors, judicial authorities, and high-ranking law enforcement officials on cross-border criminal cases. There are 25 members of EUROJUST, one representative from each of the member states.

EUROPE AGREEMENTS. Between December 1991 and June 1996, 10 **Central and Eastern European countries** (**Bulgaria**, **Czech Republic**, **Estonia**, **Hungary**, **Latvia**, **Lithuania**, **Poland**, **Romania**, **Slovakia**, and **Slovenia**) signed Europe Agreements with the **European Union** (EU). Unique association agreements, Europe Agreements contain express acknowledgment of possible future EU membership for these countries, and provide a framework for preparation and convergence to reach this ultimate goal. In addition to the liberalization of trade geared toward the eventual creation of **free trade areas** between the EU and the associated countries, the Europe Agreements also include provisions for political dialogue, **cultural cooperation**, and the harmonization of **single market** legislation. Three key instruments aid in the implementation of the Europe Agreements: Association Councils (ministerial bilateral meetings); Association Committees (senior official level meetings); and Joint Parliamentary Committees (meetings of members of the national parliaments of the associated states and members of the **European Parliament**). **PHARE** is the principle financial instrument for assistance in meeting the objectives of the Europe Agreements, including preparation for EU accession.

EUROPEAID COOPERATION OFFICE. In order to reform and streamline the administration of the **European Commission**'s external aid, the Commission inaugurated the EuropeAid Cooperation Office on 1 January 2001. This office implements all of the Commission's external aid instruments that are funded by the **European Community budget** and the **European Development Fund**. The EuropeAid Cooperation Office is involved in all aspects of external aid projects including programming, implementation, and evaluation with the objective of trying to increase the effectiveness of these external initiatives. *See also* DEVELOPMENT POLICY; FOREIGN AND SECURITY POLICY.

EUROPEAN AGENCY FOR RECONSTRUCTION. Established in 2000 and located in Thessaloniki, **Greece**, the European Agency for Reconstruction is an **agency of the European Union** (EU) responsible for managing the EU's assistance programs in **Serbia and Montenegro** and the **Former Yugoslav Republic of Macedonia** (FYROM). The Agency works under the **Community Assistance for Reconstruction, Development, and Stabilization** (CARDS) program and has centers in Pristina, Belgrade, Podgorica, and Skopje. Since the Agency's inauguration it has managed approximately €2.3 billion in aid funding to help support the objectives of the CARDS program.

EUROPEAN AGENCY FOR SAFETY AND HEALTH AT WORK. Established in 1993 and located in Bilbao, **Spain**, the European Agency for Safety and Health at Work is an **agency of the European Union** (EU) that collects, analyzes, and disseminates information with the goal of making workplaces throughout the EU safer, healthier, and more productive. The Agency's information network is composed of so-called Focal Points, or country representatives in each one of the EU member states, in the **European Free Trade Association** countries, and in the candidate countries.

EUROPEAN AGRICULTURAL GUIDANCE AND GUARANTEE FUND (EAGGF). The principal financial instrument for the **Common Agricultural Policy**, the EAGGF has been since its creation the costliest element of the **European Union**'s **budget**. The fund is divided into two different sections: guidance and guarantee. The guidance section promotes structural change and rural development, particularly through modernization and conversion projects. The guarantee section provides price and income supports to the European workers in the **agricultural** sector.

EUROPEAN ANTI-FRAUD OFFICE (OLAF). Commonly known by its French acronym, OLAF, the European Anti-Fraud Office began operation in 1999. There are approximately 300 investigative agents who work in OLAF, the majority of whom come from national investigative offices in the member states. OLAF is part of the **European Commission**, yet it remains an independent office with the right to investigate potential cases of administrative fraud. In cooperation with its national partners, OLAF's main responsibility is to protect the financial interests of the **European Union**'s institutions and the European citizens against the attacks of organized crime and other illicit actors.

EUROPEAN ARREST WARRANT (EAW). The result of a decision made at the Tampere **European Council** in 1999, and the formal adoption of the **Framework Decision** in June 2002, the EAW is valid in all member states of the **European Union** (EU) and went into effect on 1 January 2004. With the exception of several documented situations, the EAW replaces extradition procedures between EU member states, and makes the surrender of nationals a quicker, easier, and more efficient process. National courts and judicial authorities with the right to issue national arrest warrants may also issue EAWs.

The EAW is based on the principle of mutual recognition of judicial decisions in criminal matters and increases judicial cooperation between the member states. It eliminates the traditional political aspect of extradition procedures. Persons subject to an EAW have their fundamental rights guaranteed through a clause in the framework decision requiring respect for the **European Convention for the Protection of Human Rights and Fundamental Freedoms**. In principle, member states can no longer refuse to surrender one of its citizens on the basis of nationality. Member states can, however, request the return of their nationals to serve sentences on their territory.

EUROPEAN ATOMIC ENERGY COMMUNITY (EURATOM).
Created through the 1957 **Treaty of Rome**, EURATOM was designed to pool the atomic energy resources and industries of the signatory countries, the same six as those that founded the **European Coal and Steel Community**. **Jean Monnet** in his role as a member of the Action Committee for a United States of Europe understood that energy was no longer as dependent on the coal and steel sectors, and therefore, he lobbied for the inclusion of additional energy sources in the process of European integration. A conduit for the peaceful use of nuclear energy, EURATOM coordinates research, safety, and safeguards and aims to guarantee a regular supply of this important resource to all **European Community** member states. The Central and Eastern European **enlargement** brought renewed attention to EURATOM as many of the accession states were required to make adjustments in order to meet adequate nuclear safety standards.

EUROPEAN AVIATION SAFETY AGENCY (EASA). Established in 2003 and located in Cologne, **Germany**, EASA is an **agency of the European Union** (EU). It is responsible for assisting the **European Commission** in preparing and monitoring the application of aviation legislation and for adopting certification specifications and conducting technical inspections. The main goal of EASA is to have a safe and **environmentally** sound civil aviation industry throughout the EU.

EUROPEAN BANK FOR RECONSTRUCTION AND DEVELOP-MENT (EBRD). Located in London, the EBRD was proposed by French President **François Mitterrand** in November 1989, following the fall of the **Berlin Wall**. It began operations in April 1991 with a priority objective of providing assistance to the **Central and Eastern European countries** directed specifically toward facilitating transitions to democracy and open market economies. Today the EBRD encourages investment and finances projects in 27 countries from central Europe to central **Asia**. In order to receive support from the EBRD, countries must adhere to democratic practices and principles. They must also commit to **environmental** protection with respect to EBRD investments. The EBRD finances projects in both the public and private sectors on the condition that the assistance will help the country progress toward a full market economy.

Although an initiative of the **European Union** (EU), the EBRD is not actually part of the EU. The EU and its member states do, however, provide just over half of the EBRD's capital. Sixty countries (including the **United States**, Canada, and **Japan**) and two intergovernmental institutions are shareholders in the bank.

EUROPEAN CENTRE FOR THE DEVELOPMENT OF VOCATIONAL TRAINING (CEDEFOP). Created in 1975, CEDEFOP was located in Berlin until 1995 when its headquarters were relocated to Thessaloniki, **Greece**. CEDEFOP is an **agency of the European Union** (EU) responsible for the promotion of vocational **education and training** throughout the EU. The products and services of CEDEFOP include information provided via Internet, in hard copy publications and journals, and in-person conferences and seminars.

EUROPEAN CENTRAL BANK (ECB). The implementation and administration of the **euro**, the main objective of the third and final stage of the **Economic and Monetary Union** (EMU), required the creation of a new **European Union** (EU) institution, the ECB. The ECB and the **European System of Central Banks** (ESCB) (the national banks of the 25 EU member states and the ECB) began operation on 1 June 1998, in preparation for the launch of the single currency in its electronic form. **Germany**'s economic dominance combined with its decision to give up one of the strongest and most respected currencies in the world, the deutschemark, for the greater European good (and its own political objectives) consolidated its considerable influence over this process. Consequently, the ECB is based on the independence of the Bundesbank, its primary goal is to maintain price stability and prevent inflation, and it is located in Frankfurt, Germany. The ECB determines the interest rate for the **euro zone** member states.

The Executive Board of the ECB is appointed by the **European Council**. It is responsible for preparing the meetings of the ESCB's Governing Council and daily implementation of the monetary policy decided by the ESCB's Governing Council. The Executive Board is a six-member body consisting of a president, vice president, and four other members. The first president of the ECB was Wim Duisenberg (June 1998 to November 2003), former finance minister of **The Netherlands** and former president of the Dutch national bank. Jean-Claude Trichet, former president of the French national bank, is the current president of the ECB (November 2003).

The ESCB's Governing Council is its main **decision-making** body. It is composed of the ECB's Executive Board as well as the governors of the national central banks of the 12 euro zone member states. The Governing Council is responsible for making decisions regarding common monetary policy and foreign exchange operations, managing foreign exchange reserves, and ensuring efficient operations of the payments system. The members of this body meet twice a month in Frankfurt.

The president and vice president of the ECB and the governors of the national central banks of the 25 EU member states compose the ESCB's General Council. Its objectives are to provide the technical and advisory support necessary for those countries that still have not made the transitions from their national currencies to the euro. Once all member states have adopted the euro, this body will cease to exist.

EUROPEAN COAL AND STEEL COMMUNITY (ECSC). The ECSC was established by the 1951 **Treaty of Paris**, and began operation in 1952. The European countries that answered the call of the **Schuman Declaration**, **Belgium**, **France**, **Germany**, **Italy**, **Luxembourg**, and **The Netherlands**, pooled their coal and steel resources under a **High Authority** and created a **common market** for these products. The overriding goal of maintaining a lasting peace on the continent was evident as coal and steel were the two main war-making materials of the time, and the lands rich in these resources had been a constant source of conflict between France and Germany.

The High Authority, the ECSC institution responsible for its policy-making and implementation, is representative of the early presence of **supranationalism** in the European integration process. Given **Jean Monnet**'s appreciation of institutions, it is not surprising that a complete institutional framework consisting of this High Authority, a

Common Assembly, **European Court of Justice**, and **Council of Ministers** was designed to support and govern the ECSC.

The ECSC was the first experiment in European integration that would develop through **deepening** and **widening** into the **European Union** as we know it today. As stipulated in the Treaty of Paris, the ECSC ceased to exist in 2002. As a testament to its legacy, its dissolution occurred during the **European Convention** proceedings to draft the **Treaty establishing a Constitution for Europe**.

EUROPEAN COMMISSION. The European Commission as it is known today was created in 1967 with the entry into force of the **Merger Treaty**. Prior to 1967, there had been three executive institutions: the **High Authority** of the **European Coal and Steel Community** (ECSC); the Commission of the **European Economic Community** (EEC); and the Commission of the **European Atomic Energy Community** (EURATOM). The European Commission is often considered the most **supranational** institution of the **European Union** (EU). Representative of the executive branch of the EU, the Commission has the sole prerogative of initiating legislation in the EU's first pillar competences.

The European Commission has five principal responsibilities: to propose EU legislation and submit it to the **Council of the EU**; as the Guardian of the Treaties, to ensure that the other EU institutions and the member states properly implement **European Community (EC) law**; to implement EC laws, although it remains highly dependent on member state governments to fulfill this responsibility; to elaborate and manage the vast majority (about 90%) of the EU **budget**; and to negotiate international trade and development agreements with third countries. In order to comply with these duties as established by the EU treaties, the EU has developed a **bureaucracy**, consisting of approximately 25,000 **civil servants** who must pass through a highly competitive process including a battery of tests to be selected to their positions.

The European Commission is subject to financial examination by the **Court of Auditors** and responsible to the **European Parliament** (EP). Since the **Treaty on European Union**, the EP has the ability, by a two-thirds vote, to remove the entire Commission but not individual

Commissioners. Implementing its institutional powers in 1999, the EP investigated and obtained significant evidence of fraud and corruption within the Commission. Prior to an EP vote on whether or not to dismiss the **Santer** Commission, the members of this institution resigned en masse, leaving the incoming **Prodi** Commission with the difficult task of improving the Commission's already tainted image.

The European Commission is headquartered in **Brussels, Belgium**. The Commissioners serve five-year renewable terms, are nominated by their member state governments, approved as an entire college (not on an individual basis) by the EP, and appointed by the **European Council**. The president of the Commission is agreed to by consensus of the European Council and approved by the EP. He or she is responsible for assigning the commissioner's portfolios which correspond to the various Directorates General that represent major EU policy areas (i.e., **external relations**, economic and financial affairs, **regional policy**, **competition**, etc.). He or she also represents the European Commission in several international organizations, meetings and negotiations; directs policy development; and encourages an apt environment for consensus-making among the possibly conflicting interests represented in the Commission.

Prior to the May 2004 **enlargement**, the Commission had 20 members; two from each of the large member states (**France, Germany, Italy, Spain**, and the **United Kingdom**), and one from each of the small member states (**Austria, Belgium, Denmark, Finland, Greece, Ireland, Luxembourg, The Netherlands, Portugal**, and **Sweden**). Beginning with the November 2004 European Commission under the presidency of **José Manuel Barroso**, the Commission has 25 members, one from each of the member states regardless of their size. According to the **Treaty of Nice**, once the EU has enlarged to 27 member states, the number of European Commissioners must be less than 27, with the specific number and a fair rotation to be decided by unanimity. Final decisions regarding the reduced number of Commissioners will take effect with the Commission's next term beginning in 2009. Refer to appendix C.

EUROPEAN COMMUNITY (EC). In 1957, two **Treaties of Rome** were adopted; one establishing the **European Atomic Energy Community** (EURATOM) and one establishing the **European Economic**

Community (EEC). Over the years, the EEC came to be referred to as simply the EC.

The EEC officially became the EC in the **Treaty on European Union** (TEU). The first, fully integrated, and most **supranational** of the **three pillars** established in the TEU is the EC which primarily includes the **Common Agricultural Policy**, **Economic and Monetary Union**, and the **single market** and all policies associated with it.

EUROPEAN COMMUNITY HUMANITARIAN AID OFFICE (ECHO). Established in 1992, ECHO is responsible for providing emergency **humanitarian aid** in the form of goods and services to the victims of natural disasters and armed conflicts, anywhere in the world outside of the **European Union**. Since its creation, ECHO has supplied humanitarian aid to more than 85 countries valued at more than €500 million every year. ECHO relies on its partners, mainly nongovernmental organizations and agencies of the United Nations, to assure that the aid quickly and efficiently reaches those in need.

EUROPEAN COMMUNITY (EC) LAW. EC law, often referred to as Community law and at times referred to as **European Union** (EU) law, is based on the treaties, secondary legislation adopted by the **Council of the EU** and the **European Parliament**, case law of the **European Court of Justice** (ECJ), and general principles of international law. Community law falls under the jurisdiction of the ECJ and must be implemented in its entirety by all of the EU member states, as Community law has **direct effect** and **supremacy** over member states' national legislation. *See also* ACQUIS COMMUNAUTAIRE.

EUROPEAN CONVENTION. The European Convention was first proposed in the **Laeken Declaration**, as a means to debate the future of Europe, and to transform the results into a Constitution for Europe. This method was first implemented during the negotiations for the **Charter of Fundamental Rights**, however, the Convention represents the first time there was a two-step process for treaty reform—the Convention, followed by the traditional **Intergovernmental Conference** (IGC). This Convention took place from February 2002 to June 2003, during the Spanish, Danish, and Greek **presidencies of**

the **European Union** (EU). **Valéry Giscard d'Estaing**, a former president of **France**, was the chairman of the Convention, and the vice-chairmen were the former prime minister of **Italy**, **Guiliano Amato**, and the former prime minister of **Belgium**, **Jean-Luc Dehaene**. The Praesidium of the convention was a body composed of 12 participants to push the Convention forward, and consisted of the chairman and vice-chairmen, two representatives of the **European Parliament** (EP), two representatives of the **European Commission**, two representatives from the national parliaments, and one representative each from the Spanish, Danish, and Greek governments. There were a total of 105 participants in the Convention, representing the heads of state or government of the member states and candidate countries, the national parliaments of the member states and candidate countries, the EP, and the European Commission.

The Convention took place in three stages: the listening phase for the exchange of ideas; the working group phase for providing detailed analysis and proposals regarding some of the most pertinent issues in the context of the debate on the future of Europe; and the writing phase during which the constitutional treaty was drafted. Discussions and documents of the Convention were open and public in an attempt to bring the European peoples closer to the process through involvement and increased transparency. The agreed upon reforms were submitted in the form of a draft constitutional treaty to the **European Council** in Thessaloniki in June 2003, for subsequent negotiations and analysis during the second stage of the treaty reform, the IGC.

EUROPEAN CONVENTION FOR THE PROTECTION OF HUMAN RIGHTS AND FUNDAMENTAL FREEDOMS. Adopted by the **Council of Europe** and signed in Rome on 4 November 1950, the European Convention for the Protection of Human Rights and Fundamental Freedoms includes minimum standards for individual rights and freedoms with which all of its signatories must comply. The Convention also instituted a dispute resolution mechanism, the European Court of Human Rights, in which cases are heard based on claims of violations of the established norms. All of the **European Union** (EU) member states have ratified and are party to the Convention, but the EU itself is not. However, the EU's respect for **hu-**

man rights and fundamental freedoms is based on this Convention as specifically recognized in the **Treaty on European Union**, and will continue to serve as the guidelines for the EU. The **Treaty establishing a Constitution for Europe** includes the EU's **Charter of Fundamental Rights**, which would provide the Charter with a legal basis if the constitutional treaty is ratified.

EUROPEAN COUNCIL. At a 1974 Paris summit of **European Community** leaders, agreement was reached on the regularization of such high level official meetings. Known as the European Council, this institution is composed of the heads of state or government of the **European Union** (EU) member states, assisted by their foreign ministers and the president of the **European Commission**. Its first meeting took place in Dublin in 1975, but it was not recognized in the treaties until the **Single European Act**.

The **Treaty on EU** requires the European Council to meet at least twice a year at the end of each six-month rotating **presidency**. Since the beginning of the **Lisbon Strategy** in 2000, mid-semester spring summits have been held to discuss its progress, and subsequently fall mid-semester summits have become common as well. The member state holding the EU presidency might also call for an extraordinary meeting of the European Council, as was the case, for example, immediately following the September 11 terrorist attacks. Regular European Council meetings last an average of two days, while extraordinary sessions are usually significantly shorter.

The main responsibilities of the European Council are to make high-level political decisions, establish long-term goals for the EU, and play a leadership role for the **Common Foreign and Security Policy**. While the Council of the EU is the main daily **decision-making** body for the EU, the European Council makes the decisions on major initiatives and changes to the EU, especially treaty and institutional reforms. Decisions of the European Council are almost always reached by consensus, its standard operating procedure.

EUROPEAN COURT OF JUSTICE (ECJ). The ECJ, officially the Court of Justice of the European Communities, is deliberately located in **Luxembourg**, distanced from the political hub of the **European Union** (EU) in **Brussels**. The ECJ is one of the EU's most independent institutions. Its primary obligation is to ensure that the EU body of law is uniformly interpreted and applied throughout all 25 EU member states.

Twenty-five judges, one from each of the EU member states, are appointed to six-year renewable terms by the **European Council**. Along with the judges, eight **advocates-general** are responsible for **preliminary rulings** and **direct actions**. Preliminary rulings are brought to the ECJ by national courts of the member states for interpretation when the case involves Community law. In direct action cases, the ECJ serves as a dispute tribunal, establishing opinions on disputes between EU institutions and between EU institutions and the member states. Cases are normally decided in Chambers of three or five judges, and only in exceptional cases and by request are cases decided by the Grand Chamber of the full Court. In indirect action cases and cases involving decisions made by EU institutions, the ECJ is assisted by the **Court of First Instance** which was created in 1989 for this express purpose.

With the ECJ's classic cases of *Costa v. ENEL* (6/64) and *Van Gend en Loos* (26/62), this tribunal established the doctrines of **supremacy** and **direct effect** of **European Community (EC) law**, respectively. Ensuring early on in the integration process that EC law would take precedence over national law and that it would be directly applicable in the EU member states has undoubtedly contributed to the continuous process of constitutionalization and integration of the EU. Refer to appendix F and appendix G.

EUROPEAN CURRENCY UNIT (ECU). An artificial currency established in March 1979, the ECU's value was based on a weighted basket of all of the national currencies of the member states of the **European Community** (EC). The weights were typically adjusted on a five-year basis to account for changes in the member states' economies. The exchange rates between the EC member states were determined in ECUs and in order to minimize fluctuations, member states in the **exchange rate mechanism** had to remain within a bandwidth of $+/- 2.25$ percent. The ECU, which no longer exists, is considered to be the precursor to the **euro** which is also based on a weighted basket of currencies but which has irrevocably fixed exchange rates as of 1 January 1999.

EUROPEAN DATA PROTECTION SUPERVISOR (EDPS). A **European Union** (EU) regulation passed in 2001 establishes standards regarding the processing of personal data, particularly of so-called sensitive information which pertains to, for example, ethnic and racial background, political opinions, religious beliefs, and health records. In order to implement these standards, the regulation calls for the creation of an independent supervisory body to oversee the EU institutions and the way in which they process personal information and its free movement. The EDPS is assisted by a deputy supervisor and works in conjunction with the data protection officers of the individual EU institutions as well as with the national supervisory authorities of the member states. In addition to monitoring, the EDPS advises institutions and investigates complaints related to the violation of the right to individuals' privacy. On 22 December 2003, Peter Johan Hustinx of **The Netherlands** was appointed the first EDPS for a period of five years and Joaquín Bayo Delgado of **Spain** was appointed as his deputy.

EUROPEAN DEFENCE COMMUNITY (EDC). The outbreak of war on the Korean Peninsula on 25 June 1950 appeared to indicate a heating up of the Cold War, and thus, the necessity for Western Europe to strengthen its defense capabilities in order to protect against a possible Soviet attack became evident. West **Germany** was the only country in Western Europe itself with the potential to reinforce its security which would, of course, require its rearmament. Wary of the idea yet conscious of its value and under pressure from its Western allies, **France** accepted West Germany's rearmament on the condition it would take place within the supervisory guarantees provided by regional institutions. In this context, in October 1950, French Prime Minister René Pleven proposed a plan for an EDC, the first attempt to integrate in this highly sensitive area. The treaty establishing the EDC was signed by the founding members of the **European Coal and Steel Community** on 27 May 1952 in Paris. In August 1954, the treaty was defeated in the ratification process, ironically by the French parliament. While European defense integration remains difficult, progress has been made in the past decade, evidenced by the evolution of the **Common Foreign and Security Policy** (CFSP) and its **European Security and Defence Policy**. *See also* DEFENSE POLICY; FOREIGN AND SECURITY POLICY.

EUROPEAN DEVELOPMENT FUND (EDF). Established in an annex to the **Treaty of Rome**, the EDF is currently the financial instrument to support economic and social development in the **African–Caribbean–Pacific** (ACP) countries. The EDF is not, however, included in the annual **budget** of the **European Union** (EU) and has always been financed by contributions from the member states. The ninth EDF (2000–2005) provides €15.2 billion toward development in the ACP countries.

EUROPEAN ECONOMIC AND SOCIAL COMMITTEE (EESC). Established by the 1957 **Treaty of Rome**, the EESC is an advisory body from which the major **European Union** (EU) institutions are obligated to solicit a non-binding opinion on the issue areas outlined in the treaty and its amendments. The EESC advises the **Council of the EU**, **European Commission**, and **European Parliament** on economic and social issues as part of a **consultation procedure**. The EESC must be consulted before the adoption of many instruments concerning the **single market**, **education**, **consumer protection**, the **environment**, regional development, and social affairs. In addition, the EESC may issue opinions at its own initiative.

There are 317 members of this institution, representative of employer, employee, professional, and consumer groups in the 25 EU member states. The members are nominated by their national governments and appointed by the Council to four-year terms. The EESC also serves as a liaison between civil society groups and the EU institutions, playing a fundamental role in attempting to bring the EU closer to its citizens.

EUROPEAN ECONOMIC AREA (EEA). An economic agreement between the **European Union** (EU) and members of the **European Free Trade Association** (EFTA), the EEA came into effect on 1 January 1994, extending the **single market** to all of the EFTA countries with the exception of **Switzerland** where the EEA was rejected in a referendum in December 1992. After **Austria**, **Finland**, and **Sweden** joined the EU on 1 January 1995, the remaining EFTA countries party to the EEA are **Iceland**, Liechtenstein, and **Norway**. This agreement associating the EEA EFTA countries with the EU is institutionalized through high level councils and committees that convene on a regular basis to discuss policies and make decisions related to the EEA, primarily regarding the single market, including the four freedoms of movement, and **competition policy**.

EUROPEAN ECONOMIC COMMUNITY (EEC). Intended to create a **single market** for goods, people, capital, and services, the EEC was created through the 1957 **Treaty of Rome**. Due to **decision-making** and other obstacles, the **European Community** (EC) **common market** was not fully complete until the provisions outlined in the **Single European Act** facilitated this process. However, the EEC was successful in many areas, especially the transformation and impetus it provided to European integration at the time of its implementation. Trade was increased between the six signatory member states, the founding members of the **European Coal and Steel Community** (**Belgium**, **France**, **Germany**, **Italy**, **Luxembourg**, and **The Netherlands**), by gradually phasing out tariffs and other barriers to trade. An EC **customs union** began operation on 1 July 1968.

French President **Charles de Gaulle** petitioned for the inclusion of **agricultural** products in the EEC to balance the perceived rewards for highly industrialized member states. Not only was this goal included in the Treaty of Rome but, in 1960, the **European Commission** proposed a **Common Agricultural Policy** that would forever change the EC's policy and **budgetary** character.

EUROPEAN ENVIRONMENT AGENCY (EEA). Located in Copenhagen, **Denmark**, the EEA is an **agency of the European Union** (EU) and began its work in 1994. The EEA is responsible for coordinating assessments of **environmental** standards from agencies throughout the EU and to make that information publicly available. The main goals of the EEA are to work toward **sustainable development** and significant improvement to the environment.

EUROPEAN FOOD SAFETY AUTHORITY (EFSA). Established in 2002 and located in Parma, **Italy**, EFSA is an **agency of the European Union** (EU). Its main objective is to provide independent scientific information and recommendations, and risk assessments to the EU institutions. The overall goal is to protect the **health** of the EU citizens in terms of **food safety** and to restore consumer confidence in the food products available for their consumption.

EUROPEAN FOUNDATION FOR THE IMPROVEMENT OF LIVING AND WORKING CONDITIONS. Established in 1975 and located in Dublin, **Ireland**, the European Foundation for the Improvement of Living and Working Conditions is an **agency of the European Union** (EU) responsible for conducting research and providing information and analysis on **employment** and working conditions, industrial relations, and social cohesion. The Foundation has developed several projects to help with its mission. The European Industrial Relations Observatory (EIRO) was established in 1997 and monitors news on European industrial relations. In its developmental stage, the European Monitoring Centre on Change (EMCC) is an information and exchange resource for economic and social changes resulting from industrial and technological developments. Also in its developmental stage, the European Working Conditions Observatory (EWCO) is composed of a network of correspondents at member state and EU level to provide regular updates and reports on working conditions throughout the EU.

EUROPEAN FREE TRADE ASSOCIATION (EFTA). Founded in 1960 through the signing of the Stockholm Convention, the EFTA was considered an **intergovernmental** alternative to the **European Community** (EC). Focused primarily on the promotion of **free trade** among its members, the original signatories of the EFTA were **Austria**, **Denmark**, **Norway**, **Portugal**, **Sweden**, **Switzerland**, and the **United Kingdom**. By 1995 five of these countries had left the organization and joined the **European Union**, leaving Norway and Switzerland, joined by **Iceland** and Lichtenstein in the EFTA.

Having strong **trade** relations with the EFTA, in the early 1990s the EC proposed a more comprehensive economic and trade agreement with its members, which resulted in the creation of the **European Economic Area** (EEA). The EEA entered into force between EFTA (all of its member countries except Switzerland, which decided against participation) and in January 1994 the EC granting **single market** access, rights, and responsibilities to the three EFTA countries.

EUROPEAN INVESTMENT BANK (EIB). Established in 1958 as a mandate of the **Treaty of Rome**, the EIB is headquartered in **Luxembourg** and has its own internal institutional framework, consisting of a Board of Governors and several other administrative bodies. It provides loans to help meet the policy objectives of the **European Union** (EU), predominantly in the area of **regional** development. The EIB also makes a more limited number of loans outside the EU to support the EU's **foreign** and **development policies**. In order for the EIB to approve a loan for a specific project, at least 50 percent of the funding for that project must come from other sources.

The EIB is self-financing in that it obtains most of its funds by borrowing on international capital markets. The EU member states are the shareholders of the bank.

EUROPEAN MARITIME SAFETY AGENCY (EMSA). Established in 2002 and located in Lisbon, **Portugal**, EMSA is an **agency of the European Union** (EU). EMSA provides technical and scientific information and recommendations to the **European Commission** in order to help this EU institution make educated decisions regarding legislation in this area. EMSA works closely with the member states in all of its work. The main goals of this agency are to reduce the risk of accidents at sea and to improve the marine **environment**.

EUROPEAN MEDICINES AGENCY (EMEA). Located in London, the EMEA is an **agency of the European Union** and began its work in 1995. It is responsible for public and animal **health**. The EMEA evaluates and supervises medicines to be administered to humans and animals.

EUROPEAN MONETARY INSTITUTE (EMI). With the launch of Stage II of **Economic and Monetary Union** (EMU) on 1 January 1994, the EMI was established in Frankfurt to undertake preparatory work for the third and final stage of EMU. The EMI's efforts included assistance with enhancing monetary policy coordination between the member states, contributions to the creation of the **European System of Central Banks**, and the development of technical support systems. On 1 June 1998, the EMI was replaced by the **European Central Bank**, the permanent independent European institution responsible for the **euro zone**'s monetary policy.

EUROPEAN MONETARY SYSTEM (EMS). After the collapse of the Bretton Woods regime in 1971 and the resulting disorder of the international capitalist economic system, the **European Community** was determined to introduce a method of encouraging greater economic and monetary stability. The EMS was introduced on 13 March 1979 with two main components: the **exchange rate mechanism** (ERM) which provided a (+/−) 2.25 percent bandwidth for exchange rate fluctuation for the participating member states, and the **European Currency Unit** (ECU) upon which the ERM was based. The EMS, dominated by the deutschemark and German economic and monetary policy, is considered a precursor to the **Economic and Monetary Union** (EMU).

Participation in the ERM was voluntary and not always sustainable by all of the member states. In what came to be known as Black Wednesday, the **United Kingdom** and **Italy** were forced to withdraw from the ERM on 16 September 1992, after which the bandwidth of the ERM was extended to (+/−) 15 percent.

In conjunction with the launch of the **euro**, a new mechanism, the ERM II, became operational on 1 January 1999 with a standard fluctuation band of (+/−) 15 percent. The objectives of ERM II are to promote EU-wide monetary stability (between **euro zone** and non–euro zone countries) and assist the non–euro zone countries with their eventual adoption of the common currency.

EUROPEAN MONITORING CENTRE FOR DRUGS AND DRUG ADDICTION (EMCDDA). The Lisbon-based EMCDDA (also referred to as the drugs observatory) was established in 1993 by the **European Union** (EU) in response to increasing drug problems in Europe. It is an **agency of the EU** and became fully operational in 1995 and its main responsibility is to provide the EU and its member states with information on drug patterns in Europe, focusing in particular on drug abuse. The EMCDDA's main tasks are data collection and analysis, methodological research, and the dissemination of information.

EUROPEAN MONITORING CENTRE ON RACISM AND XENOPHOBIA (EUMC). Established in 1998 and located in Vienna, **Austria**, the EUMC is an **agency of the European Union** (EU) responsible for collecting and disseminating information related to the causes and effects of racism and xenophobia in the EU. The EUMC also develops strategies to combat racism and xenophobia. EUMC's work is coordinated through the European Information Network on Racism and Xenophobia (RAXEN), composed of so-called Focal Points, or country representatives in each one of the member states.

EUROPEAN MOVEMENT. Originating in 1947 with several committees and organizations intent on promoting a united Europe, the European Movement was formally established in October 1948, following the **Congress of Europe** in The Hague earlier that year. Duncan Sandys, a British politician, was the first president of the European Movement. The organization's honorary presidents were Leon Blum, **Winston Churchill**, **Alcide de Gasperi**, and **Paul Henri-Spaak**. The European Movement played an instrumental role in the creation of the **Council of Europe**, the College of Europe in Bruges (**Belgium**), and the European Centre of Culture in Geneva.

Today the European Movement, with its 41 national councils and 21 member associations, is considered a study and information group as well as a pressure group. The main objective of the European Movement is to encourage greater European integration.

EUROPEAN NEIGHBORHOOD POLICY (ENP). Adopted in the context of the 2004 **enlargement**, the ENP encompasses the idea of a "wider Europe" and is meant to demonstrate that extending the external borders of the **European Union** (EU) does not mean creating divisions between the EU and its new neighboring countries. In fact, the ENP provides a framework, based largely on bilateral action plans and agreements, for increased economic and political cooperation between the EU and its neighbors (Algeria, Armenia, Azerbaijan, **Belarus**, Egypt, Georgia, Israel, Jordan, Lebanon, Libya, **Moldova**, Morocco, Palestinian Authority, Syria, Tunisia, and **Ukraine**). Some of the EU's neighboring countries such as **Russia** and **Turkey** are not included in the ENP because relations with these countries are covered under special programs (e.g., a strategic partnership) or status (e.g., that of candidate country or prospective country). Fostering democracy, respect for **human rights**, **sustainable development**, good **governance**, open market economics, and achieving greater security and stability in the region are the main objectives of the ENP.

EUROPEAN NETWORK AND INFORMATION SECURITY AGENCY (ENISA). Created in 2004 and temporarily located in **Brussels** until its permanent headquarters can be established in Heraklion, **Greece**, ENISA is responsible for the security of the **information society** and helping the EU institutions, member states, and businesses to meet the requirements to achieve network and information security. The **Agency** will provide risk assessments, collect and disseminate information, and monitor the development of higher standards for the information society.

EUROPEAN PARLIAMENT (EP). The EP was first established as the Common Assembly of the **European Coal and Steel Community** (ECSC), transformed into the European Parliamentary Assembly with the entry into force of the **Treaties of Rome** in 1958, and agreed to change its name to the European Parliament in 1962. The Common Assembly of the ECSC first met with 78 representatives on 10 September 1952. Today, 732 Europarliamentarians, or Members of the EP (MEPs), represent over 450 million citizens of 25 EU member states. The first direct elections to this institution took place in 1979, and elections are held every five years.

Unlike traditional national parliaments, the EP has no independent authority to initiate legislation, and has typically been the one major EU institution with the least amount of autonomous powers. Since the **Single European Act**, however, the EP's powers and responsibilities have been increasing incrementally with each subsequent treaty reform. The EP shares budgetary authority and **decision-making** powers (**consultation**, **assent**, and **co-decision**) with the **Council of the EU**. The EP ultimately adopts or rejects the EU's **budget** in its entirety. The **Treaties of Amsterdam** and **Nice** extended the scope and strength of the EP's legislative powers. Moreover, the EP's assent is required for association and accession agreements. It also appoints the European **Ombudsman** who is empowered to receive complaints from EU citizens concerning maladministration by EU institutions and other bodies. Finally, the EP has the right to form temporary inquiry committees to not only examine the actions of the EU institutions, but also the actions of member states as regards the implementation of EU policies.

MEPs are organized into transnational parliamentary **political groups** which are used to determine speaking times, resource allocations, and the composition of the EP's 20 permanent committees. Each political group must have at least 19 members from at least one-fifth of the EU member states. There are currently seven parliamentary political groups plus the independent MEPs. The **Group of the European People's Party (Christian Democrats) and European Democrats** and **Socialist Group** have traditionally been and remain the largest and most influential groups in the EP.

In terms of inter-institutional checks and balances, the EP must approve of the **European Commission** President and the College of Commissioners before a new Commission is able to take office, a power brought to the forefront with the controversy surrounding the 2004 **Barroso** Commission and the delay of its inauguration. Once the Commission does take office, it remains responsible to the EP, which was demonstrated with the *en masse* resignation of the **Santer** Commission in 1999 following revealing EP investigations into certain Commission mismanagement and threats from the EP that it would adopt a motion of censure, which by a vote of two-thirds of the MEPs would force the resignation of the entire Commission.

The EP itself has been the subject of criticism regarding wasteful procedures. MEPs spend three weeks of every month in committee meetings in **Brussels**, and one week of every month in plenary sessions in Strasbourg, **France**, requiring costly, time-consuming trips for thousands of people on a monthly basis, a routine that has been institutionalized into the **acquis communautaire**. Furthermore, there are 20 official **languages** of the EU, all of which are used more in the EP than in any of the other major EU institutions, necessitating the frequent use of interpretation and translation services, amounting to exceptional expenses.

Despite the EP's role as the champion of EU democracy, low interest and approval levels have resulted in a steadily declining

EU-wide turnout for the EP's direct elections. Voter participation reached a historic low of 45.5 percent; 47.1 percent in the EU-15 and only 26.4 percent in the new member states, in the 10–13 June 2004 European parliamentary elections. Refer to appendix E.

EUROPEAN POLICE OFFICE (EUROPOL). The completion of the **single market** and the free movement of goods, capital, people and services through the internal borders of the **European Union** (EU) highlighted the need for increased police cooperation between the EU member states. The **Treaty on EU** contained the idea of creating EUROPOL, and subsequently negotiations regarding the establishment and operations of this police office began. The then 15 member states of the EU signed the EUROPOL Convention in 1995 and ratified it in 1998, and EUROPOL, located in The Hague, became fully operational soon thereafter. The main responsibilities of EUROPOL are to coordinate between national police forces of the member states in an effort to combat cross-border crimes such as drug trafficking, human trafficking, and money laundering. To this end, EUROPOL is charged with maintaining a computerized database for the exchange of information related to combating such crimes in the EU.

EUROPEAN POLITICAL COOPERATION (EPC). At the **European Community** (EC) Summit of Heads of State and Government in The Hague in December 1969, the leaders advocated for increased political coordination between the member states. In October 1970, the **Council** adopted the proposed **Luxembourg, or Davignon Report**, which established EPC as an attempt to coordinate **foreign policies** through institutionalized consultation and the exchange of ideas and information on international events and policies of common European concern. EPC was conducted through regular meetings of heads of state and government, foreign ministers and their mid and high level staff members. All EPC decisions were necessarily made by consensus.

While EPC served its purpose in some instances, it was essentially deficient in its ability to quickly respond to international events and crises and to formulate common European foreign policies and actions. EPC was officially recognized in the EC treaties in the **Single European Act** after which an EPC secretariat was established in **Brussels**. However, with few concrete advances as a result of EPC and elevated motivations for deeper political integration brought about by the collapse of the Soviet Union and end of the Cold War, EPC was replaced by the **Common Foreign and Security Policy** (CFSP) in the **Treaty on European Union**.

EUROPEAN REGIONAL DEVELOPMENT FUND (ERDF). Established in 1975, the ERDF provides financial assistance to underdeveloped regions, particularly those experiencing industrial decline. The fund was largely a response to the first **enlargement** of the **European Community** to include **Denmark**, **Ireland**, and the **United Kingdom** in 1973. It accounts for approximately half of all of the Community's **structural funds**. In order to receive funding for programs, part of the cost must be paid by the member state requesting support from the ERDF. Traditionally **Greece**, Ireland, **Italy**, **Portugal**, and **Spain** have received the most support from the ERDF. After the May 2004 enlargement to the **Central and Eastern European countries**, however, these countries also become highly eligible to receive financial assistance from the ERDF.

EUROPEAN RESEARCH AREA (ERA). In 2000 the Commission launched the ERA, which will be developed through the utilization of the resources of the **European Union** (EU) in order to better coordinate research and innovation activities throughout the EU. The idea behind the ERA is to provide an environment conducive to the protected sharing of information and results as well as access to the highest quality research institutions and equipment. The ERA will thus help contribute to the completion of a truly common research policy for the EU.

EUROPEAN SECURITY AND DEFENCE IDENTITY (ESDI). Although strongly anchored in the **North Atlantic Treaty Organization** (NATO), the ESDI is an independent European identity based on the security characteristics and threats specific to Europe. The outbreak of the wars in the **former Yugoslavia** provided an impetus for the creation of the ESDI. The development of the ESDI led to the eventual adoption of **Berlin Plus** and the ability of the **European Union** to independently engage in peacekeeping and **humanitarian** missions with access to NATO command and planning capabilities and assets. *See also* DEFENSE POLICY; EUROPEAN SECURITY AND DEFENCE POLICY (ESDP).

EUROPEAN SECURITY AND DEFENCE POLICY (ESDP). Born out of the **Saint Malo Declaration** of December 1998 calling for an autonomous **European Union** (EU) defense force for crisis management, the ESDP was officially introduced as a division of the **Common Foreign and Security Policy** (CFSP) at the Cologne **European Council** on 3–4 June 1999. The main objective of the ESDP is to develop military and civilian crisis management operations to be fully competent in the execution of the **Petersberg tasks**. ESDP is intended to complement the **North American Treaty Organization** (NATO), and will only be implemented autonomously when NATO is not involved. EU–NATO relations have been strategically coordinated, and through the **Berlin Plus** agreements, the EU is guaranteed access to NATO assets and capabilities for EU-led military operations.

Three permanent bodies were created to undertake the development of the ESDP: the **Political and Security Committee**, the **European Union Military Committee**, and the **European Union Military Staff**. The **European Security Strategy** of 12 December 2003 outlines challenges and threats, strategic objectives, and policy implications for the EU. In line with this strategy and in an effort to strengthen and make ESDP more efficient, the Council adopted a **joint action** on 12 July 2004 to establish a European Defence Agency which "will aim at developing defence capabilities in the field of crisis management, promoting and enhancing European armaments cooperation, strengthening the European defence industrial and technological base (DTIB) and creating a competitive European defence equipment market, as well as promoting, in liaison with the Community's research activities where appropriate, research aimed at leadership in strategic technologies for future defence and security capabilities, thereby strengthening Europe's industrial potential in this domain" (Council Joint Action 2004/551/CFSP of 12 July 2004 on the establishment of the European Defence Agency). Building upon two former **Western European Union** (WEU) institutions, the Council also established a **European Union Institute for Security Studies** in Paris and a **European Union Satellite Centre** in Torrejón, **Spain**. The former is charged with conducting academic research and analysis to help further develop the CFSP and ESDP, and the latter collects and analyzes information based on satellite space imagery.

The EU has been working toward developing civilian elements of crisis management, particularly police, rule of law, civilian administration, and civil protection. With regard to the military aspect, since 2003, the EU has led three crisis management/peacekeeping military operations: in the **Former Yugoslav Republic of Macedonia**, in the Democratic Republic of Congo, and in **Bosnia-Herzegovina**. *See also* DEFENSE POLICY; EUROPEAN SECURITY AND DEFENCE IDENTITY (ESDI); FOREIGN AND SECURITY POLICY.

EUROPEAN SECURITY STRATEGY. To meet the goals of defending Europe's security and promoting its values the European Security Strategy of 12 December 2003 establishes three strategic objectives: addressing the key threats defined as **terrorism**, proliferation of weapons of mass destruction, regional conflicts, state failure, and organized crime through a combination of political, economic, and diplomatic pressures; building security in the neighborhood of the **European Union** (EU) including addressing the problems of the Southern Caucasus and the Mediterranean and resolution of the Arab/Israeli conflict; and an international order based on effective multilateralism. The EU will work toward the last objective through **trade**, **development** and assistance programs. *See also* FOREIGN AND SECURITY POLICY; SOLANA , JAVIER.

EUROPEAN SOCIAL FUND (ESF). Established in the 1957 **Treaty of Rome**, the purpose of the ESF is to promote job creation and worker mobility, reduce long-term unemployment, and provide training and technological programs to encourage an advanced working force. Until the May 2004 **enlargement** eastern **Germany**, **Greece**, **Ireland**, **Italy**, **Portugal**, and **Spain** received the most support from the ESF. Following the enlargement the **Central and Eastern European countries** also became highly eligible to receive financial assistance from the ESF.

EUROPEAN STRATEGIC PROGRAMME FOR RESEARCH AND DEVELOPMENT IN INFORMATION AND TECHNOLOGY (ESPRIT). Inspired by the **single market** work and convictions of **Etienne Davignon**, the European commissioner responsible for industrial affairs and vice president of the **European Commission** from 1981 to 1985, ESPRIT was proposed by the European Commission and approved by the **Council** in 1982. ESPRIT is a basic research program with projects jointly funded by the **European Community** and private contributors. Trying to make the **European Union** (EU) more competitive in the industrial and technological sectors through increased cooperation, the program is composed of major manufacturing companies, small and medium size businesses, universities, and research institutes throughout the EU.

EUROPEAN SYSTEM OF CENTRAL BANKS (ESCB). Consisting of the national central banks of the **European Union** (EU) member states and the **European Central Bank** (ECB), the ESCB was established on 1 June 1998. The main responsibility of the ESCB is to develop and implement the common monetary policy for those EU member states that are part of the **euro zone** with the primary objective of maintaining price stability. The governing council of the ESCB is independent and the highest decision-making body in terms of the monetary policy. It consists of the ECB's executive board and the governors of the national central banks of the euro zone countries. On a daily basis the ECB executive board administers the monetary policy that has been outlined by the ESCB's governing council.

EUROPEAN TRAINING FOUNDATION (ETF). Created in 1990 and located in Turin, **Italy**, the ETF is an **agency of the European Union** and center of expertise in vocational **education and training**. The ETF designs, monitors, and assesses programs of vocational education and training projects and provides analysis on the subject to the **European Union** institutions. One of the main goals of the ETF is to develop better living conditions by helping to strengthen the skills of the people living within and across particular regions. The ETF operates in the candidate countries, South Eastern Europe, Eastern Europe and Central Asia, and in the Mediterranean region.

EUROPEAN UNION (EU). The EU is a voluntary regional organization composed of 25 member states (**Austria**, **Belgium**, **Cyprus**, **Czech Republic**, **Denmark**, **Estonia**, **Finland**, **France**, **Germany**, **Greece**, **Hungary**, **Ireland**, **Italy**, **Latvia**, **Lithuania**, **Luxembourg**, **Malta**, **The Netherlands**, **Poland**, **Portugal**, **Slovakia**, **Slovenia**, **Spain**, **Sweden**, and the **United Kingdom**), together containing a population of 457 million citizens. The member states attempt to cooperate in areas of mutual interest and agree to pool their sovereignty in certain competences and place them under the jurisdiction of a higher authority—the EU institutions. Sharing these powers with institutions above the level of the state is known as **supranationalism**. There is a strong institutional structure in the EU composed of, among others, the **European Council**, the **Council of the EU**, the **European Commission**, the **European Parliament**, and the **European Court of Justice**. **Decisions** and policies made regarding the pooled competences at the supranational level are binding on the member states and in these areas EU **law** has **supremacy** over the national laws of the member states.

European integration was institutionalized through the signing of the **Treaty of Paris** in 1951, creating the **European Coal and Steel Community**. Through several different processes of **widening** its membership and **deepening** its supranational authority, the EU has developed into its current form. The EU was officially established on 1 November 1993 when the **Treaty on European Union** went into effect, incorporating all of the elements of the **European Community** and establishing tools for intergovernmental cooperation in additional areas (**Common Foreign and Security Policy** and **Justice and Home Affairs**) within a **three pillar** system.

EUROPEAN UNION INSTITUTE FOR SECURITY STUDIES (EUISS). Created on 20 July 2001 and located in Paris, **France**, the EUISS is an autonomous **agency of the European Union** (EU) **Common Foreign and Security Policy** (CFSP). Through research and analysis, the EUISS attempts to strengthen the CFSP as well as develop a transatlantic security dialogue between the EU, the **United States**, and Canada.

EUROPEAN UNION MILITARY COMMITTEE (EUMC). The EUMC was created to provide support for the **European Security and Defence Policy** (ESDP) and is composed of the defense chiefs of each one of the member states, but most often meets at a lower level when not in a crisis situation. The EUMC serves as an institutionalized arena for the exchange of information and cooperation between member states in the area of ESDP. The EUMC provides support to the **political and security committee** for decisions regarding military capabilities and options.

EUROPEAN UNION MILITARY STAFF (EUMS). Created as a support mechanism for the **European Security and Defence Policy** (ESDP), the EUMS is composed of military staff from the **European Union** (EU) member states and is part of the **Council of the EU**. The main purpose of the EUMS is to provide expert military support for the ESDP in all of its endeavors.

EUROPEAN UNION SATELLITE CENTRE (EUSC). Created on 20 July 2001 and located in Torrejón, **Spain**, the EUSC is an **agency of the European Union** that provides satellite imaging analysis to help **decision-making** for the **Common Foreign and Security Policy** (CFSP). The EUSC falls under the political supervision of the **Political and Security Committee**, and tries to particularly provide information with regard to the crisis monitoring and conflict prevention aspects of CFSP.

EUROSTAT. Created as a statistical service for the **High Authority** at the end of 1952 with a seven-person staff, Eurostat has developed into an institution of more than 600 people with the mission to "provide the **European Union** with a high-quality statistical information service." In order to coordinate statistics Eurostat relies on harmonization and strong relations with national statistical institutes as well as with international organizations. It provides information on topics such as the economy and finance; population and social conditions; industry, trade and services; **agriculture** and industry; external **trade**; **transport**; **environment** and **energy**; and science and technology. Eurostat is located in **Luxembourg** and its office falls under the jurisdiction of the Commissioner for Economic and Monetary Affairs.

EXCHANGE RATE MECHANISM (ERM). The ERM is a currency regulating instrument. It was established in 1979 as part of the **European Monetary System** and used an artificial currency (the **European Currency Unit** [ECU]) as the basis of its system of accounting. Participation in the ERM was not mandatory. Those member states that chose to participate had to maintain the value of their currencies within $(+/-)$ 2.25 percent of the value of the ECU. Economic difficulties in the member states in the early 1990s forced **Italy** and the **United Kingdom** to withdraw from the ERM and the bandwidth to be increased to $(+/-)$ 15 percent. In order for member states to adopt the **euro**, they had to maintain their national currency within the ERM for a period of at least two years. *See also* EXCHANGE RATE MECHANISM II (ERM II).

EXCHANGE RATE MECHANISM II (ERM II). In order to promote monetary stability throughout the **European Union** (EU)—between **euro zone** and non–euro zone member states—and to help the non–euro zone countries meet the requirements to eventually adopt the euro—the ERM II became operational on 1 January 1999. Some member states either continue to opt out of ERM II or have not been able to stabilize their currencies enough to join. ERM II has a standard fluctuation band of $(+/-)$ 15 percent. *See also* EXCHANGE RATE MECHANISM (ERM).

EXTERNAL RELATIONS. The **European Union** (EU) maintains an intricate network of foreign affairs with third countries, groups of countries, and other international organizations. The EU's external relations take on many different forms including **development**, **enlargement**, the **European Neighborhood Policy**, external assistance, external **trade**, **foreign policy**, and **humanitarian aid**.

The **European Commission**'s External Service has 130 offices and delegations throughout the world that control and monitor the EU's external policies and programs and serve as a liaison between the EU and foreign governments. Additionally, the EU holds institutionalized high level meetings with several individual countries such as the **United States** and **Russia**, and on a multilateral basis with, for example, **Latin America** and Caribbean countries in the form of summits of heads of state and government. Candidate countries to the

EU are given high priority on the EU foreign affairs agenda and comprehensive agreements are designed to guide relations between the EU and these countries toward eventual membership.

The EU and its member states together contribute more to development assistance than any other individual country or organization in the world, representing approximately half of the total yearly international disbursements in this area. With the EU more integrated in economic competences, its external relations have traditionally focused on trade, aid, and other international financial transactions with third countries. However, with the creation of the **Common Foreign and Security Policy**, the EU has expanded its third country relations into the political area, especially in terms of promoting peace and stability and cooperatively addressing cross-border concerns. As the EU's foreign-related political decision and policy making is essentially **intergovernmental**, this aspect of its foreign affairs remains in a developmental yet progressing stage. The EU has been successful in requiring that all of its trade and cooperation agreements include a **human rights** clause, effectively combining elements of both political and economic policies in its conduct of foreign affairs.

– F –

FEDERALISM. The classical political theory of federalism, espoused by Alexander Hamilton, John Jay, and James Madison in *The Federalist* papers to garner support for the **United States** Constitution of 1787, is based on a union in which there is a constitutionally guaranteed division of power between central and local government. There are various forms and degrees of federalism, yet in most cases it includes provisions granting the central government the sole prerogative to maintain an army and declare war, and the central and local governments shared authority to raise and/or administer revenue through **taxation**.

Today's European federalists highly endorse the evolution of the **European Union** (EU) into a "United States of Europe," a goal seen as idealistic by most and incongruent with the original objectives of the EU founding fathers by many. **Euro-skeptics**, on the other side of the debate, associate the idea of stronger federalism in the EU as a means of usurping power from the sovereign member states and concentrating it in the EU institutions in **Brussels**. There have been attempts to officially include federalist objectives in the EU, such as in the **Treaty on European Union**, but all attempts were blocked by Euro-skeptic states, particularly the **United Kingdom**. Ironically, one of the methods adopted and promoted by Euro-skeptics as a means to prevent what they most fear, is actually a federalist approach to government: **subsidiarity**, which basically means that decisions will be taken at the closest possible level to the citizen and only at the highest level necessary. Whether or not the word is used in the official documentation of the EU, there is evidence that significant aspects of federalism have developed along with the **deepening** of EU integration.

FINANCIAL INSTRUMENT FOR FISHERIES GUIDANCE (FIFG). Part of the **structural funds** of the **European Union** (EU), the FIFG provides monetary support for the **fisheries** and aquaculture sector. The main objective of the FIFG is to help achieve the goals of the EU's common fisheries policy, which include maintaining adequate levels of fish stocks, and increasing competitiveness, modernization, and diversification. There is a strong emphasis on the need to provide support in the processing and marketing of fishery and aquaculture products. Other projects that receive funding from FIFG include but are not limited to: fleet renewal and modernization of fishing vessels; protection of marine resources; fishing port facilities; and technical assistance. For the period 2000–2006, €1.1 billion were allocated to the FIFG.

FINET, PAUL. Refer to appendix B.

FINLAND. Despite decades of informal Soviet dominance and limited or no membership in key European organizations during the Cold War, the Republic of Finland was motivated to apply for membership in the **European Community** on 18 March 1992. This decision was prompted by a steady normalization of relations with Western Europe, the collapse of the Soviet Union and the economic advantages it once provided to Finland, and economic necessity in this post–Cold War period. Finland (along with **Austria** and **Sweden**) was a member of the so-called EFTA **enlargement** of 1995, characterized by traditionally neutral and relatively wealthy countries, and a smooth negotiation process lasting only 13 months.

Finland's participation in the **European Union** (EU) was questionable considering its Cold War legacy, its neutrality, and demands to retain its policy of military non-alignment. However, during 10 years of EU membership Finland has proven to be an active participant in all aspects of EU integration including the **Common Foreign and Security Policy** (CFSP). In this respect, Finland has been a strong supporter of developing military crisis management as part of the CFSP, and promoting **human rights**. In 1997, Finland introduced its **Northern Dimension** Initiative to increase cooperation between the EU, **Russia**, and other northern neighbors, and to focus on northern-specific issues. The Northern Dimension is now a pillar of the EU's **external relations**, and was also an instrumental part of the 2004 enlargement process.

Finland has come to be known as one of the compromisers in EU negotiations, attempting to arrive at policy solutions acceptable to both EU and member state actors. Not as **Euro-skeptic** as the other Nordic countries, Finland finds economic and political advantages for small states like itself in EU membership. Its economy has improved dramatically over the past few decades, and Finland is the sole Nordic EU member state to have adopted the **euro** as its national currency. *See also* EUROPEAN FREE TRADE ASSOCIATION (EFTA). Refer to appendix A.

FISHERIES. First mentioned in the **Treaty of Rome**, it was not until 1983 that the **European Community** (EC) adopted a Common Fisheries Policy (CFP). According to the CFP, there are three categories of fishing waters: those within 12 miles of the coast in which fishing rights are guaranteed to local fishermen; those between 12 and 200 miles of the coast in which fishing rights are guaranteed to all EC fishermen; and those beyond 200 miles of the coast, or international waters, in which rights and regulations are established through international agreements negotiated by the EC. Intended to ensure the security of stock supplies, protect the marine **environment**, and to develop the industry to the benefit of fishing communities and consumers, the 1983 policy was not sufficient in reaching its objectives.

With an eye toward reform, a new CFP was adopted and came into effect on 1 January 2003. While the objectives remain the same, the new CFP is designed to take a longer term approach to stock conservation rather than annual total allowable catch, to implement better enforcement mechanisms, to develop new fleet policies to ensure that fleet capacity coincides with allotted catch limits, and to include members of fishing communities and scientists in the policy-making process for the new CFP.

The **Financial Instrument for Fisheries Guidance** is the main source of funding for the CFP. Financial assistance is provided to meet the CFP objectives in different ways including research and innovation, developing aquaculture, marketing, and **sustainable development**.

FLAG. Adopted by the **European Council** the same year as the official **anthem** of the **European Union** (EU), the EU flag is a circle of 12 gold stars on a bright blue background. The same flag has represented the **Council of Europe** since 1955, and beginning in 1985 it has been the official flag of the EU and the **European Commission**. Unlike the **United States** flag, the number of stars (12) is permanent and does not change with the number of EU member states.

FONTAINE, NICOLE (1942–). A center-right French politician, Nicole Fontaine has been a member of the **European Parliament** (EP) since 1984. Having previously served as vice president of the EP and a member of the **Conciliation Committee** (established with the **co-decision procedure**), Fontaine was elected as President of the EP in 1999, a post she would hold until 2002. In the 2004–2009 EP Fontaine is serving her fifth consecutive term as MEP and is a member of the **Group of the European Peoples' Party** (Christian Democrats) **and European Democrats**. Refer to appendix D.

FOOD SAFETY. Food-related health scares in the **European Union** (EU), such as the sale of beef contaminated with Bovine Spongiform Encephalopathy (mad cow disease) from the **United Kingdom** and dioxin-contaminated food products from **Belgium**, have diminished consumer confidence in European food products. In response, the EU has developed a comprehensive strategy, "from the farm to the fork," to try and restore the trust of the European consumers.

A Regulation adopted in 2002, commonly referred to as the General Food Law, updates food safety laws throughout the EU and ensures that there is a chain of safety measures which includes feed, livestock, and final products. The EU has also established a rapid alert system in which the governments of the EU member states notify the **European Commission** in the event of any potential food-related risks, which subsequently disseminates the information throughout the EU.

In 2002, the creation of the **European Food Safety Authority** (EFSA) was approved with the responsibility of providing independent scientific advice to the European Commission. EFSA is headquartered in Parma, **Italy**.

Food safety is also subject to strict enforcement and control measures. Individual food production plants as well as member state governments can be inspected to monitor compliance with food safety rules and practices. The Food and Veterinary Office (FVO) of the European Commission, located in Grange, **Ireland**, is the office responsible for these investigations. *See also* AGRICULTURAL POLICY.

FOREIGN AND SECURITY POLICY. The idea that the **European Union** (EU) needs to have an integrated foreign and security policy to complement its international economic might has been discussed for decades. Given the special, sensitive, and security interests of each of the individual member states, however, this has been one of the most difficult tasks to achieve as was witnessed during the 2003 **United States** intervention in Iraq and the differences of opinion amongst the EU member states and the then candidate countries. Nevertheless, as uncertainty persists in the international arena, the EU continues to take deliberate steps to address such concerns and potential threats to its security.

Beginning with the **European Political Cooperation** in the 1970s, the EC member states tried to coordinate their foreign policies on pressing international issues. In the **Treaty on European Union**, the **Common Foreign and Security Policy** (CFSP) became the second pillar of the EU, remaining **intergovernmental** but having the institutionalized support and ability to develop **joint actions** and **common positions**. The post of **High Representative for the CFSP** was included in the **Treaty of Amsterdam**. Also included in this treaty are the types of cases which an EU defense and/or military force would consider undertaking; the **Petersberg tasks** which were first adopted by the **Western European Union** in 1992 and include **humanitarian** missions, peacekeeping and peacemaking, and crisis management. As part of the **European Security and Defence Policy** (ESDP), the EU conducted its first two missions in the **former Yugoslavia** in 2003, one in **Bosnia-Herzegovina** and one in the **Former Yugoslav Republic of Macedonia**. In December 2003, a **European Security Strategy** was adopted to focus on the global war on terror, the **Middle East**, and Bosnia-Herzegovina. *See also* DEFENSE POLICY; EXTERNAL RELATIONS; FOUCHET PLAN; TERRORISM.

FOUCHET PLAN. An initiative of French President **Charles de Gaulle** beginning in 1960, the Fouchet Plan was the result of a committee created to investigate and outline possibilities for enhanced political and security cooperation between the member states of the **European Community**. The chair of this committee was Christian Fouchet, the French ambassador to **Denmark**.

Lacking **supranational** characteristics, the Fouchet Plan contained an intergovernmental institutional framework outside the **Treaty of Rome** in which the states would have dominant control over foreign and defense policy cooperation. The smaller states of the EC adamantly opposed the Fouchet Plan and the project was abandoned by 1962.

FRAMEWORK DECISION. An instrument for cooperation in **justice and home affairs** (JHA) incorporated in the **Treaty of Amsterdam**, framework decisions replace **joint actions**. Framework decisions are used as a guideline for the convergence of laws and regulations between the member states in areas of JHA. The **European Commission** or a member state may propose a framework decision, which must be agreed upon unanimously and becomes binding on the member states once adopted.

FRANCE. Marking the beginning of European-style integration, on 9 May 1950, French Foreign Minister **Robert Schuman** proposed the pooling of the French and German coal and steel industries; an offer that would be open to all democratic Western European countries in the aftermath of World War II. **Jean Monnet**, who was appointed National Planning Commissioner by President **Charles de Gaulle**, is also known as the "Father of Europe" and was responsible for the first ideas regarding this type of **supranational** organization for Europe.

A founding member of the **European Coal and Steel Community** (ECSC), France has participated in all aspects of the European integration process. Traditionally, France has been considered one of the most influential **European Union** (EU) member states, playing an important leadership role in what has come to be know as the Franco–German motor of European integration.

In 1952, the six founding members of the **European Community** (EC) signed the **European Defence Community** treaty. Ironically, the country in which the initiative began and the one in which the treaty was signed, France, would within several years also cause its defeat. Due in large part to the idea of sharing sovereignty in such a highly sensitive competence, the French parliament rejected the treaty in its ratification process in 1954, effectively rendering the proposal a failure.

Charles de Gaulle, president of the French Fifth Republic from 1958 to 1969, signed the **Treaty of the Elysée** along with German Chancellor **Konrad Adenauer** in 1963, setting the precedent for Franco–German cooperation. Nevertheless, de Gaulle did not always assume this collaborative attitude, and particularly not with all of his European counterparts. Twice he vetoed the **United Kingdom**'s application for EC membership, once in 1963 and once in 1967, unable to agree on negotiations regarding the **Common Agricultural Policy** (CAP), amongst other sensitive issues and interests. The first and only so-called crisis of **governance** in the EC—the **Empty Chair Crisis**—was a direct result of de Gaulle's actions during the European Summit of June 1965 when he recalled his government's EC representatives and officials in a dispute over the funding of the CAP. De Gaulle's position on EC policies varied depending on the particular issue and favored an economically integrated Europe while leaving the political decisions, responsibilities, and competences under the sole authority of national leaders.

With quite a different perspective on European integration, another influential French leader in this process was French President **François Mitterrand**. Mitterrand encouraged enhanced economic integration, including the idea of the European common currency, supporting the **European Commission** president, Frenchman **Jacques Delors**, largely responsible for negotiating the necessary policies for the creation of the **single market** and the **euro**. In light of the changing European context, Mitterrand also came to favor increased political coordination, cooperation, and integration. Following the fall of the **Berlin Wall**, he co-authored with German Chancellor **Helmut Kohl** in 1990 a letter to the president of the **European Council** recommending and supporting European efforts toward constructing a European Political Union.

In terms of policy, with the creation of the **European Economic Community** (EEC) through the signing of the 1957 **Treaty of Rome**, France demanded that its **agricultural** sector (in which approximately 20 percent of the French population worked at that time) be compensated on a level comparable to that of the benefits Germany's manufacturing industry would reap from the EEC. Thus, with the help of the CAP, French agriculture was modernized and the economy became able to support increased industrialization. Although the percentage of French agricultural workers has considerably decreased since then, they are a well-organized, widely supported group that has successfully pressured both the French national government and the European institutions in **Brussels** to maintain the agricultural benefits associated with the CAP. While France has participated in all aspects and policies of EU integration, the CAP undoubtedly remains one of the most crucial and at times controversial EU policies for this founding member state.

France is an essential member state of the EU. In addition to its role in the policy and **decision-making** processes, its city of Strasbourg is host to the plenary sessions of the **European Parliament**. Two of the treaties were agreed to and signed in France: the 1951 **Treaty of Paris** establishing the ECSC and the more recent **Treaty of Nice**. Nevertheless, in a national referendum held on 29 May 2005, the French citizens voted against the **Treaty establishing a Constitution for Europe**, creating a significant obstacle to the completion of the ratification process. Refer to appendix A.

FREE TRADE AREA. Consisting of two or more countries or groups of countries, a free trade area exists when agreement is reached among all participants on the removal of barriers to trade in goods. In order to have a true free trade area both tariff and non-tariff barriers should be eliminated and it should be applied to all goods traded between the countries involved. In most free trade areas, however, there are at least some exceptions to these rules. *See also* EUROPEAN FREE TRADE ASSOCIATION (EFTA).

FUNCTIONALISM. A conceptual framework for trying to explain integration, functionalism asserts that cooperation between countries will be enhanced when the integration process begins gradually, in specific issue areas that can be managed by technical experts (rather than political officials). Functionalists argue that once integration becomes consolidated in these areas, it will spill-over into additional related areas.

One of the most prominent functionalists was David Mitrany who developed the concept on an international level in the hopes of creating a lasting international peace. In the early years of European integration, functionalism was often used to explain the process as it began with the pooling of the coal and steel industries (specific competences) under a higher authority and spilled over into the areas of the economy and atomic energy with the **Treaties of Rome** in 1957. Not considered a sufficient explanatory tool for much longer, considering the complex and political elements of European integration, theorists reformed the concept in the 1960s and 1970s into a neo-functionalist approach.

FURLER, HANS. Refer to appendix D.

– G –

GALILEO SATELLITE RADIO NAVIGATION SYSTEM. A joint initiative between the **European Union** (EU) and the European Space Agency, Galileo is an independent satellite navigation system. Although still in its developmental phase, Galileo will provide satellite positioning services for individual, business, and professional use in a wide variety of sectors such as **transport**, **energy**, and civil protection. The projected date for the start of commercial operations is 2008.

The EU is encouraging international cooperation and participation in this project. Thus far, **China** and Israel have signed agreements with the EU regarding their participation in this endeavor and negotiations are under way with several other countries including Australia, Brazil, and India. It is expected that this investment will have long-term returns given the projected future international demand for these public services.

GASPERI, ALCIDE DE (1881–1954). One of the strongest supporters of deeper European integration and a more federal union, Alcide de Gasperi was the Christian Democrat prime minister of **Italy** for eight consecutive governments from 1945 to 1953, during which time he accepted **Robert Schuman**'s proposal to pool the European coal and steel industries under a **high authority**. He is considered to be one of the founding fathers of the **European Community**. In May 1954, de Gasperi was elected president of the Assembly of the **European Coal and Steel Community**. Refer to appendix D.

GAULLE, CHARLES DE (1890–1970). Dedicating much of his life to a military career, Charles de Gaulle was the leader of the French resistance during World War II. He later became the first president of the French Fifth Republic (1958–1969), personally overseeing the writing of a new constitution with powers concentrated in the office of the president and a successful economic recovery. A French nationalist, de Gaulle wished for **France** to develop a strong independent foreign policy and its own nuclear weapons, a goal which was achieved by 1960.

During his tenure in the French presidency, de Gaulle considered French membership in the **European Community** (EC) as a vehicle for increased economic development in the industrial but particularly **agricultural** sector, for reestablishing France as a major actor in the international community, and for consolidating a Franco–German rapprochement.

In 1960, de Gaulle proposed a type of institutionalized intergovernmental cooperation in the area of **foreign and security policy**. His proposal was outlined in the **Fouchet Plan** but ultimately rejected by the other member states.

De Gaulle worked diligently toward improving relations with **Germany**. Largely based on de Gaulle's initiative, the **Elysée Treaty** of Franco–German Friendship and Reconciliation was signed by de Gaulle and German Chancellor **Konrad Adenauer** on 22 January 1963.

In 1963 and 1967, de Gaulle rejected the British application for EC membership based on concerns regarding Britain's strong ties with the **United States** and the possibility of the **United Kingdom** disrupting the **Common Agricultural Policy** (CAP), an issue of extreme importance to de Gaulle and the French government.

European Commission President **Walter Hallstein** in 1965 proposed changes to the funding of the CAP, increased budgetary powers for the European Commission and **European Parliament**, and greater use of the **qualified majority voting**. De Gaulle felt these initiatives to be a threat to France's national interests within the EC as well as to its sovereignty, and an unnecessary concentration of powers in **Brussels**. Failure to reach agreement on these issues resulted in one of the only institutional crises in the EC, the so-called **Empty Chair Crisis**, when de Gaulle recalled all French representatives to the EC institutions. This crisis was eventually resolved through the **Luxembourg Compromise** in January 1966.

Despite destabilizing mass protests and strikes in France in May 1968, de Gaulle survived this politically tumultuous period with overwhelming support in June elections. Nevertheless, de Gaulle retired in April 1969 and died shortly thereafter on 9 November 1970.

GENDER EQUALITY. Gender equality has been a goal and policy of the **European Union** (EU) since its inclusion in the 1957 **Treaty of Rome**. Progress in this area has remained slow yet significant steps have been taken, particularly in the 1990s in light of the United Nations Women's Conference in Beijing, **China**, in 1995, to remedy this situation. Gender mainstreaming has been growing in importance for the **European Commission** as it attempts to ensure that the gender equality goals are incorporated into all Community policies in all stages of the policy-making process. Gender equality objectives are supported by a Community Framework Strategy on Gender Equality as well as with an action program. Equal pay for men and women holding the same positions and responsibilities is the law and maternity leave is mandatory in all of the EU member states. In order to further promote gender equality throughout the EU, the European Commission proposed on 8 March 2005 the creation of a European Institute for Gender Equality.

Levels of gender equality differ amongst the member states of the EU, with the northern states tending to be more efficient in this area than the southern member states as well as some of the member states that joined the EU in 2004. Overall in the EU, there are far less women than men holding high level positions in both the public and private sectors, a problem the Commission has been trying to resolve through awareness, related legislation, and indeed, encouraging greater gender equality in the high level positions of the EU institutions. While the European Commission has the highest ever percentage of women with seven out of the college of 25 being women, there are just two female judges and two female advocates-general on the **European Court of Justice**. Two female prime ministers have represented their countries in the meetings of the **European Council**, former British Prime Minister **Margaret Thatcher** and former French Prime Minister **Edith Cresson**; both of whom in their own way, whether positively or negatively, have left their lasting respective marks on the EU.

GENERAL AFFAIRS COUNCIL (GAC). One of the nine configurations of the **Council of the European Union**, GAC is composed of the foreign ministers of each one of the member states. Along with the **Economic and Finance Council**, GAC is one of, if not the most influential of the Council formations. **European Political Cooperation** followed by **Common Foreign and Security Policy** as the second pillar of the **European Union** reinforced GAC's status. GAC is responsible for **decision-making** on proposed legislation related to **foreign policy**.

GENERAL AGREEMENT ON TARIFFS AND TRADE (GATT). GATT was established in October 1947 as a mechanism for increasing trade by incrementally lowering tariff and non-tariff barriers on the exchange of goods, and later services. There were eight rounds of trade promotion and barrier reduction talks under GATT. The **Uruguay Round**, which lasted from 1986 to 1993, was the most contentious as it dealt with an increasing number of issue areas that the **European Union** (EU) had, for the most part, previously been able to avoid. These issues included the reduction of non-tariff barriers to **trade**, including farm subsidies in the **agricultural** sector. Completion of the Uruguay Round was dependent upon the EU agreeing to reform the **Common Agricultural Policy**, a difficult task that was facilitated by the previous commitment to the **Mac-Sharry** agricultural reforms.

By the end of the Uruguay Round agreement was reached on the creation of a formal organization to supersede GATT, the **World Trade Organization**. (WTO), which began operations in 1995, headquartered in Geneva, **Switzerland**. There are 149 members of the WTO, a significant increase from the 23 founding members of GATT. In 2001, the WTO launched a new round of trade talks, the **Doha Development Round**, with the aim of increasing market liberalization and negotiating agreements better suited to the developing countries.

GENETICALLY MODIFIED ORGANISMS (GMOs). Any organism that has had its genetic composition intentionally altered is considered a GMO, and genetically modified food is any product that contains a GMO. **Trade** disputes have arisen over GMOs between the **United States**, the number one producer of genetically modified food in the world, and the **European Union** (EU), which takes a more cautionary approach to GMOs. Pressure from consumer and **environmental** groups related to widespread public concern about the possible impact on human health and the environment prompted the EU to ban the importation of new GMOs at the end of the 1990s (and also lead to a de facto moratorium on EU authorization for GMOs or products and feeds containing GMOs). After several years in effect, the **World Trade Organization** judged that preventing the importation of genetically modified food products was an altering intervention of the open market trade system. The EU now allows for the importation of GMOs under the principle of prevention; if the safety of the product has not been proven it will not be allowed, and there are strict standards for labeling these products. *See also* AGRI-CULTURAL POLICY.

GENSCHER–COLOMBO PLAN. An initiative introduced in November 1981 by German foreign minister, Hans-Dietrich Genscher, and co-supported by **Italy's** foreign minister, Emilio Colombo, the Genscher–Colombo Plan was a design to give greater priority to **external relations** in the **European Community** (EC) by giving the EC institutions increased authority over **foreign policy** issues and by easing the **decision-making** process in this area. Officially known as the **Draft European Act**, the Genscher–Colombo Plan to increase security and foreign policy cooperation was rejected by those countries wary of integration into these sensitive areas, and therefore, did not materialize into a formal policy.

GERMANY. Germany's eventual defeat in World War II left the country's future in the hands of the victorious Allied powers (**France**, the Union of Soviet Socialist Republics, the **United Kingdom**, and the **United States**). Before long, and as a result of ideological differences between the powers that occupied its territory, Germany also found itself as the symbolic epicenter of what would become a prolonged Cold War, with the Iron Curtain dividing the Federal Republic of Germany in the capitalist West and the German Democratic Republic in the Soviet East. An independent Federal Republic of Germany (West Germany) was established in 1949 through the Basic Law (the equivalent of a constitutional text) with the express consent and supervision of the United States, France, and Britain, and the Soviets responded in kind later that same year with the founding of the German Democratic Republic (East Germany), one of the key members of the Central and Eastern European Soviet bloc.

When **Robert Schuman**, the French foreign minister, proposed the pooling of the French and German coal and steel resources under a **High Authority** on 9 May 1950, **Konrad Adenauer**, the first chancellor of West Germany was convinced that participation was the means through which West Germany could recover economically and begin to regain political respectability in the international community without arousing the uncontrollable anxiety that Germany's legacy of power and unmeasured ambition had once produced. Thus, West Germany signed the **Treaty of Paris** in 1951, becoming one of the six founding members of the **European Coal and Steel Community**. This member state participates in all aspects of European integration and has generally supported a stronger and deeper integration process. Germany, in alliance with France, has traditionally been considered the "motor" driving and guiding the European integration process.

The economic miracle experienced in West Germany in the 1950s and 1960s consolidated its dominance as the economic force behind the **European Community** (EC). At the same time, however, it remained relatively difficult for West Germany to pursue its political objectives in the region, largely as a result of the collective memory of World War II. In an effort to increase its political prowess, West Germany would compromise on several economic issues in exchange for attempts at **deepening** political cooperation within the EC.

One of the most controversial foreign policies West Germany was determined to implement in the 1970s under the Chancellorship of **Willy Brandt** was *Ostpolitik*, or the normalization of relations with the **Central and Eastern European countries**, and particularly East Germany. Given the international Cold War environment at the time, this strategy evoked concern from devout anti-Communists on both sides of the Atlantic. Therefore, the German government successfully supported the creation of **European Political Cooperation** as a method of institutionalizing (albeit weakly) **EC foreign policy** cooperation, converging foreign policy perceptions, and obtaining regional rather than unilateral support.

The fall of the **Berlin Wall** in 1989, and the imminent collapse of the Soviet Union and reunification of Germany, irrevocably altered the dynamics of European and international relations. In this context, French President **François Mitterrand** and German Chancellor **Helmut Kohl** submitted a letter to the president of the **European Council** recommending and supporting European efforts toward constructing a European Political Union. Strengthening the EC's political competence would be a way to abate fears regarding Germany's power and influence in the middle of a reunified Europe.

By 3 October 1990, less than one year after the fall of the Berlin Wall, Helmut Kohl was elected the first chancellor of a reunited Germany, giving the former East Germany de facto membership in the EC. This reunification proved to be an expensive undertaking for both the EC and the German governments. In fact, the German government is still dealing with economic difficulties including low economic growth, high levels of unemployment, and the inability to meet the deficit requirements demanded by Germany itself in the **Stability and Growth Pact**. Refer to appendix A.

GIL-ROBLES, JOSE MARIA. Refer to appendix D.

GISCARD D'ESTAING, VALERY (1926–). A longtime proponent of European integration, Valéry Giscard d'Estaing is a **French** center-right politician who was elected to the French National Assembly in 1956, served as finance minister during the 1960s, and was elected president of the French Republic in 1974, a position he held until 1981. During his presidential administration, he encouraged the creation of the **European Council** and supported the creation of the **European Monetary System**. He also founded in 1978 the Union for French Democracy, a pro-Europe center-right political party.

Following his presidential term in office, Giscard d'Estaing has remained active in French and European politics. He was a member of the **European Parliament** from 1989 to 1993 and created the Institute for Democracy in Europe in 1996. From February 2002 to June 2003, Giscard d'Estaing was the chairman of the **European Convention**, an arena in which the future of Europe was debated, the most tangible result being the submission of a draft constitutional treaty to the European Council in Thessaloniki in June 2003. In 2004, Giscard d'Estaing assumed his seat on the French Constitutional Council, a right granted to all former French presidents.

GONZALEZ, FELIPE (1942–). After the victory of the Spanish Socialist Workers Party (PSOE) in the 1982 general elections, the secretary general of the PSOE, Felipe González, became the President of the Spanish government. With the PSOE winning four consecutive general elections, González remained the head of government until 5 May 1996 when he was replaced by the leader of the Popular Party, **José María Aznar**.

During González's first administration he successfully completed the negotiations for Spanish membership in the **European Community** (EC). **Spain** became an EC member state on 1 January 1986 and less than three months later a national referendum was held regarding continued Spanish participation in the **North Atlantic Treaty Organization** (NATO), a policy Prime Minister González had originally opposed but later effectively convinced the government and citizens to support. During his administrations and the **European Union** (EU) treaty negotiations that coincided with them, Felipe González became the de facto champion of the less developed EU countries (**Greece, Ireland**, **Portugal**, and Spain), consistently campaigning for more EU funding to support the **cohesion policy** and assist these countries with meeting the requirements to participate in all aspects of EU integration.

GOVERNANCE. Improving the quality of governance is one of the priorities of the **European Union** (EU) in terms of bringing the EU closer to the people and strengthening its democracy. In this respect the **European Commission** published a **White Paper** in July 2001, defining governance as "all the rules, procedures and practices affecting how powers are exercised within the European Union." The Commission established five principles of good governance—accountability, cohesion, effectiveness, openness, and participation—which the EU works toward internally as well as in its relations with other countries and regions.

GREECE. Representing the only single-member state **enlargement** of the **European Community** (EC), Greece has a long yet sporadic history of relations with this organization. In 1962, Greece and the EC entered into their first association agreement which was subsequently suspended in 1967 due to the rise of a dictatorial regime. With the transitional return to democracy in 1974, the agreement was reinstated. Soon thereafter, on 12 July 1975, Greek Prime Minister Konstantinos Karamanlis submitted the country's application for full EC membership in an effort to protect the country's security and nascent democracy, particularly after the July 1974 Turkish invasion and occupation of Northern **Cyprus**.

Initially Greece's application was not favorably considered based on its poor economic standing. However, political concerns prevailed and Greece became the 10th EC member state on 1 January 1981. Unexpectedly, a decade of strained relations ensued after **Andreas Papandreou**, who radically opposed Greek membership in the EC during his election campaign, became the Greek prime minister on 21 October 1981. During his leadership, he threatened to block **Spain** and **Portugal**'s accession if Greece was not guaranteed compensatory funding to ensure it would not be negatively affected financially as a consequence of this future enlargement process. The result was the **Integrated Mediterranean Programmes** which provided funding to the southern European countries in an effort to increase development and cohesion with the north. By the mid-1990s, Greece's attitude had shifted, and it generally encouraged deeper European integration.

Despite impressive economic growth and development since its EC membership, Greece was the only member state wanting to join the final stage of the **Economic and Monetary Union** that did not meet the requirements by 1 January 1999. However, after implementing policies to reduce its deficit to apparently comply with the **convergence criteria**, Greece became a member of the **euro zone** on 1 January 2001. Hosting the Summer Olympic Games in 2004 brought worldwide attention to Greece, but also created a financial burden including a deficit exceeding the 3 percent stipulated in the **Stability and Growth Pact**, a goal that in the 21st century has been difficult for even the most developed EU member states such as **France** and **Germany**, to achieve.

The long-lasting dispute between Greece and **Turkey** regarding the sovereignty of a divided Cyprus has naturally influenced the EU candidacies of both Turkey and Cyprus. The Greek–Cypriots rejected a United Nations peace agreement in a referendum on 24 April 2004, and therefore, only the southern Greek–Cypriot governed Republic of Cyprus became an EU member state on 1 May 2004. EU accession negotiations with Turkey remain controversial for many reasons, not least of which is this continued conflict. Refer to appendix A.

GREEN PAPER. Documents published by the **European Commission**, Green Papers are intended to encourage discussion and consultations regarding specific topics being considered for future **European Union** legislation. Positive feedback from consultations with groups and organizations that have an interest in the results of **decision-making** regarding the issues in question may lead to the publication of a **White Paper** with more formal policy proposals.

GROUP OF THE ALLIANCE OF LIBERALS AND DEMO-CRATS FOR EUROPE (ALDE). Officially established on 14 July 2004, this pro-European center parliamentary group mainly consists of former European Liberal, Democratic, and Reformist Party members, along with some significant additional membership from new member states and different political parties. ALDE is the third largest **political group in the European Parliament** with 88 members from 19 countries. All of the May 2004 **enlargement** countries are represented in this group with the exception of **Slovenia**, **Malta**, and the **Czech Republic**.

The members of ALDE support increased European integration as the means to achieve an economically strong and politically sound Europe. The group has designed a ten-point plan for Europe based on its core values of promoting freedom and democracy.

GROUP OF THE EUROPEAN PEOPLES' PARTY (CHRISTIAN DEMOCRATS) AND EUROPEAN DEMOCRATS (EPP-ED). The Christian Democrats have been a dominant European **political group** since the 1950s, consistently obtaining representation from all **European Union** member states. In 1992, the European Democratic Group joined the European Peoples' Party to form the leading center-right political party group in the **European Parliament** (EP).

In the 2004–2009 EP, the EPP-ED is the largest parliamentary group with a total of 268 members, and is the only European parliamentary group with representation from all 25 member states. The EPP-ED's five priorities during this five-year period include: promoting competitiveness; strengthening security; meeting international commitments and responsibilities; working toward **sustainable development**; and, ensuring sound financial management.

GROUP OF THE GREENS/EUROPEAN FREE ALLIANCE (GREENS/EFA). The fourth-largest **political group** of the **European Parliament** (EP) with a total of 42 Members of the European Parliament from 13 member states, the Greens/EFA joined forces after the 1999 EP elections. The group consists of members of Green parties and parties representing national (though not necessarily state) and regional interests. They have agreed upon several common principles including the promotion of the respect for fundamental **hu-**

European Central Bank, Frankfort, Germany (European Central Bank).

Covers of books with EU treaties (European Commission).

Javier Solana, Valery Giscard d'Estaing (former president of France and president of the European Convention), Romano Prodi (president of the EU Commission), and Constantin Simitis (prime minister of Greece). Courtesy the European Commission.

The EU Parliament in Brussels. Courtesy the European Parliament.

The EU Parliament in Strasburg, France. Courtesy the European Parliament.

The Berlaymont Building at the EU Commission, Brussels. Photo by J. Roy.

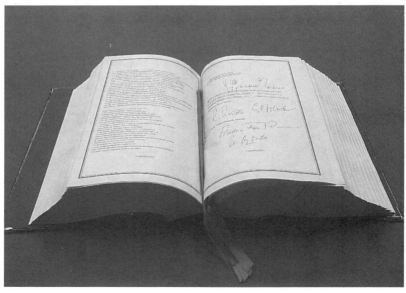

The EU Constitution. Courtesy the European Commission.

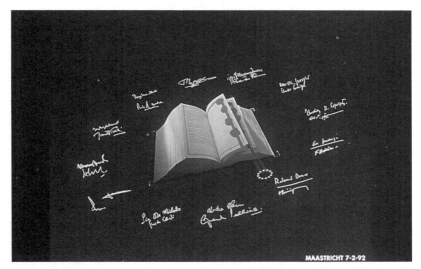

The Treaty of Maastricht, 1992. Courtesy the European Commission.

The Schuman Declaration, 9 May 1950, Salon de l'Horloge, Quai d'Orsay, Paris. Courtesy the European Commission.

Signing of the Treaty of Paris, establishing the European Community of Coal and Steel, Paris, 18 April 1951. Courtesy the European Commission.

The Treaty of Rome, establishing the European Economic Community and the European Community of Atomic Energy, 25 March 1957. Courtesy the European Commission.

Javier Solana, high representative for common foreign and security policy. Courtesy the Council of the European Union.

Konrad Adenauer, chancellor of Germany. Courtesy the European Commission.

Jose Manuel Barroso, president of the European Commission. Courtesy the European Commission.

Robert Schuman, minister of foreign affairs of France. Courtesy the European Commission.

Building of the EU Council in Brussels, by Justus Lipsius. Courtesy the Council of the European Union.

Jean Monnet and Robert Schuman of Luxemburg. Courtesy the European Commission.

Romano Prodi. Courtesy the European Commission.

Signing of the EU Constitution, 29 October 2004, Rome. Courtesy the European Commission.

Jacques Delors, president of the EU Commission, 1986–. Courtesy the European Commission.

Jean Monnet. Courtesy the European Commission.

Valery Giscard d'Estaign. Courtesy the European Commission.

Walter Hallstein, first president of the joint European Commission. Courtesy the European Commission.

Josep Borrell, the EU Parliament president. Courtesy the European Parliament.

man rights and **environmental** protection. Among other initiatives, the group supports **sustainable development**, more direct democratic participation, and the development of **foreign policies** based on methods of peaceful resolution.

– H –

HAIDER, JORG (1950–). A far right and at times very controversial **Austrian** politician, Jörg Haider was the leader of Austria's far right Freedom Party from 1986 to 2000. His political platform is nationalistic, anti-immigrant, and anti–**European Union** (EU). During his leadership, support for the Freedom Party grew significantly, to more than 20 percent in national elections. In 2000, the Freedom Party and the center-right People's Party formed a coalition government. The formation of this government gained great public and international attention, and the question surfaced as to how Haider's seemingly discriminatory and hateful remarks could be compatible with the principles and values of the EU. As a result, the 14 member states in an unprecedented response, suspended their diplomatic relations with Austria. Haider resigned from the leadership of the Freedom Party soon thereafter.

Haider was elected governor of Carinthia in 1991 but was forced to resign because of extreme comments. He was, however, reelected to this post in 1999 and 2004. In April 2005, Haider created a new political party which he leads, the Alliance for the Future of Austria.

HALLSTEIN, WALTER (1901–1982). A prominent figure in the embryonic stages of the European integration process, Walter Hallstein was **Germany**'s foreign minister during **Konrad Adenauer**'s administration, Germany's representative to the **European Coal and Steel Community** negotiations, and the first president of the **European Economic Community** (EEC) **Commission** from 1958 to 1967. Much was accomplished under Hallstein's energetic leadership including the development of the EEC, the **European Atomic Energy Community**, and the **Common Agricultural Policy**.

In one of his efforts to strengthen the **European Community**, he attempted to increase the powers of the European Commission. As a proponent of a **federal** Europe with a strong Commission and **European Parliament**, he was opposed to French President **Charles de Gaulle**'s vision of a "Europe of nations" with most powers retained by the national governments of the member states. Hallstein's plan would ultimately backfire as his unwavering stand combined with the staunch political opposition from de Gaulle resulted in the **Empty Chair Crisis** and one of the longest periods of stagnation in Europe's integration process. Refer to appendix B.

HAMMES, CHARLES LEON. Refer to appendix F.

HANSCH, KLAUS (1938–). A German politician of the Social Democratic Party, Klaus Hänsch has been a member of the **European Parliament** (EP) in the Socialist Group since 1979. From 1994 to 1997 he was president of the EP. Hänsch subsequently served as a member of the Praesidium of the **European Convention** and as an EP representative at the **intergovernmental conference** on the **Treaty establishing a Constitution for Europe**. Refer to appendix D.

HEALTH. *See* PUBLIC HEALTH.

HEATH, EDWARD (1916–2005). A conservative British politician, Edward Heath was head of the Conservative Party from 1965 to 1975 and British prime minister from 1970 to 1974. Considered to be one of the most pro-European of British politicians, Heath was responsible for negotiating the **United Kingdom**'s entry into the **European Community** (EC) in the 1960s, an effort that was at first vetoed by French President **Charles de Gaulle**. During his premiership, however, Heath successfully oversaw Britain's EC membership. Heath was first elected to the House of Commons in 1950 and did not retire from the parliament until 2001.

HIGH AUTHORITY. The institution established to manage the **European Coal and Steel Community** (ECSC), which was created through the signing of the **Treaty of Paris** by **Belgium**, **France**, **Germany**, **Italy**, **Luxembourg**, and **The Netherlands**, the High Authority was the ECSC institution responsible for its policymaking and implementation. When the Treaty of Paris came into effect in

1952 the High Authority began operations in Luxembourg with **Jean Monnet** as its first president. (In 1954, Monnet resigned from this post to dedicate more time to the promotion of the European integration project.) In 1967, based on the provisions of the **Merger Treaty**, the High Authority was combined with the Commission of the **European Economic Community** and the Commission of the **European Atomic Energy Community**, to form the Commission of the European Communities, commonly known today as the **European Commission**.

HIGH REPRESENTATIVE FOR THE COMMON FOREIGN AND SECURITY POLICY (CFSP). The position of High Representative for the CFSP was created in the **Treaty of Amsterdam** as a means of strengthening the second pillar of the **European Union** (EU) by improving internal cohesion and external perceptions. The high representative is also the secretary general of the **Council of the EU**. The first and, to date, only High Representative for the CFSP, **Javier Solana**, took office in October 1999. His main responsibilities were to assist the Council with CFSP issues, and to represent the EU in **foreign policy** matters involving third countries, along with the president of the EU and the commissioner for **External Relations** in what came to be known as the **troika**. The high representative of CFSP has control of a policy unit responsible for assessment and early warnings for crisis situations.

At the **European Council** meeting on 25 March 2004, following a proposal from Javier Solana, **Gijs de Vries** of **The Netherlands** was appointed as the first counterterrorism coordinator of the EU. The main responsibilities associated with this post are assisting the Council of the EU in combating **terrorism**, monitoring the implementation of the EU's action Plan on Combating Terrorism, and promoting the profile and awareness of the EU's policies in the global war on terror.

The **Treaty establishing a Constitution for Europe** calls for the merger of the High Representative for the CFSP and the commissioner for external affairs into a single position with dual responsibilities: vice president of the **European Commission** and union minister for foreign affairs. Although this treaty has yet to be ratified, streamlining the EU's foreign policy continues to be an objective, largely in response to the challenges posed in the **Declaration of Laeken** regarding the role of the EU in the world.

HIRSCH, ETIENNE. Refer to appendix B.

HUMAN RIGHTS. One of the core values of the **European Union** (EU), human rights was first included in the treaties in the **Single European Act**. Strengthening its commitment to the principles of human rights in subsequent treaties, the **Treaty on EU** guarantees the EU's respect for the standards on individual rights and freedoms provided for in **the European Convention for the protection of Human Rights and Fundamental Freedoms**, adopted by the **Council of Europe** in 1950. The **Treaty of Amsterdam** includes a suspension clause, outlining the appropriate actions in the case of human rights violations by any one of the EU member states. At the Nice European Council, a proclamation of the EU's own **Charter of Fundamental Rights** was proclaimed and later incorporated into the Treaty establishing a Constitution for Europe, still pending ratification.

Consideration for EU membership is based in part on the **Copenhagen criteria**, which require respect for human rights, including minority rights. The EU's overall record on the protection of human rights is strong in most areas, but work is currently being done to improve in the areas of immigrant, asylum seeker, and minority rights.

In addition to the dedication to high human rights standards in the EU, the EU promotes respect for human rights internationally. In order to support this effort, the EU funds the European Initiative for Democracy and Human Rights, which focuses on promoting democracy, good **governance**, and the rule of law, and cooperates with non-governmental organizations on projects designed to help meet these objectives. Since 1992 all of the EU's international agreements, including economic and trade agreements, contain a human rights clause.

HUMANITARIAN AID. The **European Commission** together with the 25 **European Union** (EU) member states is the largest provider of humanitarian aid in the world. In order to coordinate and control the EU's international humanitarian aid projects, the **European Community Humanitarian Aid Office** (ECHO) was established in

1992. Since then ECHO has funded more than €500 million per year in humanitarian relief and preventive projects in over 85 countries to help tens of millions of people in need. The humanitarian aid projects are implemented by the EU's partners in the field such as nongovernmental organizations, United Nations agencies, and Red Cross organizations, and provide goods and services to prevent or relieve human suffering resulting from natural disasters and violent conflict.

HUNGARY. The onset of the economic and political transitions in **Central and Eastern Europe** in 1989 inspired assistance from the west. Indicative of the priority given to Hungary, the **European Community**'s original aid program was the Poland and Hungary Assistance for the Reconstruction of the Economy (**PHARE**), which would only later be extended to other countries of the region.

Hungary was the first former Soviet bloc country to apply for **European Union** (EU) membership on 31 March 1994, and based on its relatively high level of economic development and strategic location, it was always considered to be in the lead group of Central and Eastern European candidate countries. Better treatment of the Roma minority and improved financial controls and mechanisms were among the issues addressed by the Hungarian government in conjunction with meeting the accession requirements. Negotiations were successfully completed by December 2002, and after 84 percent of Hungarians voted in favor of EU membership in a referendum on 12 April 2003, Hungary became an EU member state on 1 May 2004. Refer to appendix A.

– I –

ICELAND. Despite its close economic relations with and relative proximity to the **European Union** (EU), Iceland has never applied for membership in the EU, largely because of its large fishing industry. Iceland did, however, join the **European Free Trade Association** (EFTA) in 1970 and remains a member of this organization. As a member of EFTA Iceland has access to the EU's **single market** through the **European Economic Area**, an agreement negotiated between the EU and all of the EFTA countries except **Switzerland**. Iceland, a member of the Nordic Passport Union, also participates in the Schengen Convention and the **Schengen Information System**. *See also* FISHERIES.

IMMIGRATION POLICY. In the **Treaty of Amsterdam** the **European Union** was given competence for immigration. At the 1999 Tampere **European Council**, the guidelines for a common immigration policy were established, including a comprehensive approach to the management of migratory flows, fair treatment of third country nationals, partnerships with countries of origin, and the development of a common asylum policy. Certain additional elements are taken into consideration in the development of the common immigration policy such as the need for migratory workers in certain areas, the need to implement stricter measures against traffickers and smugglers, and the need to account for the resources and capacity of member states on an individual basis. In 2001 the European Commission proposed the adoption of an open method of coordination for the immigration policy to facilitate the exchange of information between member states and the convergence of related policies over which the EU does not have authority.

INDEPENDENCE AND DEMOCRACY GROUP (IND/DEM). Of a total of seven European Parliamentary Groups, IND/DEM is the sixth largest in the 2004–2009 **European Parliament** (EP) with 37 members from 10 **European Union** (EU) member states. The members of the IND/DEM are **Euro-skeptics** who favor a loose European association of states over a deepened European integration. The largest IND/DEM delegation is from the **United Kingdom** with 11 members, and the second largest from **Poland** with a total of 10 members. As public support for European integration continues to wane in many of the member states, including those that just joined the EU in May 2004, this **political group** has credible possibilities for growth and increased influence.

The IND/DEM was created on 20 July 2004, after the June 2004 EP elections. It was transformed from the Group for a Europe of Democracies and Diversities which had representation in the 1999–2004 EP.

INFORMATION SOCIETY. As new information and communications technologies continue to emerge, the **European Union** (EU) has made this information society a priority on its agenda. While trying to encourage its growth and the benefits it has to offer as well as the number of people who have access to it, the EU is also trying to develop policies that will ensure the security of the information society and those who use it.

INSTRUMENT FOR STRUCTURAL POLICIES FOR PRE-ACCESSION (ISPA). Established in June 1999, ISPA funds **environmental** and transportation infrastructure projects in the **Central and Eastern European** candidate countries. Prior to the May 2004 **enlargement**, 10 countries were eligible for financing under the ISPA, which was allocated €1.1 billion annually until 2003. In 2004, ISPA had a **budget** of €452 million for **Bulgaria** and **Romania**, the remaining candidate countries from the region. The main goal of the ISPA is to promote social and economic cohesion between the Central and Eastern European candidate countries and the member states of the **European Union**.

INTEGRATED MEDITERRANEAN PROGRAMMES (IMPs). A financial program designed to assist southern **France**, **Greece**, and **Italy** with the development of **agriculture**, tourism, and small businesses, the completion of the IMPs was largely a result of pressures from the Greek government under the leadership of **Andreas Papandreou**. Papandreou threatened to derail the Portuguese and Spanish **enlargement** if the IMPs were not in place to help Greece adjust to the **European Community** membership of two new "agricultural" member states. The IMPs were finally agreed to in March 1985, providing 6.6 billion ECUs to the Mediterranean region for a period of seven years.

INTERGOVERNMENTAL CONFERENCE (IGC). Once agreement has been reached regarding a significant new step in the European integration process, an IGC is held to negotiate the treaty reforms and what will become the draft treaty. The initiative for a conference comes from a member state or the **European Commission** and is convened by the **Council of the European Union**

deciding by a simple majority (after consulting the **European Parliament**). Representatives to IGCs are generally high level government officials, including cabinet ministers who try to arrive at a text acceptable to their heads of state and government who make the final decisions in the **European Council**.

The IGC has traditionally been the only method of treaty reform in the **European Union**. With the goal of more openness and transparency as stipulated in the **Declaration of Laeken**, however, the reform negotiations resulting in the **Treaty establishing a Constitution for Europe** took place in two stages; the first almost completely public **European Convention**, and the second IGC maintaining its prerogative to secrecy, albeit less so than had typically been the case in the past.

INTERGOVERNMENTALISM. A method of regional or international integration in which the participant member states preserve their national sovereignty, intergovernmentalism is characterized in part by **decision-making** based on the protection and advancement of national interests despite any ancillary benefit to the organization. In this approach to integration, intergovernmental negotiations dominate the decision-making processes in which compromises are made according to individual net cost–benefit analyses. With regard to the **European Union** (EU) there has been a constant debate concerning its nature and whether it is, and whether it should be, more intergovernmental or more **supranational**. Given the complexities of the EU, however, it is difficult to completely separate the two concepts into a zero-sum analysis.

INTERNATIONAL CRIMINAL COURT (ICC). Created by the adoption of the Rome Statute on 17 July 1998, the ICC is located in The Hague. There are 99 countries party to the Rome Statute which went into effect on 1 July 2002. The main objectives of the ICC are to promote the rule of law throughout the world and to punish the most serious international crimes.

The **European Union** (EU) is one of the strongest supporters of the ICC. On 16 June 2003, the Council adopted a **common position** on the ICC, encouraging the EU and its member states to promote additional countries participating in the ICC, and to take potential membership in the ICC into consideration in negotiations and agreements with third countries. The **United States** is not party to the Rome Statute, however, the EU encourages the United States to associate itself and cooperate in some way with the ICC.

IOANNINA COMPROMISE. The Ioannina Compromise was the result of a decision made at a meeting of the foreign ministers of the **European Union** (EU) member states on 29 March 1994. The problem was a disagreement over the change in the qualified majority weighted **voting** in the **Council of the European Union** due to the impending EU **enlargement** to include **Austria**, **Finland**, and **Sweden** as EU member states. Some member states wanted the *number* of blocking votes (23) to remain the same despite the increase in the total number of votes, and other countries wanted the *percentage* to block a vote to remain the same, therefore, increasing the actual *number* necessary to block a vote using **qualified majority voting** (QMV). The agreement reached, known as the Ioannina Compromise, states that if the members of the Council representing between 23 and 26 (the new blocking minority) votes indicate their opposition to a proposed legislation to be decided by QMV, the Council will do everything possible to reach an agreement within a reasonable amount of time in order for the proposal to be passed by at least 65 votes out of 87 (the total number of qualified majority votes following the 1995 enlargement). The Ioannina Compromise was in place from 1 January 1995 until February 2003 when the **Treaty of Nice** came into effect and contained a re-weighting of the votes in the Council of the EU.

IRELAND. In 1961, the **United Kingdom** (UK) submitted its first application for membership in the **European Community** (EC). Traditionally linked to Britain's economy, it would have been unfeasible for Ireland not to follow suit. Ireland would benefit from the **Common Agricultural Policy**, and believed EC membership to be a means of reducing its dependence on Britain. As would become the norm in **European Union** (EU) **enlargement** processes, the applications of these two candidate countries were considered in conjunction, along with those of **Denmark** and **Norway**. Upon French President **Charles de Gaulle**'s rejection of British membership, therefore, Irish accession negotiations were also suspended. It was not until de Gaulle's retirement in 1969 that the French government lifted its objection and the accession process could resume. On 10 May 1972, 83 percent of Irish voters supported EC membership in a national referendum. Ireland, Denmark, and the UK represent the member states of the first EC enlargement, joining on 1 January 1973.

Despite Ireland's generally positive outlook toward European integration, it has delayed two treaty ratifications, and thus, their implementation. It was expected that the **Single European Act** (SEA) would take effect in January 1987. However, in a case questioning the political and **foreign policy** aspects of the treaty, the Irish Supreme Court found the SEA unconstitutional, forcing the government to hold a referendum to change the Irish constitution. After a favorable response from the Irish citizens in May 1987, the treaty finally took effect two months later in July 1987. A similar situation occurred in June 2001 when the Irish voters rejected the **Treaty of Nice** in a referendum. A public relations campaign and higher voter turnout in a second referendum resulted affirmatively, enabling the treaty to take effect in February 2003.

EU membership has undoubtedly contributed to Ireland's recent economic success. Its relatively underdeveloped, agriculturally based economy prior to the launch of the **single market** qualified Ireland for substantial **structural funding** which the government was able to implement advantageously. The country has also become quite attractive to foreign investors through a combination of EU market access and national incentives. Symbolic of the opportunities associated with EU membership, today Ireland is one of the most prosperous, fastest growing economies with one of the lowest unemployment rates in the EU.

Ireland is technically a neutral country and as such has typically opposed its involvement in deeper security and defense integration. Nevertheless, recent proposals have called for a redefinition of this international position in the context of EU membership.

In the first semester 2004, Ireland held the EU presidency, and therefore, chaired the continuation of the **intergovernmental conference** on the **Treaty establishing a Constitution for Europe**. While the Italian **presidency of the EU** was unable to produce the desired result, an agreement was reached in June 2004 under the Irish direction of the negotiations. Refer to appendix A.

ISOGLUCOSE. In one of the most institutionally important cases brought before the **European Court of Justice** (ECJ), the *Isoglucose* judgment of 1980 reinforced the powers provided to the **European Parliament** (EP) through the **consultation procedure**. Consultation requires the **Council of Ministers** to receive an opinion from the EP before passing a proposal into law. In the *Isoglucose* case the ECJ nullified a law that had been enacted by the Council prior to receiving the EP's opinion. The Council claimed the EP was intentionally delaying the legislative process, however, the consultation procedure does not include a specific time frame within which the EP must submit its opinion.

ISRAEL. *See* MIDDLE EAST.

ITALY. Alcide de Gasperi was the prime minister of Italy from 1945 to 1953, during which time he accepted **Robert Schuman**'s proposal to pool the European coal and steel industries under a **High Authority**. His signing of the **Treaty of Paris** in 1951 confirmed Italy's participation as a founding member of the **European Coal and Steel Community**. Although Italy is considered a large member state, its post–World War II political instability and economic uncertainty has limited its relative influence, particularly compared to the Franco–German motor of European integration. On the other hand, Italy has traditionally been one of the strongest supporters of the **European Union** (EU) and increased powers for its institutions, especially the **European Parliament** (EP).

Italy's economy, struggling for much of the 1990s, aroused concerns about its ability to meet the **convergence criteria** on course to participate in the first group of **Economic and Monetary Union** Stage III countries. In a concerted effort, the Italian government under the leadership of **Romano Prodi** (who would later become president of the **European Commission**) and his center-left Olive Tree coalition, implemented austerity programs to comply with the required measures, and Italy adopted the **euro**, along with 10 other **euro zone** member states on 1 January 1999.

In 2003–2004, Italy was the subject of certain controversies in the context of the EU. Immediately prior to assuming the EU presidency in June 2003, the Italian parliament approved legislation granting Italy's prime minister, **Silvio Berlusconi**, immunity from prosecution, in part to avoid a potentially politically embarrassing situation and increased anxiety regarding Berlusconi's capacity to lead the EU and chair the **intergovernmental conference** on the **Treaty establishing a Constitution for Europe**. This was of particular concern given that the Berlusconi government was previously perceived to have a **Euro-skeptic** attitude, and Berlusconi's political rivalry with the then president of the European Commission, Romano Prodi. Less than a year and a half later, Italy's nominee for the new European Commission, expected to take office on 1 November 2004, was Rocco Buttiglione. His divisive remarks about homosexuality, amongst other sensitive issues, resulted in the EP threatening to veto the College of Commissioners. In order to avoid this institutionally unprecedented eventuality, the president-elect of the European Commission, **José Manuel Durão Barroso**, suspended the official vote to reshuffle the commissioners and their portfolios. Italy's replacement was Berlusconi's foreign minister, Franco Frattini, who became the European commissioner for freedom, security, and justice. Refer to appendix A.

– J –

JAPAN. *See* ASIA.

JENKINS, ROY (1920–2003). Roy Jenkins, a career politician, entered the British House of Commons in 1948 and remained a member of Parliament until 1976. He was home secretary from 1965 to 1967; chancellor of the exchequer from 1967 to 1970; and home secretary once again from 1974 to 1976. He led the successful "yes" campaign in the ex post facto referendum on the **United Kingdom**'s membership in the **European Community** (EC).

Jenkins was the first British citizen to become president of the **European Commission** in 1976, and he held the office until 1981. Under his leadership and initiative, the **European Monetary System** was established in 1979.

A founder of the Social Democratic Party in 1981, Jenkins represented this party in the House of Commons from 1982 to 1987. Beginning in 1987, Jenkins remained in politics as a member of the House of Lords. Refer to appendix B.

JOINT ACTION. Joint actions are legal instruments to coordinate activities of the **European Union** member states in the fields of **Common Foreign and Security Policy** (CFSP) and previously in **Justice and Home Affairs** (JHA). In the case of CFSP, joint actions are used to carry out agreements made either unanimously or by **constructive abstention** to reach common objectives. Joint actions in the field of JHA were eliminated in the **Treaty of Amsterdam** and since the treaty went into effect are governed by decisions and **framework decisions.**

JOSPIN, LIONEL (1937–). A politician of the French Socialist Party, Lionel Jospin was a member of the National Assembly from the late 1970s to the early 1990s, serving as the minister of education from 1988 to 1992. The Socialist Party won the parliamentary elections called for by conservative French President **Jacques Chirac** in 1997, and in a period of cohabitation Lionel Jospin became the prime minister of **France**, a position he would hold in 2002. During his administration one of Jospin's high priorities was to reduce the unemployment rate. His efforts included instituting the 35-hour work week and promoting a stronger **employment policy** for the **European Union**. Jospin was the Socialist Party's candidate for the presidential elections in 1995 and 2002. After the 2002 elections in which he came in third, following Jacques Chirac and Jean-Marie Le Pen (the candidate of the far right National Front Party), Jospin resigned from his position as prime minister.

JUSTICE AND HOME AFFAIRS (JHA). Informal and **intergovernmental** cooperation between justice and interior ministers of the **European Community** member states began in the 1970s with the **Trevi Group** and information sharing in an effort to quash terrorist organizations and activities within Europe. It was not until the 1992 **Treaty on European Union** (TEU) that JHA cooperation was institutionalized as the third pillar of the **European Union** (EU), referring to cooperation in areas related to the internal security of the EU. This became a particular necessity following the completion of the **single market** and the free movement of people throughout the internal borders of the EU member states, and the fall of the **Berlin Wall** and collapse of the Soviet Union which facilitated the passage of Eastern and Central Europeans seeking greater economic opportunities and/or asylum in the west. The TEU's framework for JHA cooperation is based on the following "common interests": asylum, external border crossings, **immigration**, combating drug addiction, combating fraud, judicial cooperation in civil and criminal matters, customs cooperation, and police cooperation.

With minimal perceptible progress, there was a concerted effort made in the **Treaty of Amsterdam** to improve JHA. The foremost objective of JHA became the creation of an area of freedom, security, and justice for the entire EU. To this end, asylum, visas, and immigration competences were moved to the first pillar, effectively implementing a more efficient **decision-making** process for these policies. Furthermore, the **Schengen Agreement** was officially incorporated into the Treaty of Amsterdam, establishing a common external border; minimum requirements for visas, asylum, and external border checks; and the **Schengen Information System** common database to control the passage of people through the internal borders of the EU member states.

Since the incorporation of JHA in the **Treaty of Maastricht**, two European agencies have been created to support JHA objectives and policies: **EUROPOL** and **EUROJUST**. EUROPOL is the EU agency responsible for cross-border police cooperation in areas of EU competence, those involving trans-border criminal activities. Criminal justice cooperation is the primary mission of EUROJUST.

Despite this measured progress, JHA remains one of the most "flexible" EU policies. **Enhanced cooperation** has been a viable option as evidenced by the decision of **Ireland** and the **United Kingdom** to not participate in Schengen activities.

Since the 11 September 2001 terrorist attacks on the **United States** and the subsequent Al-Qaeda attacks on Madrid on 11 March 2004, the focus of JHA has been global **terrorism**. In this context, cooperation between the EU and the United States has intensified, particularly in the areas of intelligence, law enforcement, and transport security.

– K –

KALININGRAD. After the May 2004 **European Union** (EU) **enlargement** Kaliningrad, a **Russian** province, became completely surrounded on land by EU member states, bordering **Lithuania** to its north and east and **Poland** to its south and east. (To the west Kaliningrad is bordered by the Baltic Sea). Kaliningrad has thus become an increasingly important topic on the EU's agenda and for EU–Russian relations and cooperation.

Kaliningrad has been receiving financial assistance from the EU since 1991 through the **Technical Assistance for the Commonwealth of Independent States** (TACIS). The aid provided by the EU is primarily designated for support in the following areas: private sector development; cross border cooperation; improving **environmental** standards; and health and education.

KARAMANLIS, KONSTANTINOS (1907–1998). A prominent figure in 20th-century Greek politics, Konstantinos Karamanlis became a member of the Greek Parliament in 1935. He served three consecutive terms as the Greek prime minister from 1955 to 1958, 1958 to 1961, and 1961 to 1963. Subsequently, he lived in exile in **France** for 11 years, after which he returned to **Greece** following the fall of the military junta that had been in place since 1967. In 1974, Karamanlis once again became prime minister of Greece, and founded a leading conservative party, New Democracy. He remained prime minister until 1980 when he was elected as president of the Hellenic Republic. In 1990, he was reelected as president, a post he would hold until he retired from Greek politics in 1995.

During his 1974–1980 term as prime minister, Karamanlis and his government successfully negotiated and concluded Greece's **European Community** (EC) accession agreement. Greece became an EC member on 1 January 1981 and was the only one-country **enlargement** in the history of the **European Union**, a distinction largely due to Karamanlis being able to separate Greece's EC application from those of **Portugal** and **Spain**.

Konstantinos Karamanlis died in 1998 but his political legacy is carried on today by his nephew, Kostas Karamanlis, the current leader of the New Democracy Party and Greece's prime minister since 7 March 2004.

KLEPSCH, EGON (1930–). A politician of the Christian Democratic Party of **Germany**, Egon Klepsch was a member of the Bundestag from 1965 to 1980. From 1973 to 1980 he was simultaneously a member of the **European Parliament** (EP), part of what is known today as the **Group of the European Peoples' Party** (Christian Democrats) **and European Democrats**, formerly the European Peoples' Party. In 1992, Klepsch was elected president of the EP, a post he held until 1994 when he retired from the EP and joined the private sector. Refer to appendix D.

KOHL, HELMUT (1930–). Leader of West **Germany**'s Christian Democratic Union since 1973, Helmut Kohl became chancellor in 1982 and would maintain this executive position for the next 16 years. During his tenure the **Berlin Wall** was torn down and Kohl administrated the reunification of East and West Germany into a single sovereign entity, integrating the former German Democratic Republic not only into the Federal Republic of Germany but also into the **European Community** (EC).

A reunited Germany in the center of a Europe no longer divided by the Iron Curtain generated a perceived advantage to increasing the EC's political integration. On 19 April 1990, French President **François Mitterrand** and Chancellor Kohl co-authored a letter to the president of the **European Council** in support of increased European efforts toward constructing a European Political Union (EPU). EPU, which was developed into the **Common Foreign and Security Policy**, would complement the **Economic and Monetary Union**, another avant-garde EC initiative supported by Kohl, a strong believer in the merits of European integration.

KOSOVO. A traditionally autonomous mostly **Albanian** entity within Serbia, after years of conflict and subsequent peacekeeping missions, Kosovo continues to be a province of **Serbia and Montenegro**. The Serbian Parliament suspended the longstanding autonomy of Kosovo in 1989 and after years of Serbian domination the Kosovo Liberation Army began to fight for its independence. The Serbs responded with military action and after the terms of a 1998 cease-fire were disregarded, the **North Atlantic Treaty Organization** intervened in 1999 to end the fighting. On 10 June 1999, the United Nations Interim Administration in Kosovo (UNMIK) was established with the **European Union** (EU) responsible for one of its four pillars—reconstruction and economic development. The EU is helping Kosovo recover through **humanitarian aid**; the financing of reconstruction and **development** programs through the **European Agency for Reconstruction**; and the EU pillar of the UNMIK which concentrates on reconstructing what was destroyed during the conflict and implementing reforms necessary to make a complete transition to an open market economy.

KUTSCHER, HANS. Refer to appendix F.

KYOTO PROTOCOL. Environmental protection has consistently been one of the internal and international policy priorities of the **European Union** (EU). Evidence of breaching greenhouse gas emission limits established in the United Nations Framework Convention on Climate Change (UNFCCC) which was adopted on 9 May 1992 led the EU, a leader in promoting international environmental standards, to encourage legally binding limits on these emissions. On 11 December 1997, this goal was achieved with the adoption of the Kyoto Protocol to the UNFCCC. The Kyoto negotiations included a clause that allows the EU to be considered as a whole and not necessarily by individual countries, and therefore, the EU's target emissions are an average of the member states.

The Kyoto Protocol went into effect on 16 February 2005, and as of 27 May 2005, 150 countries had ratified, accepted, approved, or acceded to and are bound by the Protocol, including **China**, **Japan**, and **Russia**. Conspicuously not participating is the **United States**

(U.S.), a signatory to the Protocol but with no imminent intention to ratify. Conversely, more than 100 U.S. cities, including New York and Los Angeles, support the Kyoto Protocol.

– L –

LAEKEN DECLARATION. The year after the adoption of the **Treaty of Nice**, the **European Council** signed the Declaration of Laeken outside of Brussels in December 2001. The Laeken Declaration represents the impetus toward the current state of legal affairs in the **European Union** (EU). It contains the formal decision to continue the debate on the future of Europe, to include the results agreed to during these negotiations in a new treaty, and even in a constitutional text, and to hold a **European Convention** to prepare the then forthcoming **Intergovernmental Conference**. In this declaration, 60 targeted questions are posed, relating to the division and definition of powers; the simplification of the treaties; the institutional framework; and developing a constitutional treaty. The three principle challenges established in the Laeken Declaration are: to bring the citizens and especially the young closer to the institutions of the EU; to organize the political area of the EU in an enlarged Union; and to develop the Union as a stabilizing factor and model in the new multi-polar world.

LANGUAGES. There are more than 60 official, regional, or minority languages spoken on a regular basis in Europe. Highlighting the **European Union** (EU)'s unity through diversity, there are 20 official languages of the EU, which means that all official documents must be translated into all 20 languages: Czech, Danish, Dutch, English, Estonian, Finnish, French, German, Greek, Hungarian, Italian, Latvian, Lithuanian, Maltese, Polish, Portuguese, Slovak, Slovene, Spanish, and Swedish.

The EU, through several programs and specially designed activities, encourages the learning of second and third languages. In 2001, the **European Commission** in conjunction with the **Council of Europe** sponsored the European Year of Languages to disseminate information regarding language learning. The Commission also provides ongoing resources for **education and training** programs which contain language learning elements such as the Lingua Action of the Socrates program. *See also* TRANSLATION CENTRE FOR THE BODIES OF THE EUROPEAN UNION.

LATIN AMERICA. European Union (EU) relations with Latin America are developed on three different levels: regional, sub-regional, and bilateral, and focus on economic cooperation, political dialogue, and **trade**. On the regional level, the EU has institutionalized relations with the Rio Group which includes all of the Latin American countries and is the basis of the bi-regional political dialogue between the EU and Latin America. Since 1999, Summits of the Heads of State and Government of the EU, Latin American, and Caribbean countries have been convened every few years to strengthen and provide direction to the bi-regional relations. The first summit was in Rio de Janeiro, Brazil, on 28–29 June 1999, the second in Madrid, **Spain**, on 17–18 May 2002, and the third in Guadalajara, Mexico, on 28 May 2004. Sub-regionally, the EU believes in the possible benefits of **regional integration** in Latin America, and attempts to support these projects through economic cooperation and dialogue with MERCOSUR, the Andean Community, and the Central American Common Market. In addition to these regional frameworks, the EU has developed bilateral relations with each of the individual Latin American countries. The most advanced and institutionalized of these relations are with Chile and Mexico with whom the EU has Economic and Political Association Agreements (Mexico, 1997 and Chile, 2002). These association agreements contain a democratic clause and establish the framework for institutionalized political dialogue, cooperation, and the eventual creation of a **free trade area**.

The EU is Latin America's greatest source of foreign direct investment, and its second-largest trading partner. **Development** cooperation, economic cooperation, and **humanitarian aid** are some of the ways in which the EU provides financial and technical assistance to Latin America and contributes to the strengthening of the bi-regional relations.

LATVIA. One of the Baltic states and a former republic of the Union of Soviet Socialist Republics, Latvia regained its independence on 27

August 1991. On 13 October 1995, the Republic of Latvia formally submitted its application for **European Union** (EU) membership, which has been considered a means of safeguarding Latvia's sovereignty and guaranteeing its democracy. With this in mind, in a nationwide referendum held on 20 September 2003, 69 percent of Latvians voted in favor of joining the EU. Despite the **European Commission**'s concerns regarding corruption and a weak judicial system in Latvia, the country had made enough progress to join the EU along with the other nine candidate countries on 1 May 2004. Refer to appendix A.

LAW. *See* EUROPEAN COMMUNITY LAW.

LECOURT, ROBERT. Refer to appendix F.

LEEMANS, VICTOR. Refer to appendix D.

LIBERAL INTERGOVERNMENTALISM. A conceptual framework for understanding European integration, liberal **intergovernmentalism** focuses on the role of the states in the integration process. The main idea behind liberal intergovernmentalism is that demands for integration come from different groups and actors in domestic politics and the results evolve from intergovernmental negotiations. States agree to cooperate, and even pool sovereignty in certain areas, after negotiating an acceptable compromise that appears to be in the best interest of the state. Andrew Moravcsik is one of the prominent theorists of liberal intergovernmentalism.

LISBON STRATEGY. With a view toward increasing the international economic competitiveness of the **European Union** (EU), the **Portuguese** presidency called for a special meeting of the **European Council** in spring 2000. The result was the European Council's declared goal for the EU by 2010 to "become the most competitive and dynamic knowledge-based economy in the world capable of sustainable economic growth with more and better jobs and greater social cohesion" and the launching of the Lisbon strategy to achieve these objectives. Covering a broad range of policies and focusing on completing the **single market** in all areas, the Lisbon strategy is an ambitious, comprehensive action program. A progress report is presented and analyzed at the mid-term spring meetings of the European Council, dedicated specifically to this task. Policies designed with the intention of complying with the Lisbon strategy can be adopted through the traditional **decision-making** process or through a more flexible open method of coordination between the member states themselves.

LITHUANIA. Declaring its independence from the former Soviet Union on 11 March 1990, Lithuania began the process that would enable it to autonomously participate in several international and regional organizations such as the United Nations, the **World Trade Organization**, the **North Atlantic Treaty Organization**, and the **European Union** (EU), to which it submitted its official application on 8 December 1995. Of the Baltic States, only **Estonia** was originally included in the predicted first wave of **enlargements**. Lithuania, not satisfied with its exclusion from this group, worked diligently toward economic and institutional reforms to earn a positive endorsement from the **European Commission**.

   In a referendum held on 10–11 May 2003, Lithuanian citizens voted in favor of EU membership. On 1 May 2004, Lithuania joined the EU. Initially considered one of the worst economic cases amongst the candidate countries, in 2003 Lithuania had one of the highest EU growth rates with estimated potential to continue this trend. Refer to appendix A.

LOME CONVENTION. Named after Togo's capital city where it was signed in February 1975, the Lomé Convention provides **trade** preferences and economic **development** aid to **European Union** (EU) member states' former colonies and/or current territories, known as a group as the **African–Caribbean–Pacific (ACP) countries**. The details of the agreements included in the Lomé Convention were renegotiated every five years during its existence from 1975 to 2000. Despite distinct assistance programs complemented by the introduction, particularly in later renegotiations, of auxiliary policies such as **environmental** protection, **human rights**, and debt management, the

Lomé Convention fell short of its desired results including poverty reduction and increased economic development. In 2000, the Lomé Convention was replaced by the **Cotonou Agreement**.

LUXEMBOURG. Despite the guarantee of Luxembourg's neutrality provided for in the 1867 Treaty of London, this virtually defenseless Grand Duchy was invaded and occupied by **Germany** in both World War I and World II, prompting the government to seek economic and security associations in order to protect its territory and interests. Luxembourg became a founding member of the **Benelux Customs Union** in 1948, and joined the **North Atlantic Treaty Organization** (NATO) in 1949.

Signing the **Treaty of Paris** in 1951, Luxembourg became one of the original members of the **European Coal and Steel Community**, and also the smallest member state of the **European Union** (EU) until **Malta**'s EU accession on 1 May 2004. A strong supporter of the integration process, two **European Commission** presidents have come from Luxembourg (although the outcome of the **Santer** Commission was the only *en masse* resignation of this institution), and this landlocked country is also the headquarters of the **European Court of Justice**, the **Court of Auditors**, and the **European Investment Bank**. This international financial center boasts one of the highest standards of living in Europe, joining the third stage of **Economic and Monetary Union** (EMU) with no difficulty as one of the most fiscally sound EU member states. Refer to appendix A.

LUXEMBOURG COMPROMISE. In July 1965, French President **Charles de Gaulle** recalled his country's representatives to the **European Community** institutions in protest against what he considered to be a concentration of power in the European institutions, the increased scope of **qualified majority voting** (QMV), and changes to the financing of the **Common Agricultural Policy**. The continued absence of the French officials during the entire second semester of 1965 is known as the **Empty Chair Crisis**. On 28–29 January 1966, an agreement known as the Luxembourg Compromise was reached, resolving this impasse in the integration process.

The Luxembourg Compromise effectively prolonged the practical implementation of QMV until the 1980s by consenting to the continued use of unanimous **decision-making** for sensitive national issues. This clause made it remarkably difficult to deepen integration as policy proposals could be vetoed by any member state.

By the early 1980s, French President **François Mitterrand**, a strong supporter of European integration, allowed for a shift away from the Luxembourg Compromise. It was institutionally abolished with the **Single European Act** and the essential inclusion of QMV for **single market** issues.

– M –

MACEDONIA, FORMER YUGOSLAV REPUBLIC OF (FYROM). Although the FYROM declared its independence from the **former Yugoslavia** in 1991, it was not officially recognized by the **European Union** or the United Nations until 1993. Macedonia is also the name of a northern region in **Greece** and a controversy over the use of the name "Macedonia" ensued. In an effort to quickly and peacefully resolve this issue, international mediators named the independent country FYROM.

The FYROM experienced an escalation in ethnic tensions this same year and the EU aided in the negotiation and acceptance of a Framework Agreement to prevent further conflict. The **North Atlantic Treaty Organization** (NATO) was first responsible for the peacekeeping mission to monitor the agreement but was later replaced by the first EU **Berlin Plus** military mission, Operation Concordia.

On 9 April 2001, the EU and the FYROM signed a **Stabilization and Association Agreement** providing a comprehensive framework for their economic and political relations. The FYROM receives EU funding from the **Community Assistance for Reconstruction, Development, and Stability** (CARDS) program as well as from other EU specialized programs. This funding supports, among other issue areas, democracy and the rule of law; economic and social **development**; police reform and the fight against organized crime; Integrated Border Management; and development of local infrastructure. On 22

March 2004, the FYROM officially applied for membership in the EU and is awaiting formal candidate status and the start of membership negotiations.

MACKENZIE STUART, ALEXANDER JOHN. Refer to appendix F.

MACMILLAN, HAROLD (1894–1986). A British politician of the Conservative Party, Harold Macmillan was a member of the House of Commons from 1924 until 1963, except for several short interruptions. He served in several different cabinet positions in successive governments from 1951 to 1957. He became the British prime minister in 1957 and remained in office until 1963. During his administration the British government submitted an application for membership in the **European Community**, a request that was vetoed by French President **Charles de Gaulle** on 29 January 1963. Macmillan resigned from politics in October 1963 and went to work in his family's publishing company. In 1984, just two years before his death, Macmillan became the Earl of Stockton.

MACSHARRY REFORMS. In an effort to quell internal controversy regarding the costs and sustainability of the **Common Agricultural Policy** as well as to facilitate progress in the **Uruguay Round** of the **General Agreement on Tariffs and Trade** (GATT), negotiations to reform the **agricultural policy** of the **European Community** (EC) began in the early 1990s. Named after the European commissioner for agriculture, Ray MacSharry of **Ireland**, the MacSharry reforms cut the intervention price (the price at which surplus agricultural products are purchased) in exchange for direct income subsidies to European farmers. They also included guidelines for farming practices that would be less damaging to the **environment**. The acceptance of the MacSharry Reforms by the member states of the EC in 1992 was the basis for agreement between the EC and the **United States** on **trade** in agriculture and ultimately the conclusion of the Uruguay Round of GATT.

MADARIAGA, SALVADOR DE (1886–1978). A strong supporter of European integration and an active participant in the **Congress of Europe** in The Hague in 1948, Salvador de Madariaga was a **Span-**

ish politician and diplomat. In 1931 he was appointed ambassador to the **United States** and subsequently became ambassador to **France**. He was elected to the Spanish Congress of Deputies in 1933, briefly served on the government as Minister of Education, and later became Minister of Justice. During the Spanish civil war Madariaga went into exile in the **United Kingdom**, where he remained a strong opponent of Spanish dictator Francisco Franco.

The most tangible and lasting result of Madariaga's work in the Congress of Europe was his founding in 1949 of the College of Europe, a truly European institution of higher education. Located in Bruges, **Belgium**, with a second campus in Natolin, **Poland**, the College of Europe provides the opportunity for students from all across Europe as well as other parts of the world to pursue postgraduate European studies. College alumni founded the Madariaga European Foundation in 1998 to support Madariaga's ideals for European integration. The president of the foundation is **Javier Solana**, Madariaga's grandson and the **High Representative for the Common Foreign and Security Policy**.

MAJOR, JOHN (1943–). A conservative member of the House of Commons since 1979, foreign secretary for a short period in 1989, and Chancellor of the Exchequer in 1989–1990, John Major replaced **Margaret Thatcher** as Britain's prime minister on 28 November 1990. Given that he brought the British pound into the **exchange rate mechanism** (ERM) in October 1990 and claimed that his goal was to place Britain at the heart of Europe, there were expectations of a more pro-European British attitude after this change of government. Nevertheless, and albeit with a generally more congenial attitude, the economic and political positions of Major were generally a continuation of those adopted under the Thatcher administration. Major negotiated a British **opt-out** from the final stage of **Economic and Monetary Union** (EMU), rejected the inclusion of a social chapter in the **Treaty on European Union** (TEU), insisted on eliminating all references to **federalism** in the TEU, and in 1994 vetoed the **European Commission** presidential nomination of Belgian Prime Minister **Jean-Luc Dehaene** because he considered him to be too much of a federalist.

Despite attempts to reverse economic problems, Prime Minister Major was forced to withdraw from the ERM on Black Wednesday,

16 September 1992. This was seen by many in Britain as an indication of the risks associated with European integration.

It was during Major's administration that the Bovine Spongiform Encephalopathy (BSE), or mad cow disease, crisis escalated. **European Union** (EU) scientists declared British beef unsafe for human consumption and a ban was placed on British beef exports to the other EU member states, causing a period of tension between the EU and the British government.

On 2 May 1997, following general elections, Labour Prime Minister **Tony Blair** succeeded John Major. Major retired from political life in 2001 and currently works in the private sector.

MALFATTI, FRANCO MARIA. Refer to appendix B.

MALTA. One of the two Mediterranean island countries to join the **European Union** (EU) as part of the May 2004 **enlargement**, the Republic of Malta has had an ongoing relationship with the EU having signed an Association Agreement (one of the first of its kind) with the EU as early as 1970. Malta's original application for EU membership was submitted on 16 July 1990 by the prime minister and Nationalist Party leader, Eddie Fenech Adami. The country remained on the long-term waiting list until 1996 when its application was suspended following the election of the Labour government, led by Alfred Sant. However, upon Adami's elected return to power in 1998, Malta's application was renewed, and negotiations began soon thereafter.

Malta was one of the first May 2004 candidate countries to complete its accession treaty ratification process through a referendum held in March 2003 and subsequent parliamentary approval in July of the same year. With a population of barely 400,000 people, Malta is the smallest of the 10 countries that joined the EU in May 2004, and the smallest of all the EU member states. Refer to appendix A.

MALVESTITI, PIERO. Refer to appendix B.

MANSHOLT, SICCO. Refer to appendix B.

MARIN, MANUEL. Refer to appendix B.

MARSHALL PLAN. Officially the European Recovery Program, the Marshall Plan was proposed by **United States** (U.S.) Secretary of State George Marshall in 1947 as a means of providing U.S. financial assistance to the European countries for their economic and physical recovery following the destruction caused during World War II. Between 1948 and 1951, the United States provided approximately $12.5 billion to 16 European countries.

One requirement of the Marshall Plan was that the European countries cooperate in the administration of the program's funding. Thus, in April 1948, the European governments established the **Organization for European Economic Cooperation** (OEEC), responsible for requesting and distributing the financial aid.

MARTINO, GAETANO. Refer to appendix D.

MAYER, RENE. Refer to appendix B.

MERGER TREATY. The Treaty Establishing a Single Council and a Single Commission of the European Communities was signed by the founding members of the **European Community** in 1965 and is commonly referred to as the Merger Treaty. This treaty, which reflects an institutional consolidation of the European integration process, went into effect in 1967 and created one **Council of Ministers** for the **European Coal and Steel Community** (ECSC), the **European Economic Community** (EEC), and the **European Atomic Energy Community** (EURATOM). The treaty also merged the **High Authority** of the ECSC and the Commissions of the EEC and EURATOM to form one Commission of the European Communities.

MERTENS DE WILMARS, JOSSE J. Refer to appendix F.

MESSINA CONFERENCE. In June 1955, the foreign ministers of the member states of the **European Coal and Steel Community** met in Messina, **Italy**, to discuss the future progression of European integration. The ministers decided to establish a committee headed by former Belgian Prime Minister **Paul-Henri Spaak** responsible for drafting such proposals. The final report submitted by the so-called

Spaak Committee included designs for the creation of the **European Economic Community** and the **European Atomic Energy Community**.

MIDDLE EAST. Peace and stability in the Middle East is a strategic concern of the **European Union** (EU) considering its long history and current economic and political relations with this neighboring region. Therefore, the EU is committed to active participation in the Middle East Peace Process (MEPP), and as such is a member of the International Quartet (together with **Russia**, the United Nations, and the **United States**) committed to assisting with the implementation of the Road Map for a settlement of the Israeli–Palestinian conflict by 2005. The EU's position as established in the Seville Declaration of 22 June 2002 is the "negotiation of a settlement with the objective of establishing an independent, democratic, and viable Palestinian state, living in peace and security with Israel." The EU emphasizes the potential of intense negotiation and persistently condemns **terrorism**.

In order to support its objectives, the EU engages in regional dialogue through the **Euro–Mediterranean Partnership** in which both Israel and the Palestinian Authority participate. In 1996, the EU established the ambassadorial post of Special Representative (EUSR) for the MEPP to support EU actions and initiatives in the region. Miguel Angel Moratinos (currently **Spain**'s foreign minister) served in this position from 1996 to 2003 when he was replaced by the current EUSR, Marc Otte. Furthermore, the EU's Partnership for Peace program provides support to civil society projects that promote peace, tolerance, and non-violence.

The EU and Israel signed an Association Agreement which entered into force on 1 June 2000 and establishes the framework for free **trade**, political dialogue, and economic and cultural cooperation. Bilateral economic cooperation between the EU and all MEPP parties is administered through the MEDA program. In addition, the EU provides **humanitarian aid** and financial assistance, conditioned on reform, to the Palestinians. On 1 July 1997, an Interim Association Agreement on Trade and Cooperation between the EU and the Palestinian Authority entered into force, although it has been difficult to implement given the continuous conflict in the first few years of the 21st century.

MITTERRAND, FRANÇOIS (1916–1996). François Mitterrand, a veteran French politician, was elected president of **France** for two consecutive terms which he served from 1981 to 1995. He had been involved in French politics since World War II, and had run for president twice (once against **Charles de Gaulle** and once against **Valéry Giscard d'Estaing**) before winning the elections in 1981, becoming the first Socialist president of the Fifth Republic.

Mitterrand, unlike his political rival Charles de Gaulle, was a strong supporter of the European integration process. After assuming the French presidency, Mitterrand supported the increased **qualified majority voting** necessary to complete the **single market**. In the second semester 1989, France held the rotating **presidency of the European Union** (EU), and Mitterrand was able to successfully manage an unexpected and unprecedented situation during the fall of the **Berlin Wall** and the start of the transitions in **Central and Eastern Europe**.

Despite his previous actions and appreciation of friendly Franco–German relations, especially with **Helmut Kohl** in the German chancellery, Mitterrand was initially against the reunification of **Germany**. However, once the process became an imminent reality, Mitterrand's options were limited. Rather than obstruct this history-making event, he advocated deeper economic integration to allow France increased influence over the economic policies that had been dominated by Germany in both the **European Monetary System** and the **exchange rate mechanism**. Almost simultaneously, Mitterrand and Kohl co-authored a letter to the president of the **European Council** recommending and supporting European efforts toward constructing a European Political Union.

MOLDOVA. The only parliamentary democracy in the **Commonwealth of Independent States** (CIS), Moldova signed a **Partnership and Cooperation Agreement** (PCA) with the **European Union** (EU) on 28 November 1994 which went into effect on 1 July 1998. The PCA establishes a framework for comprehensive economic and political relations administered through bilateral institutions created expressly for this purpose. The EU–Moldova PCA contains a clause that addresses the possibility of developing a **free trade area** between the EU and Moldova in the future. Moldova receives funding from the EU under the **Technical Assistance for the Common-**

wealth of Independent States (TACIS) program as well as from direct **humanitarian assistance**. Moldova is also a member of the **Stability Pact for South Eastern Europe**.

The EU closely monitors an unresolved issue in Moldova; that of the separatist region, Transnistria, which has claimed its independence since Moldova became independent in 1991. Despite agreements to the contrary **Russia** continues to maintain forces in the area. Due to the unruly nature of the situation, this region has become an area prone to illegal activities and organized crime. This is of increased importance to the EU as Moldova will border the EU upon **Romania**'s EU membership scheduled for 2007.

MONNET, JEAN (1888–1979). A French businessman and government-appointed official and advisor, Jean Monnet is affectionately remembered by many as the "father of Europe." Monnet had traveled widely in both his private and public roles and was appointed to develop a plan for the modernization of the French economy following the end of World War II. Based on his experience, he came to believe the only way to achieve peace and progress on the continent was through European unity. Monnet, the inspiration behind what has developed into today's **European Union** (EU), proposed the pooling of the French and German coal and steel industries, an idea that was accepted by the French Foreign Minister **Robert Schuman** and West German Chancellor **Konrad Adenauer**.

On 9 May 1950, Robert Schuman made his now-famous declaration based on Monnet's proposal. In addition to West **Germany** and **France**, **Belgium**, **Italy**, **Luxembourg**, and the **Netherlands** accepted the historic offer made by Schuman on that date, now know as Europe Day. A strong believer in **functional** integration and the power of institutions, Monnet subsequently chaired the **intergovernmental conference** that would lead to the signing of the **Treaty of Paris** in 1951 and the creation of the **European Coal and Steel Community** (ECSC) the following year. The ECSC was managed by an executive-type body, the **High Authority**, whose first president was Jean Monnet.

Frustrated with the progress of European integration, particularly after the rejection of the **European Defence Community** in the French parliament, Monnet resigned from the High Authority in 1954 to have more time and liberty to dedicate to his cause. The next year he founded the Action Committee for a United States of Europe, composed mainly of political party and trade union leaders, who would lobby those that could influence and/or make decisions regarding the future of Europe. These efforts, in part, led to the signing of the **Treaties of Rome** and the creation of the **European Economic Community** and the **European Atomic Energy Community**. Until his death in 1979, Monnet remained a strong defender of his ideals for European integration. Refer to appendix B and the introduction.

MULTI-LEVEL GOVERNANCE. A conceptual approach used to help explain **regional integration**, and particularly European integration, multi-level **governance** questions the state-centric focus espoused by intergovernmentalists and liberal intergovernmentalists. Supporters of multi-level governance contend that although national governments play a significant and irreplaceable role in the integration process, that networks of interconnected actors and institutions at the **supranational** and sub-national levels also influence the **decision-making** and policy-making processes in the **European Union**. Two of the thinkers helping to develop the framework of multi-level governance are Liesbet Hooghe and Gary Marks.

MUTUAL RECOGNITION. First established with the 1979 *Cassis de Dijon* case, mutual recognition is one of the fundamental principles of the **European Union**'s **single market**. Basically, mutual recognition means that national standards of production are accepted by all member states and cannot be further regulated. European standards were established with the help of European standardization bodies. As long as products meet the stipulated standards national authorities of the member states may not place additional health, safety, or technical standards on these products or in any way impede their importation.

– N –

NEO-FUNCTIONALISM. A theory used to explain European integration, neo-functionalism has its roots in the functionalist theory first developed by David Mitrany. Ernst Haas and Leon Lindberg were two of the pioneers of neo-functionalism. Proponents of this theory claim that integration is largely a result of economic and political spillover; after integration begins in one competence it will spread to additional competences and include a greater number of political actors and supporters at both the national and European levels. Neo-functionalism largely fell out of favor during the seeming stagnation of the European integration process in the 1970s but was revived and revised following the completion of the single European market.

THE NETHERLANDS. A constitutional monarchy known for its liberal policies and high standard of living, The Netherlands was one of the six founding members of the **European Community**. Two major **European Union** (EU) treaties were agreed to and signed in The Netherlands; the **Treaty on European Union** (also known as the Treaty of Maastricht), and the **Treaty of Amsterdam**. Today, The Netherlands is one of the strongest proponents of requiring higher **environmental** standards in the EU.

The Hague, The Netherlands' administrative capital, is often referred to as the legal capital of the world. This city hosts amongst other international organizations, the International Court of Justice, the **International Criminal Court**, the Organization for the Prohibition of Chemical Weapons, the United Nations International Criminal Tribunal for the **Former Yugoslavia** (UNICTY), and the headquarters of **EUROPOL** and **EUROJUST**.

In a national referendum on 1 June 2005 Dutch citizens decisively rejected the **Treaty establishing a Constitution for Europe**, creating a significant obstacle to the completion of the ratification process. Refer to appendix A.

NEWLY INDEPENDENT STATES (NIS). Composed of **Russia** and the other successor states of the former Union of Soviet Socialist Republics, the **European Union** (EU) has significant interest in and is working toward developing strong relations with the NIS. Following the collapse of the Soviet Union, the EU negotiated **Partnership and Cooperation Agreements** that establish a framework for comprehensive relations between the EU and the individual NIS. The EU also provides financial assistance to the NIS through the **Technical Assistance for the Commonwealth of Independent States** (TACIS), largely supporting Russia and the **Ukraine** but also including the rest of central Europe, the Caucasus, and Central Asia.

NORTH ATLANTIC TREATY ORGANIZATION (NATO). Signed in April 1949 by **Belgium**, Canada, **Denmark**, **France**, **Iceland**, **Italy**, **Luxembourg**, **The Netherlands**, **Norway**, **Portugal**, the **United Kingdom**, and the **United States** (U.S.), the North Atlantic Treaty establishes a mutual defense alliance between its signatory members in NATO. Article 5 of the North Atlantic Treaty affirms that an attack on any one of the NATO members would be considered as and responded to as an attack on all its members. This organization, primarily military in nature but with significant political aspects as well, has enlarged over the years, granting membership to **Greece** and **Turkey** in 1952; West **Germany** in 1955; **Spain** in 1982; the **Czech Republic**, **Poland**, and **Hungary** in 1999; and **Bulgaria**, **Estonia**, **Latvia**, **Lithuania**, **Romania**, **Slovakia**, and **Slovenia** in 2004.

During the Cold War, NATO served as a means of thwarting a Soviet incursion into Western Europe. Complementarily, it also facilitated Germany's rearmament and U.S. involvement in European affairs, both deemed necessary to prevent the perceived Soviet threat. Following the end of the Cold War and the **enlargements** of both the **European Union** (EU) and NATO to include former Soviet bloc members of **Central and Eastern Europe** and former Soviet republics, the rationale for maintaining NATO was reinvented as a political–military organization to "promote peace and stability in problem areas in Europe itself." Today, after the 11 September attacks on the United States and the 11 March attacks on Madrid, NATO is trying to consolidate its role in the international fight against **terrorism**.

As the EU continues to develop its security dimension, questions have been raised regarding the relations between NATO (a North Atlantic organization including the United States and the EU (a regional organization of which the United States is not a member). Many members of the EU are also members of NATO; however there are members of NATO that are not members of the EU and vice versa, which has brought into question the sharing of resources. Nevertheless, official statements reflect that NATO and EU are meant to be complementary, that neither one is a threat to the other, and that there is much work to be done in terms of maintaining peace and security in Europe, which means there is no redundancy in maintaining the security aspects of both organizations. *See also* BERLIN PLUS; DEFENSE POLICY.

NORTHERN DIMENSION. The Northern Dimension became a significant component of the **external relations** of the **European Union** (EU) since the so-called EFTA **enlargement** (**Austria**, **Finland**, and **Sweden**) of 1995. It encompasses the area spanning from **Iceland** to Northwest **Russia** between the seas to the north of the Nordic countries to the southern coasts of the Baltic Sea. The overriding goal of the Northern Dimension is to address the interests and challenges particular to the region. Areas of cooperation between its members include the **environment**, nuclear safety, **energy** cooperation, **Kaliningrad**, infrastructure, and social development. One of the major successes of the Northern Dimension was the support it provided to the **Central and Eastern European countries** of the region in their quest for EU membership.

NORWAY. Participation in the method of European integration inspired by **Jean Monnet** and based on the pooling of national sovereignty under a **High Authority**, has long been a controversial topic in Norway. In the 1960s, this Scandinavian country applied twice for membership in the **European Community** (EC), alongside the bids of **Denmark**, **Ireland**, and the **United Kingdom**. Having completed its accession negotiations, a public referendum was held on 24–25 September 1972 in which 53.5 percent of the Norwegian people voted against EC membership. A similar scenario unfolded in the 1990s when Norway once again submitted an application on the eve of the completion of the **single market** and in light of the pending applications of **Austria**, **Finland**, **Sweden**, and **Switzerland**. After the conclusion of membership negotiations on 30 March 1994, another referendum was held in which once again the Norwegian people rejected this integration proposal.

Issues related to the protection of Norway's **fishing** and **agricultural** industries, as well as its national sovereignty have remained the most highly contested amongst members of the Norwegian government and general population. Although Norway is not a member of the **European Union** (EU), it does participate in the **Schengen Agreement** as a member of the Nordic Passport Union. The country also has access to the EU market through the **European Economic Area** but has no policy-making or **decision-making** rights. The Norwegian economy is quite successful, even more so than many of the EU member states, supported by its oil and gas resources and the development of these industries.

– O –

OFFICE FOR HARMONIZATION IN THE INTERNAL MARKET (TRADEMARKS AND DESIGNS) (OHIM). Established in 1994 and located in Alicante, **Spain**, the OHIM is an **agency of the European Union** (EU). It is responsible for registering Community trademarks and designs. These trademarks and designs provide their owners with rights valid in all of the member states in the EU.

OMBUDSMAN. A new institutionalized position created in the **Treaty on European Union** (EU), the European Ombudsman is a liaison between the citizens and legal residents of the EU and EU institutions. The ombudsman is appointed by the **European Parliament** (EP) and serves during its full term in office, with the possibility of reappointment. Responsible for receiving complaints from European legal residents and citizens regarding maladministration in the European institutions (except the **European Court of Justice** and the **Court of First Instance**), the ombudsman investigates these claims and tries to resolve the problem with the institution in question. A report is submitted to the EP by the ombudsman on an annual basis. The current European Ombudsman is P. Nikiforos Diamandouros, the former national ombudsman of **Greece**, who has held this position since April 2003.

OPT-OUT. The opt-out is an exemption granted to a **European Union** (EU) member state that has substantiated reasons not to participate in a particular area of Community competence. The opt-out is a way of encouraging progress in the European integration process when only a few member states oppose a particular policy.

The **United Kingdom** was granted an opt-out of the third stage of **Economic and Monetary Union** (EMU), which was considered a condition for the British government to approve the **Treaty on European Union** (TEU) as a whole. Opt-outs in the areas of **defense policy**, the third stage of EMU, legal cooperation under the **Schengen Agreement**, and some **Justice and Home Affairs** cooperation were similarly negotiated with **Denmark** after the Danish people rejected the TEU in the first public referendum held on this issue. Denmark and the UK might decide to opt into these policy areas, including the EMU, if they meet and maintain the **convergence criteria**.

ORGANIZATION FOR EUROPEAN ECONOMIC COOPERATION (OEEC). Created in April 1948, the OEEC was one of the first attempts at post–World War II institutionalized European cooperation. The OEEC was headquartered in Paris and had 16 founding member states. Its main objective was to encourage European economic cooperation and to coordinate the funding available through the **United States**' European Recovery Program, commonly known as the **Marshall Plan**. By 1961, the OEEC was transformed into the Organization for Economic Cooperation and Development (OECD), an international organization for the study of global social and economic issues.

ORGANIZATION FOR SECURITY AND COOPERATION IN EUROPE (OSCE). The Conference on Security and Cooperation in Europe process was founded by the 1975 Helsinki Final Act, and was developed into the Organization for Security and Cooperation in Europe in 1995. Originally created in order to reduce tensions and increase cooperation between the West and the Soviet bloc, the OSCE currently has 55 members from Europe, Central **Asia**, and North America, and addresses security issues, including but not limited to arms control, **human** and minority **rights**, and election monitoring. Providing a peaceful arena for political dialogue and cooperation in areas of mutual interest, the main focus of the OSCE is conflict prevention and crisis management.

The **European Union** (EU) is represented at OSCE meetings by representatives of the country holding the **presidency of the EU** and by representatives of the **European Commission**. Having many of the same objectives, the EU and the OSCE cooperate on many projects, and with the developments in the EU's **Common Foreign and Security Policy** and **European Security and Defence Policy**, they are working toward building an efficient complementary relationship.

ORTOLI, FRANÇOIS-XAVIER. Refer to appendix B.

– P –

PAPANDREOU, ANDREAS (1919–1996). A Greek politician from a family of Greek politicians, Andreas Papandreou was elected to the Greek parliament in 1964 and took part in the cabinet of his father, George Papandreou who had become prime minister in 1963. Although having previously lived, studied, and worked in the **United States** (U.S.), and even becoming a U.S. citizen, upon entering political office in **Greece** he renounced his U.S. citizenship and ironically developed an anti-U.S. political stance.

During the military dictatorship in Greece from 1967 to 1974, Papandreou went into exile and formed an organization in opposition to the military regime. When it collapsed in 1974, Papandreou returned to Greece and formed a new political party, the Panhellenic Socialist Movement (PASOK). His party won the 1981 elections and Papandreou became prime minister. Coming into office only shortly after Greece joined the **European Community** (EC) on 1 January 1981, and having campaigned against the EC, Papandreou was one of the most difficult heads of government to deal with in the EC. He threatened to veto the EC membership of **Portugal** and **Spain** if there was not first a guarantee of **agricultural** and other economic concessions for Greece, a demand that was answered in the form of the **Integrated Mediterranean Programmes**.

Papandreou remained prime minister until 1989 and assumed the position once again from 1993 to 1996 when he retired due to health problems and died later that year. His son, George Papandreou succeeds him as leader of the PASOK party.

PARTNERSHIP AND COOPERATION AGREEMENTS (PCAs). Following the collapse of the Soviet Union, the **European Union** (EU) negotiated PCAs that establish a framework for comprehensive relations between the EU and the individual **newly independent states** (NIS) of the former Soviet Union. The PCAs contain clauses that refer to the adherence to democratic principles and the respect of **human rights**, and they establish the legal basis for bilateral political, economic, and **trade** relations between the EU and each one of these countries. There are nine PCAs in effect between the EU and the following countries: Armenia, Azerbaijan, Georgia, Kazakhstan, Kyrgyzstan, **Moldova**, **Russia**, **Ukraine**, and Uzbekistan. There is a Trade and Cooperation Agreement in effect between the EU and Mongolia, and PCAs have been signed but not yet entered into force between the EU and **Belarus** and the EU and Turkmenistan.

PELLA, GIUSEPPE. Refer to appendix D.

PETERSBERG TASKS. In June 1992, the foreign and defense ministers of the **Western European Union** issued a declaration outlining the types of military missions in which its members would become involved: **humanitarian**, rescue, peacekeeping, peacemaking, and crisis management, known as the Petersberg tasks after the Hotel Petersberg near Bonn, **Germany**, where they were endorsed. In 1997, the Petersberg tasks were adopted by the **European Union** (EU) and included in the **Treaty of Amsterdam**, and they are the basis of the EU's **European Security and Defence Policy**.

PFLIMLIN, PIERRE (1907–2000). A French Christian Democratic politician, Pierre Pflimlin served as prime minister for a few weeks in 1958, directly prior to **Charles de Gaulle** assuming this position. He was a member of the **European Parliament** (EP) from 1962 to 1967. He was later elected in the first direct elections of the EP in 1979 and served as EP president from 1984 to 1987. Refer to appendix D.

PHARE PROGRAMME. Originally the Poland and Hungary Assistance for the Reconstruction of the Economy and now referred to as the Programme of Community Aid to the **Countries of Central and Eastern Europe** (CEECs), or simply PHARE, this is the main financial instrument for the **pre-accession strategy** of the **European Union** (EU). PHARE was launched in 1989 and at that time provided technical and financial assistance to **Poland** and **Hungary**. Within just a few years, the program was extended in number and scope to include most of the CEECs (**Bulgaria, Czech Republic, Estonia,** Hungary, **Latvia, Lithuania**, Poland, **Romania, Slovakia,** and **Slovenia**) and to address key issues associated with pre-accession, including but not limited to incorporating the **acquis communautaire** into national legislation, meeting **environmental** standards, improving infrastructure, and addressing **justice and home affairs** related issues. Between 2000 and 2006, the **budget** for the PHARE programme exceeded €10 billion. After countries accede to the EU they can no longer receive assistance from the PHARE programme, but they do become eligible for other internal funding programs.

PILLARS, THREE. The **Treaty on European Union** (TEU) reorganized European integration into a figurative temple with three pillars. The first pillar represents the **European Community**, and is the only fully integrated pillar of the **European Union** and considered to be its most **supranational** pillar. The second and third pillars are the **Common Foreign and Security Policy** and **Justice and Home Affairs**, respectively, both of which remain principally **intergovernmental**, based on cooperation and generally requiring all member states' support for policy and **decision-making**.

During the negotiation phase of the TEU some European leaders unsuccessfully argued for a more unitary approach to integration. The symbolic pillar architectural design has come to be considered by many as an impediment to integration, particularly in the competences encompassed by the second and third pillars. If the **Treaty establishing a Constitution for Europe** is ratified in the future, the three pillar system would be eliminated in an effort to form a more cohesive Union.

PILLOTTI, MASSIMO. Refer to appendix F.

PLEVEN PLAN. In October 1950 French Prime Minister René Pleven revealed his plan for a **European Defense Community** (EDC). This was the first attempt to integrate in this highly sensitive area, and the

EDC was designed to encourage European **defense** cooperation as well as to allow for the rearmament of **Germany** within the context of a regional organization. The treaty establishing the EDC was signed by the founding members of the **European Coal and Steel Community** on 27 May 1952 in Paris. In August 1954, the treaty was defeated in the ratification process, ironically by the French parliament.

PLUMB, CHARLES HENRY (1925–). A British politician of the Conservative party, Lord Plumb was a member of the **European Parliament** (EP) from 1979 until 1999. He was part of what is known today as the **Group of the European Peoples' Party** (Christian Democrats) **and European Democrats**, formerly the European Peoples' Party. Plumb was president of the EP from 1987 to 1989. Refer to appendix D.

POHER, ALAIN. Refer to appendix D.

POLAND. The first Soviet bloc country to form a non-Communist government in 1989, Poland submitted its application for membership in the **European Union** (EU) on 5 April 1994. Being the largest of the 10 candidate states approved to participate in the 1 May 2004 **enlargement** process, negotiations proved tense, particularly over the **agricultural** issue. Poland's relatively large agricultural sector which is in need of modernization and increased productivity, combined with its relatively low levels of economic development, would have placed an impracticable burden on the EU's **Common Agricultural Policy**. Nevertheless, a compromise was reached and accession negotiations were completed by 2002, after which Poland was invited to become an EU member state in 2004.

Poland is considered a medium country with a population size similar to that of **Spain**. In fact, during the **Intergovernmental Conference** (IGC) on the **Treaty establishing a Constitution for Europe**, Spain and Poland allied with each other to demand weighted influence in **decision-making** processes, comparable to what they had obtained in the **Treaty of Nice**. This united diplomatic stance contributed to the delay in the approval of the treaty and prolonging the IGC into the Irish presidency of the first semester 2004. Refer to appendix A.

POLICY PLANNING AND EARLY WARNING UNIT. Created in the **Treaty of Amsterdam**, the Policy Planning and Early Warning Unit is an office responsible to the **High Representative for the Common Foreign and Security Policy** (CFSP). The main responsibilities of this unit are to monitor and assess international situations and provide early warnings to the High Representative of CFSP in order to try and respond in terms of crisis prevention rather than after the fact.

POLITICAL AND SECURITY COMMITTEE. The main committee of the **Council of the European Union** for the **Common Foreign and Security Policy**, the Political and Security Committee was created in 2001 to manage the **European Security and Defence Policy**. The committee is composed of senior officials from the Permanent Representations of the member states, but often meets at other levels as well. The main responsibilities of the political and security committee are to monitor international situations and to help guide and define security policies and possible responses to crisis situations.

POLITICAL GROUPS IN THE EUROPEAN PARLIAMENT. Political activity in the **European Parliament** (EP) is organized by political groups which are obligatorily transnational and based on political affinity. Political groups must have at least 19 Members of the EP (MEPs) from at least one-fifth of the **European Union** member states. Levels of political cohesion with regard to issues and values vary amongst the different political groups.

Committee formations, speaking times, and administrative funding is determined by political groups, including independent MEPs who are "grouped" together for organizational purposes and have the same rights as the other political groups. Representing the European citizens and not the member states, during parliamentary sessions MEPs do not sit in national delegations but rather with their political groups. In addition to the independents, the 2004–2009 EP has seven political groups: **Confederal Group of the European United Left-Nordic Green Left**, **Group of the Alliance of Liberal and Democrats for Europe**, **Group of the European Peoples' Party** (Christian Democrats) **and European Democrats**, **Group of the Greens/European Free Alliance**, **Independence and Democracy**

Group, Socialist Group in the European Parliament, and **Union for Europe of the Nations Group**. Refer to appendix E.

POMPIDOU, GEORGES (1911–1974). With a distinct change of position from **Charles de Gaulle**'s administration, French President Pompidou consented to the **United Kingdom**'s membership in the **European Community** (EC), allowing accession negotiations to resume following de Gaulle's suspension of them. In a strategic domestic political move, he called for a French referendum on the issue which was held on 23 April 1972 and, with approval from the French public, the first EC **enlargement** including **Denmark**, **Ireland**, and the UK took place on 1 January 1973. Pompidou also proposed the December 1969 Hague Summit where the EC leaders advocated for increased political coordination between the member states providing the impetus for **European Political Cooperation**, which was established the following year.

    Georges Pompidou was prime minister of the French Government from 1962 to 1968 when he was dismissed by President Charles de Gaulle. He was subsequently elected to the French presidency in 1969 following de Gaulle's resignation. Pompidou's presidential term ended prematurely as he died from cancer in 1974 while in office.

PORTUGAL. A small and nationally homogenous country on Europe's Atlantic periphery, Portugal was governed by the dictatorship of the *Estado Novo* from 1933 to 1974. Following the Carnation Revolution and the transition to democracy, **European Community** (EC) integration became a priority as a means of maintaining and stabilizing the new democratic regime.

    Prior to EC accession, Portugal was one of the poorest countries in Western Europe with minimal foreign investment, a highly **agricultural** and inefficient economy, and an overall low level of economic development. On the morning of 1 January 1986, Portugal officially entered the EC and became eligible for **structural** and regional **funding** that has enabled this relatively poor country to make significant progress. Intent on participating in all aspects of the European integration process, the Portuguese government implemented strict, and not always publicly favorable, economic policies to meet the **con-**

vergence criteria and participate in the third stage of **Economic and Monetary Union** (EMU). Portugal's ability to meet the requirements necessary to adopt the **euro** demonstrates the considerable economic improvements experienced by the country since its EC membership.

Portugal and **Spain** joined the EC on the same day, and this Iberian **enlargement** has led to greater economic and political cooperation between these two countries that had previously maintained a suspicious attitude toward one another. They have similar interests in terms of the **European Union** (EU) agenda such as **cohesion policy**, **immigration**, **Latin America**, and the Mediterranean.

PRE-ACCESSION STRATEGY. The historic decision to open its doors to the **Central and Eastern European countries** of the former Soviet bloc upon their fulfillment of the **Copenhagen criteria** was made at the Copenhagen **European Council** in 1993, potentially doubling the number of **European Union** (EU) member states. In a concerted effort to ensure that the upcoming **enlargements** would not merely be characterized by their quantity but also by their quality, a pre-accession strategy was defined at the Essen European Council in 1994.

In order to assist the candidate countries with their preparation for membership the EU finances three pre-accession instruments: the **PHARE** Programme, the **Instrument for Structural Policies for Pre-accession** (ISPA), and the **Special Accession Programme for Agriculture and Rural Development** (SAPARD). Originally the PHARE Programme had two main priorities: to support institution building, and the ability to incorporate the **acquis communautaire** into national legislation and to sustain and implement this **European Community law**. In the programming period closest to the actual first enlargement processes (2000–2006), the PHARE Programme was expanded to address **cohesion** and **structural funds**. During this period the two other instruments were created; ISPA dedicated to large infrastructure projects related to transportation and the **environment**, and SAPARD, which focused on the acquis in terms of **agriculture** and rural development.

While the financial measures associated with the pre-accession strategy are some of its key elements, this is a comprehensive plan that includes technical expertise and institutionalized dialogue and negotiations. Furthermore, the candidate countries participate in specified EU programs and agencies prior to their full membership in order to gain experience and be better prepared for the accession process and the all important adoption of the acquis communautaire into their national legislation.

PRELIMINARY RULINGS. Preliminary rulings are one of the ways, in addition to **direct actions**, to bring a case to the **European Court of Justice** (ECJ). The majority of the cases filed in the ECJ are preliminary rulings, and other than certain extremely limited clearly and specifically outlined preliminary rulings, the ECJ handles all of these requests without assistance from the **Court of First Instance**.

The only entities capable of requesting a preliminary ruling are national courts of the member states of the **European Union** (EU), and they can do so when a case brought before the national court involves issues included in the EU treaties and laws. Under these circumstances the ECJ provides an interpretative ruling on the points of the case involving EU law which the national courts must subsequently recognize and apply.

PRESIDENCY OF THE EUROPEAN UNION (EU). The presidency of the EU sets the EU agenda for six months, attempts to garner consensus for legislative packages, answers to the **European Parliament**, and speaks on behalf of the EU in international meetings. The presidency is held on a six-month rotating basis by each of the EU member states. During this period, meetings of the **Council of the EU** are chaired by the minister from the member state holding the presidency, and **European Council** meetings are chaired by the head of state or government of that member state. Member states that acceded to the EU in the 1 May 2004 **enlargement** will enter the rotation in 2008 in order to provide them with a transitionary period for acclimation and preparation. Given the increase in the number of member states, the **Treaty establishing a Constitution for Europe** includes a reform of the presidency in which the European Council elects a president of the EU who has no national political commitment by a qualified majority for a period of two-and-a-half years, renewable once. If the constitutional treaty is ratified, this presidential reform would be implemented.

PRODI, ROMANO (1939–). From April 1996 to November 1998, Romano Prodi was the prime minister of **Italy**, leading the Olive Tree center-left coalition. During his time as prime minister, Prodi was instrumental in passing economic policy-related legislation to ensure that, despite all odds, Italy would become a founding member of the **euro zone**.

With major reforms in mind, Prodi was appointed as president of the **European Commission** in 1999. He assumed this position at a most inauspicious moment, when **public opinion** regarding the Commission was at one of its lowest points in history, following the *en masse* resignation of the **Santer** Commission due to allegations of fraud and mismanagement.

Although Prodi's performance as president of the Commission can be debated, the fact is that long-term and decisive integration objectives were attained under his leadership of this institution: implementing the **euro** as the common currency of 12 **European Union** (EU) member states; completing the largest **enlargement** process in the history of the EU; and reaching agreement on the **Treaty establishing a Constitution for Europe**, allowing for the ratification process to begin. While his political enemies consider him to be dull and a poor communicator, supporters might argue that his ability to compromise and his negotiating skills were the basis of his achievements as Commission president.

Romano Prodi and the Italian prime minister coinciding with Prodi's term as Commission president, **Silvio Berlusconi**, are political rivals. Concerns were raised regarding the impact of this relationship on European politics, especially when Italy held the rotating **presidency of the EU** in the second semester 2003, at the same time chairing the **Intergovernmental Conference** responsible for deciding the fate of the constitutional treaty. Nevertheless, there were no overt confrontations between the two. At the end of his term as president of the European Commission in November

2004, Prodi returned to Italy to once again dedicate himself to Italian politics and his political opposition to Berlusconi. Refer to appendix B.

PUBLIC HEALTH. Although health care is primarily a member state competence, the **European Union** (EU) has adopted a public health strategy which focuses on a more coordinated approach to EU-wide and cross-border health concerns. The EU's public health strategy is based on improving the quality and dissemination of information about health, creating a mechanism for quickly responding to health threats, and better understanding factors that affect health. One of the objectives is to have the same safety and quality health standards throughout the EU.

A European Centre for Disease Prevention and Control, a centralized agency to coordinate measures to stop the spread of communicable diseases, began operations in Stockholm in 2005. The EU also provides financial support for general health research and funds studies to determine links between **environmental** factors and health problems. Given the known health risks, the EU additionally works toward preventing the use of tobacco and drug products.

PUBLIC OPINION. For more than 30 years the **European Commission** has monitored the public opinion of the European citizens, in large part through the Eurobarometer which conducts surveys and provides reports on the attitudes of the European people toward different European issues. In general, citizens of the **European Union** are divided in their feelings toward European integration, divisions that while based on the individual are also apparent in different member states and political groups. The Eurobarometer evaluates attitudes on a number of issue areas including most recently the **Treaty establishing a Constitution for Europe**, the **environment**, **development** aid, and the **euro**.

– Q –

QUALIFIED MAJORITY VOTING (QMV). *See* VOTING.

– R –

REGIONAL INTEGRATION. An institutionalized association of countries within a defined geographical territory, regional integration varies in scope from the removal of economic barriers to economic, political, and military cooperation between all of the members of the organization. There are generally considered to be four stages of economic integration: **free trade area**, **customs union**, **common market**, and economic union. Considered as one of the most successful attempts at regional integration, the **European Union** (EU) is working toward completing its economic and monetary union and has begun institutionalized cooperation in the political, security, and military fields as well.

Recognizing the benefits regional integration has provided to the European continent—lasting peace, overall economic recovery and growth, and greater international influence, particularly in the areas of development and **humanitarian aid**—other regions around the world have opted to implement their own versions of regional integration. In its **external relations** with third countries and groups of countries, the EU prefers to deal and negotiate with other regional organizations. The EU considers regional integration to be a viable means of reducing and eventually eliminating many of the problems in developing countries and, therefore, provides funding to regional organizations directed toward strengthening their institutions, rules, and coordinating mechanisms. Different forms of regional integration exist in Europe, North America, **Latin America**, the Caribbean, **Asia**, the **Middle East** and Africa. Refer to appendix H.

REGIONAL POLICY. *See* COHESION POLICY; STRUCTURAL FUNDS.

REGULATIONS. A type of **European Community (EC) law** that is binding on all member states of the **European Union** both in terms of the methods to be implemented and the final results to be achieved. Regulations have **direct effect** in all of the member states.

RESEARCH AND DEVELOPMENT. An important element for increased productivity, competition, and safety, research and development in the **European Union** is in part financed and coordinated by the **European Commission**. The Commission sponsors its own research initiatives conducted by the Joint Research Centre, mainly on issues related to nuclear **energy**, the **environment**, and industrial research. It also shares costs and coordinates activities between research institutes in different European member states.

In 1984, a multi-annual framework program for research was established. The sixth framework program which covers 2000–2006 was allocated €17.5 billion, part of which is to be used toward the completion of the **European Research Area**.

REY, JEAN. Refer to appendix B.

RODRIGUEZ IGLESIAS, GIL CARLOS. Refer to appendix F.

RODRIGUEZ ZAPATERO, JOSE LUIS (1960–). José Luis Rodríguez Zapatero has served as a member of the Spanish Congress of Deputies since 1986 and the general secretary of the Spanish Socialist Workers' Party (PSOE) since 2000. After the PSOE won the general elections of 14 March 2004, Zapatero became the prime minister of the government of **Spain**, sworn in on 17 April 2004. A relatively young politician with third-way tendencies, he complied with his campaign promise of ordering the Spanish troops home from Iraq soon after his assumption of power, emphasizing respect for Spain's democracy and Spain's return to Europe. Approximately 90 percent of the public had disagreed with Prime Minister **José María Aznar**'s policy to support the 2003 **United States** intervention in Iraq and the deployment of Spanish troops to aid the Coalition of the Willing, which also went against the position of the governments of **France** and **Germany**, the traditional motor of the European integration process.

On 11 March 2004, only three days prior to the general elections, an al-Qaeda terrorist attack on Madrid killed 191 people and injured more than 1500. While it has been argued that Zapatero's Iraq policy reversal is a demonstration of being a weak player in the war against **terrorism**, the Spanish prime minister claims that his government will persistently continue the fight both domestically and internationally.

ROMANIA. On 22 June 1995, Romania, formerly a Soviet bloc country, submitted its application for membership in the **European Union** (EU), but was one of the candidate states not invited to join the EU in 2004. Corruption, continuing discrimination against the Roma minority, and the inability to satisfactorily reform the police forces and judicial branch of government had been the main obstacles to Romania's membership. However, accession negotiations were concluded in December 2004. Along with **Bulgaria**, Romania's expected date of accession is 1 January 2007. Maintaining a traditionally close bilateral relationship, **France** has been one of the strongest supporters of Romania's EU membership. Refer to appendix A.

RUSSIA. Following the collapse of the Union of Soviet Socialist Republics, the **European Union** (EU) has developed its relations with Russia based on promoting political and economic stability in this newly democratic regime. Since it was initiated in 1991, the EU's **Technical Assistance for the Commonwealth of Independent States** (TACIS) program has provided billions of **euros** in assistance geared toward completing the transition to an open market economy, consolidating democratic institutions and processes, and encouraging respect for the rule of law.

EU–Russian relations have become a heightened priority with successive **enlargements** that have extended the EU's borders to those of Russia. There are five EU member states that border Russia: **Estonia**, **Finland**, **Latvia**, **Lithuania**, and **Poland**.

Bilateral relations between the EU and Russia are regulated by their **Partnership and Cooperation Agreement** that entered into force in December 1997 for a period of 10 years. This agreement commits the signatories to political dialogue and cooperation in **trade**, **justice and home affairs**, and several sectoral areas. It also establishes the institutional framework for these relations including biannual summits, a newly created Permanent Partnership Council at the ministerial level, a Cooperation Committee at the senior official level, sub-committees, and a Parliamentary Cooperation Committee.

At the May 2003 St. Petersburg Summit, the EU and Russia agreed to reinforce their cooperation by working toward the creation of four common spaces: a Common European Economic Space; a common **area of freedom, security, and justice**; a space of coordination in the field of external security; and a space of **research** and **education**. These common spaces and a strategy for their implementation was also the focus of the 25 November 2004 EU–Russia Summit in The Hague.

The EU–Russia agenda is quite comprehensive and several additional areas of interest include but are not limited to the EU–Russia Energy Dialogue, Chechnya, and **Kaliningrad**. EU is dependent on the import of **energy** products and is attempting to consolidate its energy cooperation with Russia, finalize long-term supply contracts, and ensure **environmental** protection. In terms of Chechnya, the EU unreservedly condemns **terrorism**, demands the respect for **human rights**, and advocates a peaceful solution to the conflict and the creation of an environment conducive to long-term security. Since the 1 May 2004 enlargement the Russian exclave of Kaliningrad has been completely surrounded by EU territory on its land borders, requiring new regulations and the facilitation of the transit of goods and people through this territory.

– S –

SAINT-MALO DECLARATION. Announced in December 1998, the Saint-Malo Declaration of British Prime Minister **Tony Blair** and French President **Jacques Chirac** is a declaration on European **defense**. It calls for a strengthened **Common Foreign and Security Policy** and developing an increased capacity for autonomous military action by European forces. The declaration is considered to be a decisive moment in European defense cooperation.

SANTER, JACQUES (1937–). A center-right politician in **Luxembourg** and Europe for decades, Jacques Santer was a member of the **European Parliament** (EP) from 1974 to 1979, prime minister of Luxembourg from 1985 to 1995, and president of the **European Commission** from 1995 to 1999. Following in the footsteps of **Jacques Delors** (president of the European Commission from 1985 to 1995), considered one of the most influential presidents of this institutions, was already a difficult proposition, made more so by the fact that Santer was the compromise candidate for the position. While the Santer Commission certainly achieved some success, it is most remembered for its en masse resignation in March 1999 following the publication of an independent report accusing the Commission of corruption and maladministration. Following the resignation, Santer was once again elected to the EP, where he served from 1999 to 2004. Since 2004, Santer has worked in the private sector as chairman of the board of CLT-UFA, an international film licensor and distributor, replacing **Gaston Thorn**, another former president of the European Commission.

SCELBA, MARIO. Refer to appendix D.

SCHENGEN AGREEMENT. The Schengen Agreement creates a single **European Union** (EU) external border (with no internal borders) for citizens of both EU and several non-EU member states, thus contributing to one of the fundamental objectives associated with completing the EU's **single market**—the free movement of persons. The first steps toward the creation of this territory were taken in 1985 when five of the EU member states, **Belgium**, **France**, **Germany**, **Luxembourg**, and **The Netherlands**, agreed to participate **intergovernmentally** in this endeavor. With slow and steady progress, it was not until 1997 that the Schengen Agreement officially became part of the EU with its incorporation in the **Treaty of Amsterdam**, yet it remains a policy of **enhanced cooperation** as **Ireland** and the **United Kingdom** do not participate. (Interestingly, **Norway** and **Iceland** as members of the Nordic Passport Union are included in the Schengen Agreement despite the fact that they are not EU member states, and Switzerland's membership was ratified by referendum in June 2005).

Allowing the free movement of people within the EU's internal borders required the harmonization of certain policies by all signatory member states. Minimum rules regarding visa requirements, asylum policies, and external border checks had to be commonly adopted in order for Schengen to work efficiently. Of course, this free movement of people created additional security concerns for the Schengen countries, and thus, in terms of creating an Area of Freedom, Security and Justice as outlined in the Treaty of Amsterdam, police and judicial cooperation was enhanced, especially within the context of combating typically cross-border crimes. In this regard, the **Schengen Information System** was designed as a common database that allows national authorities to consult and update this automated system with descriptions of "undesirable" persons and objects when passing through the internal borders of the member states.

All of the 2004 candidate states were required to adopt the Schengen "acquis" as part of their terms of accession. The development of the **Schengen Information System II** is currently underway, completion of which is a prerequisite for the May 2004 **enlargement** member states to eventually become part of the Schengen territory.

SCHENGEN INFORMATION SYSTEM (SIS). The SIS, part of the Schengen "acquis," is a common database network maintained by each one of the Schengen member states with a technical support unit in Strasbourg, **France**. The 13 member states of the EU signatories to the Schengen Convention as well as **Iceland**, **Norway**, and **Switzerland** participate in this system.

The SIS allows national law enforcement and consular authorities the ability to contribute to and consult this automated system to obtain descriptions of lost or stolen objects and kidnapped and wanted persons when passing through the internal borders of the member states. The SIS is intended to protect the single European market which includes the free movement of goods and people. There were concerns regarding the SIS with respect to the protection of personal information which were addressed through the passage of privacy laws. The implementation of the SIS was delayed due to technical difficulties.

SCHENGEN INFORMATION SYSTEM II (SIS II). Designed to increase the capacity of the original Schengen Information System (SIS) to include the member states that joined the **European Union** in May 2004 as well as those that will join in expected forthcoming enlargements, SIS II, also known as the second generation SIS, is in its developmental stage. It includes updated technological and information gathering potential in line with judicial and police cooperation and common immigration and visa policies.

SCHMIDT, HELMUT (1918–). Helmut Schmidt's West German chancellorship from 1974 to 1982 coincided with **Valéry Giscard**

d'Estaing's term as the president of **France**. The two leaders of the traditional "motor" of European integration embraced this role not only as a means of maintaining solidarity during the **European Community** decade characterized by Eurosclerosis but also of reinforcing the Franco–German rapprochement.

Although not always assuming a favorable stance, Schmidt eventually came to support the **European Monetary System** (EMS), the precursor to **Economic and Monetary Union** (EMU). Without this German approval the EMS would not have become a reality in 1979.

SCHRÖDER, GERHARD (1944–). A member of the Social Democratic Party (SPD), Gerhard Schröder has been chancellor of the Federal Republic of **Germany** since 1998, serving in his second term since 2002. He is the head of a coalition government that includes the SPD and the German Green Party. In order to focus on politically sensitive reforms based on his Agenda 2010, Schröder resigned as chairman of the SPD in February 2004.

Along with French President **Jacques Chirac**, Chancellor Schröder was one of the European leaders most adamantly opposed to the 2003 **United States** intervention in Iraq. In other areas, however, Schröder has been a German military pioneer, the first post–World War II Chancellor to send German peacekeeping troops outside of **NATO** territory, to Afghanistan, **Kosovo**, and the **Former Yugoslav Republic of Macedonia**.

Some of the policies Schröder supports have caused conflict within the **European Union** (EU), within Germany itself, and even within his own party. Given Germany's sustained economic difficulties in the early 21st century, Chancellor Schröder has called for greater flexibility in applying the rules of the **Stability and Growth Pact** which Germany has breached for more than three consecutive years. The chancellor also supports lifting the arms embargo against **China**, and has been a strong supporter of **Turkey**'s bid for EU membership.

SCHUMAN, ROBERT (1886–1963). A member of the French Resistance during World War II and a career Christian Democrat politician in **France** from 1919 until two years prior to his death, Robert Schuman was a long-serving member of the French parliament, prime minister from 1947 to 1948, and foreign minister from 1948 to 1953.

During his term in office as foreign minister, Schuman made the historic decision, based on his personal and political beliefs, to accept the proposal made by **Jean Monnet** to pool the French and German coal and steel industries. On 9 May 1950, now known as Europe Day, he made the now-famous declaration that bears his name. The offer included in the **Schuman Declaration** was accepted not only by France and West **Germany** but also by **Belgium, Italy, Luxembourg**, and the **Netherlands**, who signed the **Treaty of Paris** in 1951 and became the founding members of the **European Coal and Steel Community**. From 1958 to 1960, Schuman served as the president of the European Parliamentary Assembly. He is remembered as one of the founders of the **European Union**. Refer to appendix D.

SCHUMAN DECLARATION. On 9 May 1950 (officially Europe Day since 1985), **Robert Schuman**, the minister of foreign affairs of **France**, made an announcement of historical proportions. The document he read has been labeled by some scholars as a "Declaration of Interdependence."

The Declaration focused on creating a lasting peace on the continent which would be achieved through incremental steps starting with the pooling of the French and German coal and steel industries under a **High Authority**. This project was open to other European countries but primarily addressed the need to eliminate the longstanding animosities between **France** and **Germany**. The Schuman Declaration led to the signing of the 1951 **Treaty of Paris**, establishing the **European Coal and Steel Community** (ECSC).

SERBIA AND MONTENEGRO. For most of the 1990s the Western Balkans region experienced ethnic and religious conflict. Part of the **former Yugoslavia**, Serbia entered into military conflict with **Croatia**, **Bosnia-Herzegovina**, and **Kosovo** under the leadership of Slobodan Milosevic in successive wars throughout the 1990s, resulting in hundreds of thousands of deaths and millions of displaced people. After the failure of several attempts at resolution of the conflict including peace conferences organized by the **European Union** (EU), the **North Atlantic Treaty Organization** (NATO) attacked Serbia in 1995 over Bosnia and in 1999 over Kosovo, and set up subsequent peacekeeping missions.

Former Serbian President Milosevic was charged with war crimes in Croatia and Kosovo and genocide in Bosnia-Herzegovina and was on trial by the United Nations International Criminal Tribunal for the Former Yugoslavia (UNICTY) when he was found dead in March 2006.

Serbia and Montenegro is composed of Serbia, Montenegro, and Kosovo, a fact that could cause additional problems in the future considering this is a temporary resolution and claims for independence from Montenegro and Kosovo have not been sufficiently addressed in any of the peace agreements. Nevertheless, after Milosevic was removed from power, the EU lifted the sanctions it had placed on the country and renewed its intention to develop strong relations with this possible future EU member state. Serbia and Montenegro receives EU funding in the form of **Community Assistance for Reconstruction, Development, and Stability** (CARDS) as well as **humanitarian aid**, totaling more than €2 billion since October 2000. The three main objectives of this funding are conflict management, post-conflict reconstruction and stabilization, and aiding with transitions and reforms necessary to form a closer association between Serbia and the EU and eventual EU membership for Serbia and Montenegro. On 12 April 2005, the **European Commission** announced that Serbia and Montenegro had made enough progress, including cooperation with the UNICTY, to begin negotiations for a **Stabilization and Association Agreement**.

SINGLE EUROPEAN ACT (SEA). After years of relative stagnation in the European integration process, there was a general consensus amongst the European leadership that another treaty reform was necessary; one that would address institutional reforms and the completion of the **single market**. Naturally there were conflicts over the extent and scope of the reforms as well as over several of the more controversial details. Nevertheless, after being signed in 1986, the SEA was ratified and came into force on 1 July 1987.

One of the main goals of the SEA was to complete the single market by 31 December 1992, facilitating the free movement of persons, goods, capital, and services across the internal borders of the **European Community** (EC). In an attempt to avoid the traditional obstacles to reaching this goal, **qualified majority voting** was introduced for more issue areas in the SEA, particularly those dealing with removing barriers to **trade** and harmonization and regulations necessary to complete the single market according to the established schedule. Recognizing the potential financial benefit of this integration project, European businesses took advantage of the possibilities and engaged in increased acquisitions and mergers.

The SEA was the first treaty reform since the implementation of direct elections to the **European Parliament** (EP), and the increase in power for this institution was small but significant. The EP was given the opportunity to have the final approval over future **enlargement** countries. Furthermore, the **cooperation procedure** was introduced in the SEA, making it mandatory for proposed legislation in specific issue areas to be submitted to the EP for its opinion. Although the **Council of Ministers** still had the ability to overrule the EP in this procedure, the EP gained influence in the legislative process through its ability to amend and delay proposed legislation.

For the first time **European Political Cooperation** was officially recognized in the SEA. The institutionalization of political cooperation would eventually lead to its transformation into the **Common Foreign and Security Policy** in the **Treaty on European Union**.

The **cohesion policy** and **structural funds** were also an important part of the SEA. Unofficially led by Spanish Prime Minister **Felipe Gonzalez**, the less developed EC member states lobbied for the inclusion of these funds in the SEA, basically transferring EC contributions from the wealthiest member states to the poorest member states under EC supervision and through the EC institutions. The objective of these policies in terms of the single market was to make its completion as equally beneficial to all member states as possible and to prevent the emergence of a two-speed Europe.

SINGLE MARKET. On 1 January 1993 the **European Community**'s single market became fully operational. Although the completion of a **common market** was one of the primary goals of the 1957 **Treaty of Rome** establishing the **European Economic Community**, obstacles such as the principles of the **Luxembourg Compromise**, hindered its development. By the early 1980s during which European goods had difficulty competing in international markets and governments were struggling economically in general, many leaders, including **Margaret Thatcher**, optimistically considered the idea of the single market and the benefits that would theoretically accompany this increased liberalization. **Jacques Delors**, president of the **European Commission** from 1985 to 1995, played an indispensable role in convincing national leaders of the merits of the single market as well as negotiating terms that would become acceptable to all parties to the resultant treaty. The **Single European Act** went into effect on 1 July 1987.

The removal of barriers to trade, investment, and other intra-state economic and financial transactions was enhanced through the harmonization of laws, the implementation of new regulations, and the elimination of a substantial amount of paperwork. The free movement of goods, persons, services, and capital through the internal borders of the European Community member states was greatly improved. Despite the unquestionable progress that has been achieved in terms of the European single market, it still has yet to be perfectly completed.

SKOURIS, VASSILIOS. Refer to appendix F.

SLOVAKIA. Gaining its sovereignty in 1993 following Czechoslovakia's "Velvet Divorce," the Slovak Republic submitted its application for membership in the **European Union** (EU) on 27 June 1995. Relations between Slovakia and the EU were complicated by the isolationist positions of Slovakia's Prime Minister Vladimir Meciar (1994–1998), and as a result accession negotiations were delayed until 15 February 2000. Despite the limited time frame, Slovakia had successfully completed the talks in time to participate in the 1 May 2004 **enlargement** process. In a public referendum held on the issue on 16–17 May 2003, 92.4 percent of Slovakians overwhelmingly approved of their country's EU membership. *See also* CZECH REPUBLIC. Refer to appendix A.

SLOVENIA. The Republic of Slovenia applied for **European Union** (EU) membership on 10 June 1996, began accession negotiations on 31 March 1998, and was officially invited to join the EU at the

Copenhagen **European Council** on 13 December 2002. In a March 2003 referendum, 91 percent of Slovenes supported EU membership. Slovenia is the smallest continental 2004 **enlargement** country and has a relatively stable economy.

Slovenia, the most prosperous region of the **former Republic of Yugoslavia**, gained its independence in 1991. Today Slovenia is the only EU member state among the former Yugoslav republics. It is hoped that Slovenia will serve as a "bridge" between the EU and the other former Yugoslav republics wanting and expected to eventually join the EU. Refer to appendix A.

SOCIAL CHARTER. Officially the Community Charter of the Fundamental Social Rights of Workers, the Social Charter was proposed in the late 1980s to promote a **social policy** for the **European Community** (EC) in light of the imminent completion of the single European market. The Charter contains 12 categories of fundamental social rights including freedom of movement, freedom of association, equal treatment for men and women, and the protection of children. In December 1989, 11 of the then 12 heads of state or government, all except that of the government of British Conservative Prime Minister **Margaret Thatcher**, adopted the Social Charter. The Charter remained outside the legal framework of the EC until it became the basis for the Social Protocol which was annexed to the **Treaty on European Union** by the same 11 member states. The **Charter of Fundamental Rights** included in the **Treaty establishing a Constitution for Europe** contains all of the rights originally provided by the Social Charter, and will gain legal status if the constitutional treaty is ratified.

SOCIAL POLICY. *See* EMPLOYMENT AND SOCIAL POLICY.

SOCIALIST GROUP IN THE EUROPEAN PARLIAMENT (PES). One of the two most prominent **political groups in the European Parliament** (EP), the PES was the largest EP political group from 1979 to 1999, with Members of the EP (MEPs) from all of the **European Union** (EU) member states. The results of the June 2004 EP elections show that the PES is currently the second-largest European parliamentary group with a total of 200 MEPs from 23 member states, all except **Latvia** and **Cyprus**. Characterized as a center-left political group, the PES promotes an agenda including but not limited to issues of **employment**, social security, equal rights, and **environmental** protection.

SOLANA, JAVIER (1942–). The grandson of **Salvador de Madariaga**, an active supporter of European integration and founder of the College of Europe, Javier Solana was educated as a physicist but is a **Spanish** politician and diplomat by profession. He has been involved in Spanish and European politics since the 1960s, when he joined the Spanish Socialist Workers' Party, illegal at the time under the dictatorship of Francisco Franco. Solana first entered the Spanish Congress of Deputies in 1977, where he would remain until 1995. During this time he served in several positions in the government of **Felipe González** (1982–1996), including Minister of Culture, Education, and Foreign Affairs. As the Minister of Foreign Affairs during the Spanish presidency of the **European Union** (EU) in 1995, Solana played a major role in the beginning of the **Euro-Mediterranean Partnership**. Ironically, having previously been opposed to Spanish membership in its ranks, Solana became the Secretary General of the **North Atlantic Treaty Organization** in 1995.

In 1999 Solana was appointed by the **European Council** to a position that was created in the **Treaty of Amsterdam**, the **High Representative for the Common Foreign and Security Policy** (CFSP). He is also the Secretary-General of the **Council of the EU**. As the High Representative for the CFSP, Solana is responsible for coordinating foreign policies of the member states and representing the EU in international negotiations and organizations. In this position, he has been involved in peacemaking in the Balkans, the **Middle East** peace process, and numerous negotiations for bilateral and regional agreements with the EU. He also drafted the current **European Security Strategy** in 2003 and created the new position of Counter-Terrorism Coordinator in 2004.

In June 2004, the European Council agreed that Solana would be the first Union Minister for Foreign Affairs, a position created in the **Treaty Establishing a Constitution for Europe**. While the current stalemate in the treaty ratification process prevents him from assuming this position, he continues as the High Representative of the

CFSP, as in June 2004 the European Council also reappointed him to this post.

SPAAK, PAUL-HENRI (1899–1972). A member of Belgium's socialist Labour Party, Prime Minister of **Belgium** four times between 1938 and 1949, Belgian foreign minister during several administrations including his own, and secretary general of the **North Atlantic Treaty Organization** from 1957 to 1961, Paul-Henri Spaak was truly devoted to the cause of European integration. Spaak not only presided over the **Messina Conference** in 1955 but also chaired the committee that drafted the final report in preparation for the 1957 **Treaties of Rome** and the creation of the **European Economic Community** and the **European Atomic Energy Community**. Refer to appendix D.

SPAIN. The transition to democracy in the late 1970s opened the door to European integration, and on 28 July 1977, Spain applied for membership in the **European Community** (EC). From the time Spain's accession application was favorably accepted by the EC in 1977 until the treaty was signed, Spain's political parties worked together toward EC membership. For politicians and community leaders, EC integration was not merely a goal in and of itself but rather a guarantee of the consolidation of the key internal changes in Spain, above all the transition to democracy, and of the reestablishment of international respectability.

France and **Italy** were concerned about the economic implications of Spanish membership, particularly how they might be affected by this Iberian country's inclusion in certain policy frameworks and funding allocations. **Agriculture** and **fisheries** were the most difficult aspects of the Spanish accession negotiation process. On the other hand, Spain was able to include its special relations with **Latin America** in its accession treaty, ensuring that this region would become a lasting element of the EC agenda.

On 1 January 1986, after six years of intense negotiations, Spain finally became an EC member state. Since becoming an EC member state, Spain has played an active role in European institutions, decisions, and policy-making. The **cohesion policy**, European **citizenship**, and the **Committee of the Regions** are just some of the successful policies supported by Spain. The post of **High Representative for the Common Foreign and Security Policy** has been filled thus far by only person, former secretary general of **NATO**, **Javier Solana** of Spain.

Leading up to and during the **Intergovernmental Conference** (IGC) on the **Treaty establishing a Constitution for Europe**, Spain demanded the same or similar weighted **decision-making** power as it was able to so effectively negotiate in the **Treaty of Nice**. With no resolution on this matter by December 2003, the IGC was extended to the Irish presidency of the first semester 2004, when an acceptable compromise was reached.

In March 2004, Madrid fell victim to an Al-Qaeda terrorist attack, three days prior to the country's general elections. Not only were there internal repercussions with a change in the government, but the urgent need for the **European Union** to commonly address the issue of **terrorism** was accentuated. *See also* AZNAR, JOSE MARIA; GONZALEZ, FELIPE; RODRIGUEZ ZAPATERO, JOSE LUIS. Refer to appendix A.

SPECIAL ACCESSION PROGRAMME FOR AGRICULTURE AND RURAL DEVELOPMENT (SAPARD). Established in 1999 as part of **Agenda 2000**, SAPARD focuses on providing financial assistance exclusively for the **agricultural** sector and rural areas of the 10 **Central and Eastern European countries**. Until 2003 the annual **budget** for all 10 countries was €560 million. In 2004, **Bulgaria** and **Romania**, the then two remaining candidate countries from the region, received approximately €225 million from SAPARD.

SPENALE, GEORGES. Refer to appendix D.

SPINELLI, ALTIERO (1907–1986). A European federalist, Altiero Spinelli significantly contributed to the development of the **European Union** (EU). He was not only an activist but also an avid thinker on the subject. While imprisoned on the island of Ventotene for participating in the Italian Resistance during World War II, he co-authored what has come to be known as the Ventotene Manifesto in support of a federal Europe as a means of creating peace on the continent.

From 1970 to 1976, Spinelli was one of the Italian representatives to the **European Commission**. For the next ten years he was an active member of the **European Parliament** (EP), during which time he founded the **Crocodile Club**, known as such for the restaurant where it first started meeting. Within a short period of time this club, focused on making reforms to the **European Community**, not only increased its membership but also transformed into the EP Committee on Institutional Affairs. In 1983 the committee presented a draft treaty on EU, which although not ratified by the member states was adopted by the EP in 1984. Spinelli was also a strong supporter and lobbyist for the adoption of the **Single European Act**.

STABILITY AND GROWTH PACT (SGP). The SGP was adopted in 1997 as a means of ensuring continuous fiscal discipline in the third and final stage of **Economic and Monetary Union** (EMU). Considered to be the key element in obtaining price stability, a strong (**euro**) currency, and sustainable growth, **budgetary** soundness has proven difficult for many of the **European Union** (EU) member states, including the strongest supporter of the SGP, **Germany**. One of the most controversial aspects upon which the SGP is based is the excessive deficit procedure which requires member states to maintain their government deficits within 3 percent of their respective gross domestic products (GDP) and government debt within 60 percent of their respective GDPs. If these obligations are breached the Council, based on reports from the **European Commission**, may eventually impose sanctions against a member state if it is determined that the member state has not made serious attempts and progress toward attaining the established goals.

Over the past few years many of the EU countries, including those with the typically strongest economies, have had significant difficulties meeting the deficit criteria. Due to prolonged breaches, the European Commission has recommended (unsuccessfully) giving notice to some countries including **France** and **Germany**, which has caused interstate and inter-institutional tensions. Thus, while the precise future of the Pact is uncertain, there seems to be greater agreement toward flexibility in its implementation.

STABILITY PACT FOR SOUTHEASTERN EUROPE. Proposed by French Prime Minister Edouard Balladur in 1993, and also known as the Balladur Plan, the Stability Pact for Southeastern Europe is an attempt to encourage good relations and increased cooperation between the **Central and Eastern European countries** (CEECs). The Pact is intended to reduce the potential for conflict in this region, particularly relevant following the outbreak of war in the **former Yugoslavia** in the early 1990s. A particular focus is on the resolution of border and minority disputes, a requirement for membership in the **European Union** (EU).

The EU provided positive support for the Balladur Plan in 1994, and it was signed in Paris in March 1995. After the launch of the Stability Pact for Southeastern Europe, the management of the implementation of its bilateral agreements was transferred to the authority of the **Organization for Security and Cooperation in Europe** (OSCE).

STABILIZATION AND ASSOCIATION AGREEMENTS (SAAs). A significant part of the process to strengthen relations between the **European Union** (EU) and the countries of the Western Balkans region (**Albania**, **Bosnia and Herzegovina**, **Croatia**, **Serbia and Montenegro**, and the **Former Yugoslav Republic of Macedonia**) which are considered to be future potential candidate countries, SAAs are bilateral mechanisms through which the countries of the region begin to adopt the necessary reforms to achieve a formal association with the EU. The agreements include adherence to democratic principles and the gradual development of **free trade areas** between the EU and the individual country signatories from the region. They also include a commitment to increase regional cooperation between the countries of the region itself. **The Community Assistance for Reconstruction, Development, and Stabilization** financial instrument provides funding to meet the objectives established in the SAAs.

STRUCTURAL FUNDS. Cohesion, or narrowing the gap between the rich and poor member states, has been a general strategy since the creation of the European Communities in 1957. With the **Single**

European Act of 1987, and its goal of completing the **single market** by 1993, increased emphasis and concern emerged in regard to the **cohesion policy**. The structural funds are the instruments that financially support this cohesion policy.

The main objective of the structural funds is to provide financial support to underdeveloped regions of the **European Union** (EU), and particularly to projects that incorporate elements of long-term planning and its resulting development. There are four types of structural funds: **European Regional Development Fund**, **European Social Fund**, **European Agricultural Guidance and Guarantee Fund**, and **Financial Instrument for Fisheries Guidance**. Based on the principle of additionality, this EU funding is intended to complement and not substitute for national funding allocated to development plans.

SUBSIDIARITY. The principle of subsidiarity refers to the idea that decisions will be taken at the lowest level possible and only at the highest level when necessary. It was first included in the legal framework of the **European Union** (EU) in the **Treaty on EU**. This means that the EU will take actions and make decisions only when it is considered that optimal effectiveness in a specific area cannot be adequately addressed by the national or local governments of the member states and must, therefore, be handled at the EU level. One of the problems associated with the principle of subsidiarity is the ambiguity associated with it and its application.

SUPRANATIONALISM. An approach to integration in which there is a pooling of national sovereignty under a **higher authority**, supranationalism contends that member states are not the only influential actors, but that **European Union** (EU) institutions and interests also play a decisive role in the policy-making process. Through the series of treaties and treaty reforms governing this method of integration, member states have provided the EU institutions with policy and **decision-making** powers in certain competences that are binding on all member states. Supranationalism is unique to the EU as a regional organization and represents integration as a step beyond traditional **intergovernmental** international cooperation.

SUPREMACY. A fundamental principle of **European Community (EC) law** firmly established in the 1964 *Costa v. ENEL* case, supremacy means that EC law takes precedence over the national laws of the member states. If there is a conflict between EC law and national laws, the national laws are to be modified.

SUSTAINABLE DEVELOPMENT. As defined by the United Nations World Commission on Environment and Development, sustainable development "meets the needs of the present without compromising the ability of future generations to meet their needs." According to the **European Commission**, sustainable development refers to: "balanced and equitable economic development; high levels of **employment**, social cohesion and inclusiveness; a high level of **environmental** protection and responsible use of natural resources; coherent policy making in an open, transparent and accountable political system; and effective international cooperation to promote sustainable development globally." Sustainable development is a vital concern of the **European Union** which it tries to promote both internally and externally through strategies developed by the European Commission.

SWEDEN. The Kingdom of Sweden, a founding member of the **European Free Trade Association** (EFTA) and the **Council of Europe**, formally submitted its application for membership in the **European Community** on 1 July 1991. Due in part to Sweden's neutrality, extensive welfare state, and high **environmental** standards, **European Union** (EU) membership had been and remains widely controversial in this Nordic country. However, motivated by economic considerations, Sweden became a member state in 1995, as part of the first **enlargement** of the EU.

Despite its well-known **Euro-skepticism**, Sweden has played an instrumental role in promoting (along with **Finland**) the development of the EU's capacity for crisis management and **humanitarian** endeavors. Support for higher EU environmental standards and establishing **gender equality** as one of the Union's goals are some of Sweden's EU priorities.

Sweden remains one of the pre–May 2004 member states (along with **Denmark** and the **United Kingdom**) to not use the **euro** as its legal tender. While there is some strong government backing for Sweden to adopt the euro as its national currency, the public has not been supportive as voters rejected this possibility in a referendum in September 2003. However, the country continues to prepare for potential entry into the **euro zone** in the event of a change in public sentiment. Refer to appendix A.

SWITZERLAND. Completely encircled by European member states since the 1995 accession of **Austria** to the **European Union** (EU), Switzerland has a long tradition of close relations with the EU. After signing the **European Economic Area** (EEA) agreement, the Swiss government applied for membership in the **European Community** (EC) on 20 May 1992. A referendum was held on 6 December 1992 in which the Swiss citizens rejected ratification of the EEA agreement, and the Swiss government subsequently indefinitely suspended EC accession negotiations.

Switzerland is the only member of the **European Free Trade Association** (EFTA) that does not participate in the EEA. Nevertheless, the EU and Switzerland are amongst each others' most important trading partners, and Switzerland has signed more agreements with the EU than any other third country. Seven agreements pertaining to the free movement of people, **agricultural** trade, public procurement, technical barriers to trade, air transport, land transport, and **research** entered into force on 1 June 2002. In October 2004, nine additional agreements were signed and await the ratification process. These agreements include issues of **taxation**, fraud, asylum, agriculture, the **environment**, the free movement of people, and Switzerland's participation in the **Schengen Agreement**, the European Statistical System, and the EU Media program.

– T –

TAXATION. Large tax differentials between **European Union** (EU) member states can significantly debilitate the **single market** and fair competition. Therefore, although tax policy remains a member state competence in terms of income and corporate taxes, the EU attempts to coordinate the harmonization of indirect taxes to prevent substantial distortions. In this regard, this **intergovernmental** EU issue has been addressed through unanimous agreement on the setting of minimum and maximum excise tax and value-added tax (VAT). The standard VAT is 15 percent, although this remains flexible depending on specific circumstances in different member states, and subject to exemptions. The main goal of the **European Commission** is to achieve as much single market related tax harmonization as possible without interfering in the prerogatives of the member state governments.

TECHNICAL ASSISTANCE FOR THE COMMONWEALTH OF INDEPENDENT STATES (TACIS). Begun in 1991, TACIS provides technical financial assistance to 12 countries of Eastern Europe and Central Asia: Armenia, Azerbaijan, **Belarus**, Georgia, Kazakhstan, Kyrgyzstan, **Moldova**, **Russia**, Tajikistan, Turkmenistan, **Ukraine**, and Uzbekistan), mainly to support their transitions to democracy and open market economies. The 2000–2006 TACIS regulation's principal goal is to help achieve the objectives of the **Partnership and Association Agreements** by providing support for, among other issue areas, institutional and legal reforms, economic development, and **environmental** protection.

TERRORISM. Terrorism has long existed in post–World War II Western Europe, in **Ireland**, **Italy**, and **Spain**, to name just a few of the countries that have experienced repeated violent terrorist (post–September 11 definition) acts. In 1975, the **Trevi Group**, composed of senior officials from justice and interior ministries of the **European Community** member states, was established to cooperate on issues of **justice and home affairs**, particularly the fight against terrorism. With the creation of the third **pillar** on Justice and Home Affairs in the **Treaty on European Union**, this coordination became legally institutionalized.

Following the terrorist attacks on the United States on 11 September 2001, the **European Union** (EU) responded with declarations of their solidarity and support to build a strong coalition against global terrorism. On 11 March 2004, the international terrorist group, al-Qaeda struck Europe itself, with bombings in the capital city of

Madrid that killed 191 people and wounded more than 1500. This incident instigated even greater EU cooperation and dedication to combating global terrorism, evidenced by the creation of a counter-terrorism coordinator in the office of the Council Secretary General/**High Representative for the Common Foreign and Security Policy**. The counter-terrorism coordinator is responsible for helping to coordinate anti-terrorism initiatives between the member states as well as managing the EU's anti-terrorism agenda. Obviously even more work needs to be done in this area as on 7 July 2005 the **United Kingdom** was the target of a terrorist attack on its public transportation system, killing 56 people and injuring 700.

THATCHER, MARGARET (1925–). With an aggressive, suspicious, and uncompromising attitude toward the **European Community** (EC), Margaret Thatcher became the prime minister of the **United Kingdom** (UK) on 4 May 1979 as the head of the Conservative Party. Thatcher was the first female to hold this executive post, and the first woman to participate as government representative in the **European Council**.

Thatcher strongly believed that the basis of European integration should be **intergovernmentalism**, often questioning the merits and intentions of the EC government in **Brussels**. A now infamous speech she made at the College of Europe in Bruges in September 1988 accentuated her standpoint by addressing the need to avoid being dominated by an overriding European government.

After Thatcher assumed the premiership she immediately campaigned to rectify the injustices regarding Britain's EC budgetary contribution. Due to Britain's export and import patterns, particularly in **agricultural** products, the UK's payments to the EC **budget** far exceeded the financial benefits it received in return. Outraged (and for the most part rightly so) by the continuation of these unfair practices, Thatcher demanded a British budgetary rebate, a topic that would dominate European Council agendas until an agreement was reached in June 1984.

Despite her generally negative attitude toward the European integration process, Thatcher was one of the strongest proponents of the **single market**. She fully understood and appreciated how advantageous this liberalization program could be for Britain's economy. She considered the single market to be a sufficient end to the EC's economic integration and, in contrast to her position on that policy, wholeheartedly opposed the **Economic and Monetary Union**.

With regard to the events transpiring in **Central and Eastern Europe** close to the end of her term in office, Thatcher opposed such a quick and complete reunification of **Germany** so soon after the fall of the **Berlin Wall**. However, unable to delay or influence this process which she witnessed one month prior to the end of her executive administration, she supported **enlargement** to the former Soviet bloc countries as a means of moderating Germany's leading influence in the region, and promoting a significantly wider EC, practically ensuring a more gradual **deepening** of EC integration.

For the most part, Thatcher's term in office (1979–1990) coincided with that of the Republican president of the **United States**, Ronald Reagan (1980–1988). These two leaders are often referred to as each other's ideological soul mates, and during the 1980s the special Atlantic relationship between the United States and the UK was reinforced. Thatcher was sure to include provisions or declarations confirming these relations in European policy proposals and organizations such as the **European Union** (EU) and **Western European Union** (WEU).

On 28 November 1990, after Thatcher's own Conservative Party forced her resignation, she was replaced by her finance minister, **John Major**. It is believed that a combination of controversial proposed domestic policies as well as her Europessimism contributed to Thatcher's political downfall.

THORN, GASTON EDMONT. Refer to appendix B.

TRADE POLICY. The EU Community has exclusive competence over the trade policy of the **European Union** (EU), which means that the EU member states, represented by the **European Commission**, must act commonly in all trade negotiations. The European Commission almost always represents the EU member states with a single voice in the **World Trade Organization** (WTO).

The EU is a **customs union** and has a **common external tariff** and a common commercial policy, all of which are the key elements of its trade policy. The EU's position on this issue is to progressively liberalize all trade, and it plays a significant role in the WTO and its rounds of trade liberalization negotiations. Indeed, almost all barriers to trade amongst the EU member states have been eliminated, and reducing these barriers between the EU and third countries is one of the priorities of the trade policy. Thus, the EU has negotiated and signed bilateral trade agreements with many countries and regions throughout the world and has developed, or is in the process of developing, **free trade areas** with others. Since the early 1990s, all cooperation and association agreements between the EU and third countries, including those based predominantly on trade, contain a **human rights** clause.

One of the EU's strongest trading partners is the **United States**. Although much news attention is given to the trade disputes that arise between these two significant trading partners and actors in international trade, only two percent of their total trade is actually contested, and many of these disputes have been resolved in the framework of the WTO.

The EU gives special trade preferences to many of the world's developing countries, including the **African–Caribbean–Pacific (ACP) countries**, through its Generalized System of Preferences, allowing duty-free entry of industrial and most agricultural products from these countries into the EU. The Everything But Arms program, adopted in 2001, gives the world's least developed countries unlimited access to the EU market, with the only exception being the importation of arms. *See also* DEVELOPMENT POLICY.

TRANS-EUROPEAN NETWORKS (TENs). The completion of the single European market has accentuated the need for interconnection and interoperability between the national infrastructure networks of the **European Union** (EU) member states. TENs are intended to address this issue through three sectors in which projects are developed: transportation, **energy**, and telecommunications. Funding for TENs comes from various sources; the EU **budget** which allocated €4.6 billion to the TENs from 2000–2006, the **European Investment Bank**, private investors, national and regional government contributions, and other EU funds such as the **cohesion** fund. Although the EU is dedicated to TENs-related projects, there are several difficulties associated with TENs including that they are generally long-term projects that require large amounts of investments, investment that is not always readily available.

TRANSLATION CENTRE FOR THE BODIES OF THE EURO-PEAN UNION. Established in 1994 and located in **Luxembourg**, the Translation Center is an **agency of the European Union** (EU) and provides for the translating needs of all of the other agencies of the EU. *See also* LANGUAGES.

TRANSPORT POLICY. The free movement of people, capital, goods, and services through the **single market** of the **European Union** (EU) requires an open and fair transport policy to support this increased movement. A once highly regulated industry, legislation has been passed in the EU to open transportation to competition, particularly for road and air travel, in an effort to make it more efficient. The EU also supports large infrastructure projects, **Trans-European Networks**, to help address some of the problems associated with transportation in the EU, including congestion and pollution.

TREATIES OF ROME. Following the defeat of the **European Defence Community**, **Jean Monnet** resigned as the president of the **High Authority** in order to dedicate his time and energy to promoting increased European integration. He founded the Action Committee for a United States of Europe, an association composed of high ranking members of political parties and trade unions, to lobby the cause. Monnet's efforts, in part, resulted in the signing of the Treaties of Rome in 1957.

  Paul-Henri Spaak, **Belgium**'s foreign minister, directed the negotiations and drafting of the treaties for what came to be known as the **European Community**. The Treaties of Rome were signed by the six founding members of the **European Coal and Steel Community**, establishing both the **European Atomic Energy Community** and the **European Economic Community**. In 1965, the **Merger Treaty** was signed, effectively fusing the institutional frameworks of the three existing communities into one, all of which would be subsequently referred to as the European Communities.

TREATY ESTABLISHING A CONSTITUTION FOR EUROPE. The **European Convention**, the entity created to debate the future of Europe and incorporate its conclusions in a constitutional text, adopted by consensus the draft constitutional treaty in June 2003, subsequently submitting it to the **European Council** in Thessaloniki, **Greece**. After an **Intergovernmental Conference** spanning both the Italian and Irish **European Union** (EU) presidencies (second semester 2003 and first semester 2004, respectively), the European Council approved the final version of this treaty in **Brussels** in June 2004.

Signed in Rome on 29 October 2004, the Treaty establishing a Constitution for Europe (also referred to as the constitutional treaty) primarily eliminates the need to negotiate treaty reforms on a regular basis, and incorporates all of the previous treaties governing the EU into a single legal document. Included in this treaty are the institutional and **decision-making** reforms necessary to accommodate not only the May 2004 **enlargement** but future enlargements as well. In an effort to meet the objectives established in the **Laeken Declaration**, the treaty contains the **Charter of Fundamental Rights**, creates the post of Union Minister for Foreign Affairs, and collapses the **three pillar** structure which had eventually come to be considered an impediment to integration progress in many of the issue areas of the second and third pillars. Furthermore, there is an increased focus on **subsidiarity** which ensures that decisions are made at the closest level to the citizen as possible and that there is a proper exercise of power.

The constitutional treaty is dedicated to the fundamental theme of achieving unity through diversity as specifically elaborated in its preamble:

> Convinced that, while remaining proud of their own national identities and history, the peoples of Europe are determined to transcend their ancient divisions and, united ever more closely, to forge a common destiny,
>
> Convinced that, thus "united in its diversity," Europe offers them the best chance of pursuing, with due regard for the rights of each individual and in awareness of their responsibilities towards future generations and the Earth, the great venture which makes of it a special area of human hope.
>
> Unity through diversity is the motto of the EU.

Despite agreement amongst European heads of state or governments to approve this constitutional treaty, it still had to pass through what proved to be a challenging ratification process; either through established internal parliamentary procedure, or through public national referenda.

As of October 2005, 14 member states had ratified the Treaty establishing a Constitution for Europe: **Austria**, **Belgium**, **Cyprus**, **Germany**, Greece, **Hungary**, **Italy**, **Latvia**, **Lithuania**, **Luxembourg**, **Malta**, **Slovakia**, **Slovenia**, and **Spain**. The citizens of **France** and **The Netherlands** rejected the Treaty establishing a Constitution for Europe in national referendums held on 29 May 2005 and 1 June 2005, respectively. The Treaty must be ratified by all member states before it can take effect. The ratification process has been postponed and the EU and its member states are currently engaged in period of reflection and discussion regarding the treaty.

TREATY ESTABLISHING A SINGLE COUNCIL AND A SINGLE COMMISSION OF THE EUROPEAN COMMUNITIES. *See* MERGER TREATY.

TREATY OF AMSTERDAM. Improvements to the **Treaty on European Union** (particularly the second and third **pillars**), and the need for institutional and **decision-making** modifications to accommodate what would become the largest **enlargement** in **European Union** (EU) history, inspired the 1996/1997 **Intergovernmental Conference** and the treaty reform resulting in the 1997 **Treaty of Amsterdam**. The proposed institutional reforms were postponed, however, as agreement could not be reached on the size and composition of the **European Commission** or on the system of **qualified majority voting** in the **Council of the EU**. Two of the most highly contested topics leading up to the enlargement, they would be revisited and remain controversial in both the **Treaty of Nice** and the **Treaty establishing a Constitution for Europe**.

The Treaty of Amsterdam was nevertheless a relative success, providing for the creation of a **High Representative for the Common Foreign and Security Policy** (CFSP) as one means of meeting the established goal of economically and politically strengthening the CFSP, and for the creation of an **area of freedom, security, and jus-**

tice to enhance **Justice and Home Affairs**. The institutional changes that were agreed upon were largely to the benefit of the **European Parliament**, increasing the number of decisions to be made by the **co-decision procedure** and clarifying the procedure itself. The Treaty of Amsterdam also institutionalized flexibility as a working method of the EU in the form of **enhanced cooperation**.

TREATY OF MAASTRICHT. *See* TREATY ON EUROPEAN UNION.

TREATY OF NICE. The decision to approve **European Union** (EU) **enlargement** to the **Central and Eastern European countries** implied extensive change for the EU itself in order to accommodate this considerable increase in its membership. Unable to reach agreement regarding the institutional reforms in the **intergovernmental conference** that prepared the **Treaty of Amsterdam**, this pre-enlargement necessity became the focus of the Treaty of Nice.

Unlike the previous attempt, the Treaty of Nice contained tangible results. **Qualified majority voting** will be used as the **decision-making** method, although more complex, for additional policy areas. There was also a redistribution of the weighted votes in the **Council of the EU** to account for the candidate countries. In addition, the qualified majority must represent the majority of the member states and at least 62 percent of the EU's population. The **European Commission** will have one representative per member state regardless of its size until the EU reaches 27 member states at which time the number of commissioners will be less than that of the member states, based on a rotation to be decided by the Council. The number of possible European parliamentarians was increased to 732, and the number of seats for each member state was reallocated accordingly. Following the enlargement, all required **European Council** meetings will be held in Brussels.

Despite the apparent progress, the institutional and decision-making reforms included in the Treaty of Nice remained limited, particularly in terms of simplifying the EU and bringing it closer to the people. The treaty was rejected in an Irish referendum held in June 2001, and it was not until the Irish government implemented an intense public relations campaign that this decision was reversed in a second referendum held in October 2002. By the time the treaty entered into force on 1 February 2003, the **European Convention** was in its third and final stage of drafting the **Treaty establishing a Constitution for Europe**. Since this constitutional treaty has not been ratified by all 25 EU member states, the EU will continue to follow the negotiated agreements of the Treaty of Nice.

TREATY OF PARIS. In response to the 9 May 1950 **Schuman Declaration** proposing to pool the French and German coal and steel industries, an invitation that was accepted by several other Western European countries, **Belgium**, **France**, **Germany**, **Italy**, **Luxembourg**, and **The Netherlands** signed the **Treaty of Paris** on 18 April 1951, creating the **European Coal and Steel Community** (ECSC) which came into effect in August 1952. As per its original stipulations, the Treaty of Paris was in effect for 50 years, expiring on 23 July 2002. This initial Community treaty paved the way for the European integration process as it is known today, providing for the pooling of sovereignty into the ECSC's **High Authority** as well as for a highly institutionalized organization.

TREATY ON EUROPEAN UNION (TEU). Otherwise known as the Treaty of Maastricht for the Dutch city in which it was signed in 1992, the TEU marks a significant transition in the history of European integration. Due to its comprehensive and complex nature, negotiations leading to an agreement on this treaty were some of the most intense and extensive in the history of **European Union** (EU) treaty reforms.

Basically the TEU reorganized European integration into a **three-pillar** system. The first and fully integrated pillar is the **European Community** (EC). The second and third pillars, **Common Foreign and Security Policy** (CFSP) and **Justice and Home Affairs** (JHA), respectively, are based on **intergovernmental** cooperation between the member states. Most decisions in the first pillar can be made by **qualified majority voting** and relate to all policies previously considered part of the EC such as **single market**, economic, **agricultural**, and **competition policies**. The Maastricht Treaty also provided for the economic stages and **convergence criteria** necessary to complete the **Economic and Monetary Union** (EMU). Based on a range of broad international objectives, the EU member states agreed to more closely coordinate their **foreign policies** through **common positions** and **joint actions** while the competence remains the responsibility of the member state governments. Therefore, all decisions must be made unanimously as is the case with JHA. This third pillar orignally focused on the EU's internal security and the coordination of policies related to visas, **immigration**, and asylum policies, as well as police and judicial cooperation (visas, immigration, and asylum were subsequently moved to the first pillar). This pillar structure served as a foundation for the **deepening** of integration but will cease to exist if the **Treaty establishing a Constitution for Europe** is ratified.

Some of the institutional changes that accompanied the general reorganization within the treaty include the introduction of the **European System of Central Banks** and the **European Central Bank** (ECB), the creation of the **Committee of the Regions**, and additional **decision-making** powers for the **European Parliament** (EP). In order to successfully complete all stages of EMU, establishment of the ECB was necessary as an autonomous and independent institution responsible for the management of the single monetary policy and common currency. The Committee of the Regions was, in part, a response to the fact that the majority of EU laws and **regulations** are implemented at the local and national regional levels, creating a real need for this consultative body as an outlet for those responsible to have their interests heard and considered. The EP, the only EU institution directly elected by the people, has traditionally held the least amount of power, but was granted **co-decision** legislative power (along with the **Council of the EU**).

TREVI GROUP. An informal group of senior officials from justice and home ministries of the **European Community** (EC) member states, the Trevi Group was formed in response to series of **terrorist** attacks in Europe in the 1970s. Although not within the legal framework of the EC, the Trevi Group began work in 1975 to exchange information and try to coordinate responses to acts affecting the internal security of the EC member states. Over time, the Trevi Group began to address additional security-related issues such as organized crime. With the completion of the single European market, the free movement of people, goods, services, and capital, there was a need to strengthen security on the external borders of the **European Union**. **Justice and Home Affairs** was legally institutionalized in the third **pillar** of the **Treaty on European Union**.

TRICHET, JEAN-CLAUDE. *See* EUROPEAN CENTRAL BANK.

TROIKA. There are two troikas in the **European Union** (EU): one in the context of the rotating **presidency** and one in the context of **external relations**. The troika related to the presidency is a system in which the ministers from the member states holding the outgoing, current, and future presidencies collaborate in order to maintain at least minimal continuity in what are otherwise very rapid presidency rotations. In the area of external relations, the troika refers to the international representation of the **Common Foreign and Security Policy** (CFSP) by representatives of the member state holding the EU presidency, the **High Representative for the CFSP**, and representatives of the **European Commission**.

TURKEY. Engaged in a prolonged battle for acceptance by Europe, an association agreement between the **European Economic Community** (EEC) and Turkey first entered into force in 1964. The Turkish government officially applied for full membership in 1987, several years prior to the **Central and Eastern European countries** that were invited to join the **European Union** (EU) on 1 May 2004. It was not until the Helsinki Summit in 1999 that Turkey was officially granted candidate status.

Although Turkey became a member of **North Atlantic Treaty Organization** (NATO) in 1952, relations with the **European Community** (EC) have been marked by controversy. One question concerns whether or not Turkey is actually a European country in that only approximately 3 percent of its territory is considered to be geographically part of the European continent. Another involves the long-standing hostility between **Greece** and Turkey that was magnified by the Turkish invasion and occupation of northern **Cyprus** in 1974. After Greece's EC accession in 1981, this small southern Mediterranean member state gained the power to influence and, in fact, obstruct the development of closer relations between Turkey and the EC. Turkey's **human rights** record has also caused contention, both in terms of the questionable practices of a systematically entrenched military and of the treatment of the large ethnic Kurdish minority.

Furthermore, the internal economic and political dynamic would be considerably altered as a result of Turkish EU membership. Currently, Turkey would have one of the largest populations in the EU, second only to **Germany**, which means that with no prior experience in the integration process it would have significant weighted influence in the **decision-making** process in the **Council of the EU**. Finally, Turkey's population is approximately 99 percent Muslim, which has caused reservations regarding the traditional religious characteristics of the EU member states and how they may be changed upon Turkish membership.

At the same time, Turkey has demonstrated its willingness to accept and apply the EU membership requirements. While additional work is still necessary, significant progress has been made toward democratization and greater respect for human rights. The Turkish government has amended its penal code and a multitude of laws have been transformed in order to comply with EU criteria. Furthermore, it is argued that Turkey can serve as a bridge between Europe and the **Middle East**, as it shares borders with **Bulgaria**, Greece, Georgia, Armenia, Iran, Iraq, and Syria. Based on the undeniable effort made to meet EU standards and the positive political and social reforms reinforced by potential EU membership, in December 2004, the **European Council** made the decision to commence formal accession negotiations with Turkey. On 3 October 2005, this process was formally initiated. Refer to appendix A.

– U –

UKRAINE. Part of the Union of Soviet Socialist Republics until it declared its independence in 1991, Ukraine has made a transition to democracy and a developing market economy. Ukraine, bordering three of the May 2004 enlargement countries (**Hungary**, **Poland**, and **Slovakia**) as well as candidate country, **Romania**, is of key strategic importance to the **European Union** (EU). In this context, Ukraine is considered a priority country in the **European Neighborhood Policy**. A **Partnership and Cooperation Agreement** was signed between the EU and Ukraine on 14 June 1994 which went into effect on 1 March 1998. Ukraine (along with **Russia**) receives the most funding from the **Technical Assistance for the Commonwealth of Independent States** (TACIS) program, and a joint EU–Ukraine Action plan was adopted on 21 February 2005. The main policy areas addressed in EU–Ukraine relations and included in the Action Plan are: the approximation of Ukraine's legislation with that of the EU; **energy**; **environmental** protection; **trade** and investment; **transport** and infrastructure; cross-border cooperation; science and technology; and **justice and home affairs**. Political dialogue between the EU and Ukraine focuses on four general issue areas: security threats; democracy and **human rights**; regional and international issues; and disarmament and non-proliferation.

With opposition public protests and a political crisis in Ukraine emerging after the presidential elections held on 21 November 2004, and reports from international organizations that the elections did not meet democratic standards, the EU played a major role in trying to ensure a peaceful resolution to the conflict. The EU monitored the electoral process in Ukraine and financially supported the Election Observation Mission to the repeat elections on 26 December 2004. Following a smooth and peaceful resolution of this short-lived crisis, relations between the EU and Ukraine were enhanced, particularly with the adoption of the EU–Ukraine Action Plan.

UNION FOR EUROPE OF THE NATIONS GROUP (UEN). The UEN is the smallest of the parliamentary groups in the 2004–2009 **European Parliament** (EP) with 27 members of the EP from six member states: **Denmark**, **Ireland**, **Italy**, **Latvia**, **Lithuania**, and **Poland**. The main interests of this political group are preserving regional identities, as well as protecting and respecting rural populations and their ways of life.

UNITED KINGDOM (UK). While the six founding members of European integration were developing the original European Communities and even attempting to create a **European Defence Community**, the British had a different idea regarding how this process should evolve. Favoring a more **intergovernmental**, free trade–based approach rather than the **supranational** style of integration espoused by the **European Community** (EC), the UK founded the **European Free Trade Association** (EFTA) through the signing of the Stockholm Convention on 4 January 1960, with the participation of six other European countries (**Austria**, **Denmark**, **Norway**, **Portugal**, **Sweden**, and **Switzerland**). With only a few years experience, however, it became apparent that the advantages of membership in the European Communities greatly surpassed those of the EFTA, and by 9 August 1961, the UK had submitted its first application for membership in the EC.

The UK's economic commitments to EFTA and the Commonwealth along with its strong ties to the **United States** complicated the accession negotiations, and British membership was vetoed by French President **Charles de Gaulle** in January 1963. Insistent upon gaining access to the **trade** and investment benefits associated with EC membership, the UK submitted its second application for membership in May 1967, which was subsequently rejected once again by de Gaulle. It was not until his resignation and the election of **Georges Pompidou** to the French presidency in 1969 that Britain's application was accepted on terms leading to approval. On 1 January 1973, the UK (along with Denmark and **Ireland**) joined the EC; a large state whose membership would continuously be characterized by its resolute **Euro-skepticism**.

When **Margaret Thatcher** became British prime minister in May 1979, concerns regarding Britain's EC **budgetary** responsibility became a consistent component of the EC agenda. Due to the UK's import and export patterns, particularly in the **agricultural** sector, its contributions far exceeded its compensation. The undeniably valid British claims were resolved in 1984 by a 66 percent rebate on its yearly budgetary payment. Recent suggestions to reopen discussions regarding the rebate have been flatly rejected by the British government.

In the 1990s, Britain's outbreak of Bovine Spongiform Encephalopathy (BSE), commonly known as mad cow disease, created a **public health** crisis throughout the **European Union** (EU) and, on 27 March 1996, the EU imposed a ban on British beef in an effort to prevent the spread of BSE. Although the **European Commission** formally lifted the ban in 1999, **France** tried to unilaterally maintain it on claims that British beef still represented a health risk. After years of disputes, embittered relations, and a case brought to the **European Court of Justice** (ECJ), on 2 October 2002, France finally agreed to resume importation of British beef and beef products.

As the EC moved toward a **single market** and its transformation into the EU in the 1980s and 1990s, there has been a series of policies in which the UK has opted not to participate. As a result of the UK's staunch opposition, the proposed **Social Charter** was not included in the **Treaty on the European Union** (TEU) despite the support of the 11 other member states. (These member states were able to engage in policy and **decision-making** under the auspices of the EU institutions as the UK allowed for the Social Protocol to be attached to but not included in the TEU as long as it would not be subject to its regulations.) It was not until a transition to the Labour-led British government in May 1997 that the Social Protocol was approved by the UK, enabling its full inclusion in the **Treaty of Amsterdam**. The UK, along with Ireland, does not belong to the **Schengen Agreement**, and therefore is not part of the common travel and visa zone that exists between the continental EU member states.

Finally, and perhaps most visibly, the UK did not adopt the **euro** as its national currency, and along with other pre-2004 enlargement EU member states, Denmark and Sweden, remains outside of the **euro zone**. There are five internal tests that must be passed before the UK will apply for the third stage of **Economic and Monetary Union** (EMU). In an assessment conducted in June 2003, the British Treasury determined that while the UK was making progress, there were no clear indications that the test criteria were sustainable or that adopting the euro was in the best national interest at that time. This general British reluctance has disconcerted many who believe the integration process should evolve uniformly. Refer to appendix A.

UNITED STATES (U.S.). Since the end of World War II, the United States has been involved in European affairs economically, politically and militarily. In the early postwar period, the United States allocated billions of dollars in aid for postwar European recovery through the **Marshall Plan**, which required the European recipients to jointly develop and elaborate projects in order to receive the funding. The United States controlled one of the four German occupied zones that were established through the Potsdam Agreement until the western allies permitted the creation of the Federal Republic of **Germany** in 1949. U.S. membership in the **North Atlantic Treaty Organization** (NATO) ensured its consistent military involvement in the region, providing a guaranteed force of security in the case of an attack during the Cold War, and focusing on peacekeeping, peace-making, and crisis management in the post–Cold War period.

Given U.S. strategic interests in the region and its strong bilateral relations with many of the European countries, the United States closely followed the developments of the **European Community** (EC) and established diplomatic relations early on in the integration process. The **European Commission** has been represented by a delegation in Washington, D.C., since 1954, and was granted full diplomatic privileges comparable to any nation-state's embassy by 1971. The U.S. Mission to the European Communities in **Brussels** was established in 1961.

Close relations and cooperation between the United States and the **European Union** (EU) have not been absent of conflicts; from the early years of the EC to the present, **trade** disputes have been unavoidable and differing positions on some international crises and issues have caused political tensions. While the trade dispute over steel and the conflict regarding the 2003 U.S. intervention in Iraq receive the most media exposure, trade disputes between the United States and the EU concern less than 2 percent of their overall trade volume, and in terms of foreign policy both the EU and the United States uphold similar values regarding open markets, democracy, and **human rights** but do not always agree on the methods of achieving their mutual international goals. It has often been difficult, and perhaps confusing, for U.S. representatives to deal with the EU in this area given the **intergovernmental** nature of the EU's **foreign policy** competence and the number of officials involved in the policy-making process. In many cases the United States relies on its alliances with individual member states and the relative ease of negotiations with their governments to consult and cooperate in foreign policy issues.

Transatlantic relations are sustained and cultivated through regular presidential EU–U.S. summits. Economic relations are extensive with the EU and the United States which are each others' main trading partner and primary source of foreign direct investment. On 3 December 1995, the New Transatlantic Agenda (NTA) was signed at the EU–U.S. Summit in Madrid. Supplemented by a Joint EU–U.S. Action Plan, the NTA is designed to enhance bilateral relations and commit to active cooperation in four major areas: promoting peace, stability, development, and democracy throughout the world; responding to global challenges, contributing to the expansion of world trade and closer economic relations; and building bridges across the Atlantic. At the EU–U.S. Summit of May 1998, agreements were made on new initiatives for the Transatlantic Economic Partnership, focusing on bilateral trade agreements and institutionalized discourse on multilateral trade issues. A Joint Statement on "People to People" links was issued at the December 1998 EU–U.S. Summit, resulting in Transatlantic Dialogues between legislators, the business community, consumer organizations, **environmental** organizations, and between the European Trade Union College (ETUCO) and the American Federation of Labor and Congress of Industrial Organizations (AFL-CIO). In addition, in 1998, the **European Commission** launched a program to establish a network of **European Union** Centers in the United States Providing information, improving education, and promoting transatlantic understanding through research and programs; there are 10 of these Centers located at different universities throughout the country.

URUGUAY ROUND. One of the most complex and comprehensive negotiating rounds of the **General Agreement on Tariffs and Trade** (GATT), the Uruguay Round originally contained 15 subjects for discussion including tariffs, non-tariff barriers, **trade** in textiles, and anti-dumping measures. Negotiations on an issue particularly sensitive to the **European Union** (EU), which the EU had previously been successful in omitting from GATT negotiating rounds, trade in **agricultural** products, were also on the Uruguay Round agenda, and encouraged reforms to the **Common Agricultural Policy**. During the Uruguay Round, agreement was reached on the General Agreement on Trade in Services (GATS), the Agreement on Trade-Related

Aspects of Intellectual Property Rights (TRIPS), and the establishment of the **World Trade Organization** (WTO) to include formal and binding dispute settlement procedures. The Uruguay Round was launched in September 1986 in Uruguay, concluded in December 1993 in **Switzerland**, and signed by the trade ministers in April 1994 in Morocco. By the time of conclusion of the round, 123 countries were participating in the negotiations.

– V –

VAN GEND EN LOOS. In this 1963 case brought before the Dutch national court, one of the main principles of **EC law** was established — the principle of **direct effect**. The Dutch company brought the case against the Dutch government claiming its rights under the **Treaty of Rome** had been violated when the Dutch government imposed a new tariff on a product van Gend en Loos was importing into **The Netherlands**. The Dutch court referred the case to the **European Court of Justice** (ECJ) for a preliminary ruling. The ECJ ruled that indeed the tariff was illegal according to the treaty which called for a transition period in the development of the **free trade area** and **customs union** during which no new tariffs were allowed to be imposed. Furthermore, and having the greatest impact, the ECJ ruled that EC law had a direct effect, and therefore, was directly applicable and entitled individuals, companies, and governments and other legal entities within the EC with certain rights and responsibilities under its treaties.

VEIL, SIMONE (1927–). The first female cabinet minister in **France**, Simone Veil was minister of health from 1974 to 1979. In 1979, Veil became the first president of the directly elected **European Parliament** (EP), a post she held until 1982. She served three consecutive terms in the EP, from 1979 to 1993, when she was appointed minister of state for social affairs, health, and urban affairs, maintaining this position until 1995. The president of the French Senate appointed Veil to the Constitutional Council in February 1998, where she now serves as one of France's highest judges. Refer to appendix D.

VISA POLICY. The completion of the single European market, and particularly the free movement of people, emphasized the need to have a common visa policy. This would be particularly important for those member countries of the **Schengen Agreements**. For these countries there is a common list of countries from which citizens are required to obtain a visa for entry into the **European Union** (EU) and common requirements for people from those countries to meet in order to be granted a visa for travel to the EU.

VOTING. In the **Council of the European Union** (EU), the main **decision-making** institution of the EU, the two principal official forms of voting on the adoption of proposed legislation are unanimity and **qualified majority voting** (QMV). In practice, however, the great majority of the decisions made in the EU, regardless of the issue at hand, are made by consensus.

In general, unanimity is required for issues related to the more **intergovernmental** second and third **pillars** of the EU, **Common Foreign and Security Policy** and **Justice and Home Affairs**, respectively. QMV is used for issues related to the **single market**, **competition policy**, and most other issues of the first pillar of the EU, the **European Community**. In QMV, each country, relatively based on the size of its population, is assigned a number of votes. Legislation is passed when the minimum number of total possible votes is attained. Prior to the **Treaty of Nice**, a qualified majority was reached with 62 out of a total 87 votes, with the member state vote distribution as follows:

Germany, France, Italy, United Kingdom	10
Spain	8
Belgium, Greece, The Netherlands, Portugal	5
Austria, Sweden	4
Denmark, Ireland, Finland	3
Luxembourg	2
Total	**87**

In order to accommodate the 2004 **enlargement** process, a redistribution of votes was incorporated in the Treaty of Nice. In addition to the new member state weightings, a qualified majority would also require support from the majority of the member states, as well as verification that the qualified majority votes represent at least 62 percent of the overall EU population if specifically requested. In effect since 1 November 2004, a qualified majority based on the Nice agreement is reached with 232 votes out of a total of 321, with the member state vote distribution as follows:

Germany, France, Italy, United Kingdom	29
Spain, Poland	27
The Netherlands	13
Belgium, Czech Republic, Greece, Hungary, Portugal	12
Austria, Sweden	10
Denmark, Ireland, Lithuania, Slovakia, Finland	7
Cyprus, Estonia, Latvia, Luxembourg, Slovenia	4
Malta	3
Total	**321**

One of the most controversial topics of negotiations for the **Treaty establishing a Constitution for Europe** was the allocation of votes in the qualified majority voting system. The final compromise was one of "double majority" voting to begin in 2009, in which 55 percent of the member states representing more than 65 percent of the population would be needed to pass legislation. The transition to this system in 2009 remains contingent upon future ratification and implementation of this constitutional treaty.

VRIES, GIJS DE. A Dutch politician of the Dutch People's Party for Freedom and Democracy, Gijs de Vries was a member of the **European Parliament** in what is known today as the **Group of the Alliance of Liberals and Democrats for Europe**. He served in his government as deputy interior minister from 1998 to 2002. He was also a member of the **European Convention** responsible for drafting the **Treaty establishing a Constitution for Europe**. On 25 March 2004, Gijs de Vries was appointed to the newly created post of counterterrorism coordinator for the **European Union** (EU), responsible for coordinating information and responses between member states and the EU and proposing better and more efficient options for the EU in its fight against **terrorism**.

– W –

WERNER REPORT. On 8 October 1970, Pierre Werner, who was the prime minister of **Luxembourg** from 1959 to 1974 and 1979 to 1984, proposed the completion of **Economic and Monetary Union** (EMU) for the **European Community** (EC) by 1980 in what is known as the Werner Report. Werner's plan called for a three-stage process in which economic and monetary policy would become a competence of the EC, a single currency would be created with the fixing of exchange rates between the currencies of the member states, and a **European system of central banks** would be created. At the time, the plan was unsuccessful and its goals were abandoned in the early 1970s. Nevertheless, the **Delors Report**, which did lead to Economic and Monetary Union in the 1990s, was based in part on the Werner Report.

WESTERN EUROPEAN UNION (WEU). Created through the signing of the Brussels Treaty on Economic, Social and Cultural Collaboration and Collective Self-Defense by **Belgium**, **France**, **Luxembourg**, **The Netherlands** and the **United Kingdom** (UK) on 17 March 1948, the WEU was an instrument for closer cooperation between its signatories as well as a mutual **defense** mechanism. On 23 October 1954, the Paris Agreements were signed, amending the Brussels Treaty, reestablishing the WEU, and including **Italy** and West **Germany** in this organization. For the first half of the 1950s, it had been expected that the Federal Republic of Germany would be reintegrated into the western security structure through the **European Defence Community** (EDC). However, upon the rejection of the EDC by the French parliament in August 1954, the WEU became an alternative option. The WEU was the means through which West Germany became a member of the **North Atlantic Treaty Organization** (NATO) in May 1955. It also served as a liaison between the

European Community (EC) and the UK until the latter became an EC member state on 1 January 1973. From that point until 1984, the WEU was essentially inactive.

The adoption of the Rome Declaration at a meeting of the foreign and defense ministers on 26–27 October 1984 reactivated the WEU. The objectives of this renewed agreement include the institutionalization of consultation on defense matters, strengthening of western European security, and working toward harmonizing defense policies among its members.

Throughout the 1990s, there were some significant developments within the WEU and between the WEU and the **European Union** (EU). In 1993, WEU headquarters were moved from London to **Brussels**, the host city of both NATO and many of the EU institutions. The option of the **Council** to unanimously request the WEU to carry out EU policies with defense implications was included in the **Treaty on European Union**. In 1992, the WEU adopted the Petersberg Declaration outlining the types of tasks (**humanitarian**, peacekeeping, peacemaking, and crisis management missions) in which the organization would become involved. These **Petersberg tasks** were adopted by the EU and incorporated in the 1997 **Treaty of Amsterdam**. When the **Treaty of Nice** went into effect on 1 February 2003, the WEU was fully incorporated into the EU as a part of the EU's **defense policy**.

WHITE PAPER. White Papers are documents published by the **European Commission** that contain proposals for incorporating additional issue areas into the **European Union** agenda. If the proposals outlined in the White Paper are accepted by the Council, they may be the basis for EU action programs in that particular area.

WIDENING. Widening is a term used to refer to the **enlargement** of the **European Union** to include new member states.

WILSON, HAROLD (1916–1995). A British Labour politician, Harold Wilson was a member of the House of Commons from 1945 to 1983. He was British prime minister from 1964 to 1970 and from 1974 to 1976, when he resigned from this position.

In 1967, while Wilson held the premiership, the **United Kingdom** (UK) submitted its second application for membership in the **Euro-**

pean Community (EC), a petition that was vetoed by French President **Charles de Gaulle**. While **Edward Heath**, Wilson's political rival, was head of government from 1970 to 1974, Heath successfully negotiated the UK's membership in the EC. When Wilson resumed office in 1974, he pledged to renegotiate the terms of the UK's membership and to hold a referendum on the results of the renegotiation. This referendum asking whether or not the UK should remain in the EC was held on 5 June 1975 with more than 60 percent of the electorate turning out to vote and more than 60 percent of the voters favoring continued UK membership in the EC.

After Wilson resigned as prime minister in 1976, he remained a member of the House of Commons until 1983. He was subsequently named Lord Wilson of Rievaulx. Harold Wilson died on 24 May 1995.

WORLD TRADE ORGANIZATION (WTO). Although proposed in the aftermath of World War II, the **General Agreement on Tariffs and Trade** (GATT) served as the world's predominant arena for international **trade** negotiations until the WTO was finally established following the end of the Uruguay Round in 1995. The WTO is now the only international organization responsible for setting the rules of global trade. Located in Geneva, **Switzerland**, the WTO has 149 members. Since 2005, the Director-General of the WTO is Pascal Lamy, a former European Commissioner for trade.

In addition to incorporating agreements on services and intellectual property rights, the WTO is distinct from the GATT in that it contains a permanent Dispute Settlement Body and an Appellate Body, and can enforce the rules of its dispute decisions by allowing for trade sanctions if there is not compliance with the rules. The WTO also has a Ministerial Conference, its main decision-making body, which is composed of representatives of all of the WTO's members.

The **European Commission** almost always represents the member states of the EU with a single voice in the WTO. At the same time the EU has been pushing for greater global trade liberalization, it has been pushed to make changes to some protectionist measures, particularly in the **agricultural** industry, in order to comply with WTO rules. The EU has been both the claimant and defendant in several high-profile trade dispute cases. It plays a leading role in the WTO and the trade liberalization negotiations including the current Doha Round.

– Y –

YAOUNDE AGREEMENT. Former colonies of the **European Union** (EU) member states maintain close relations with the EU through **development** aid and preferential trade agreements signed between these countries, or groups of countries, and the EU and its member states. The first of these agreements, the Yaoundé Agreement, was negotiated in 1963 between the **European Community** (EC) and 17 francophone countries of the Associated African States and by Madagascar. A second Yaoundé Agreement was signed in 1969. By 1975, the Yaoundé Agreements were succeeded by the more comprehensive **Lomé Convention** between the EC and, at the time, 46 **African–Caribbean–Pacific countries**.

YUGOSLAVIA (FORMER). In 1991, after 40 years of relative peace and stability in Europe, a violent conflict erupted in Yugoslavia that would last until after the turn of the century. From brief independent secessionist movements to **humanitarian** crises, the Yugoslav wars posed serious concerns for regional security and stability. As an indication of the need to improve its **foreign policy** and enhance the instruments with which to carry it out, the **European Union** (EU) was independently unable to successfully respond to this crisis on its borders. In 1995, the **North Atlantic Treaty Organization** (NATO) initiated a peacemaking mission in **Bosnia-Herzegovina**, and, following the settlement agreed to in the Dayton Accords, led the subsequent peacekeeping and stabilization forces.

By mid-1999, the EU was able to assume a more consolidated approach toward the former Yugoslavia. Considering the Western Balkan republics as potential future EU candidate countries, the EU developed the **Stability Pact for Southeastern Europe** and agreed to begin **Stabilization and Association Agreements** with these countries. In this context, in 2001, the **Community Assistance for Reconstruction, Development, and Stability** in the Balkans (CARDS) program was established in order to provide these countries with financial assistance aimed at increasing their capacity to meet economic, political, and **human rights** candidacy criteria.

Demonstrating that it is no longer restricted to diplomatic and economic instruments to respond to regional conflict, in 2003, the EU implemented its first two missions as part of the **European Security and Defence Policy** in the former Yugoslavia, one in Bosnia-Herzegovina, and one in the **Former Yugoslav Republic of Macedonia**. On 2 December 2004, the EU replaced NATO as the primary peacekeeping force in Bosnia-Herzegovina.

In June 2003, the **European Council** declared that all of the Western Balkan countries would be eligible for EU membership upon progress and reforms in specified areas including economic development, democracy, stability, and the rule of law. One of the former Yugoslav republics, **Slovenia**, became an EU member state on 1 May 2004. **Croatia** submitted an application for membership in the EU in February 2003, and was officially granted candidacy status at the European Council meeting in June 2004. The Former Yugoslav Republic of Macedonia submitted its application for EU membership on 22 March 2004 and is awaiting official candidate status. While there is still no timetable established for the other Western Balkan countries, the EU has reiterated its pledge for partnership, and eventually membership, for these former Yugoslav republics.

Appendix A

European Union Member States and Candidate Countries

Member States	Territory (Km²)	Population	GDP per Capital in Purchasing Power Standards
Austria	83,870	8,174,762	27,910
Belgium	30, 528	10,348,276	26,830
Cyprus	9,250	775,927	19,550
Czech Republic	78,866	10,246,178	16,230
Denmark	43,094	5,413,392	28,400
Estonia	45,226	1,341,664	11,480
Finland	338,145	5,214,512	25,500
France	547,030	60,424,213	26,150
Germany	357,021	82,424,609	24,900
Greece	131,940	10,647,529	18,880
Hungary	93,030	10,032,375	14,130
Ireland	70,280	3,969,558	30,370
Italy	301,230	58,057,477	24,600
Latvia	64,589	2,306,306	9,680
Lithuania	65,200	3,607,899	11,610
Luxembourg	2,586	462,690	47,920
Malta	316	396,851	17,170
The Netherlands	41,526	16,318,199	27,270
Poland	312,685	38,626,349	10,940
Portugal	92,391	10,524,145	17,110
Slovakia	48,845	5,423,567	12,240
Slovenia	20,273	2,011,473	18,070
Spain	504,782	40,280,780	22,190
Sweden	449,964	8,986,400	26,260
United Kingdom	244,820	60,270,708	27,820

Candidate Countries	Territory (Km²)	Population	GDP per Capital in Purchasing Power Standards
Bulgaria	110,910	7,517,973	Unavailable
Croatia	56,542	4,496,869	Unavailable
Romania	237,500	22,355,551	Unavailable
Turkey	780,580	68,893,918	Unavailable

Sources: CIA World Fact Book website, www.cia.gov/cia/publications/factbook (territory); CIA World Fact Book website, www.cia.gov/cia/publications/factbook (population); and GDP Per Capita in Purchasing Power Standards: Eurostat website, www.europa.eu.int/comm/eurostat/.

Appendix B
Presidents of the European Commission

Presidents of the High Authority of the ECSC

Name	Country	Term
Jean Monnet	France	1952–1955
René Mayer	France	1955–1958
Paul Finet	Belgium	1958–1959
Piero Malvestiti	Italy	1959–1963
Dino Del Bo	Italy	1963–1967
Albert Coppé	Belgium	1967

President of the EEC Commission

Name	Country	Term
Walter Hallstein	West Germany	1958–1967

Presidents of the EURATOM Commission

Name	Country	Term
Louis Armand	France	1958–1959
Etienne Hirsch	France	1959–1962
Pierre Chatenet	France	1962–1967

Presidents of the European Commission

Name	Country	Term
Jean Rey	Belgium	1967–1970
Franco Maria Malfatti	Italy	1970–1972
Sicco L. Mansholt	Netherlands	1972–1972
François-Xavier Ortoli	France	1973–1976
Roy Jenkins	United Kingdom	1977–1980
Gaston Edmont Thorn	Luxembourg	1981–1984

Presidents of the European Commission (*continued*)

Name	Country	Term
Jacques Delors	France	1985–1995
Jacques Santer	Luxembourg	1995–1999 (resigned)
Manuel Marín (Interim President)	Spain	July–September 1999
Romano Prodi	Italy	1999–2004
José Manuel Barroso	Portugal	2004–

Source: Official Website of the European Union: EUROPA—Presidents of the European Commission, www.europa.eu.int/comm/commissionpresidents.

Appendix C
The European Commission, 2004–2009

Name	Country	Portfolio
Almunia, Joaquín	Spain	Economic and Monetary Affairs
Barroso, José Manuel (President)	Portugal	Commission Administration
Barrot, Jacques (Vice President)	France	Transport
Borg, Joe	Malta	Fisheries and Maritime Affairs
Dimas, Stavros	Greece	Environment
Ferrero-Waldner, Benita	Austria	External Relations and European Neighbourhood Policy
Figel', Ján	Slovakia	Education, Training, Culture, and Multilingualism
Fischer Boel, Mariann	Denmark	Agriculture and Rural Development
Frattini, Franco (Vice President)	Italy	Justice, Freedom, and Security
Grybauskaitė, Dalia	Lithuania	Financial Programming and Budget
Hübner, Danuta	Poland	Regional Affairs
Kallas, Siim (Vice President)	Estonia	Administrative Affairs, Audit, and Anti-Fraud
Kovács, László	Hungary	Taxation and Customs Union
Kroes, Neelie	The Netherlands	Competition
Kyprianou, Markos	Cyprus	Health and Consumer Protection
McCreevy, Charlie	Ireland	Internal Market and Services
Mandelson, Peter	United Kingdom	Trade
Michel, Louis	Belgium	Development and Humanitarian Aid
Piebalgs, Andris	Latvia	Energy
Potočnik, Janez	Slovenia	Science and Research
Reding, Viviane	Luxembourg	Information Society and Media
Rehn, Olli	Finland	Enlargement

Name	Country	Portfolio
Špidla, Vladimir	Czech Republic	Employment, Social Affairs, and Equal Opportunities
Verheugen, Günter (Vice President)	Germany	Enterprise and Industry
Wallström, Margot (Vice President)	Sweden	Institutional Relations and Communication Strategy

Source: Official Website of the European Union: EUROPA, The Commissioners—Profiles, Portfolios and Homepages, www.europa.eu.int/comm/commission.

Appendix D

Presidents of the European Parliament

Presidents of the Common Assembly of the ECSC

Name	Country	Term	Party
Paul-Henri Spaak	Belgium	1952–1954	Socialists
Alcide de Gasperi	Italy	1954	Christian Democrats
Giuseppe Pella	Italy	1954–1956	Christian Democrats
Hans Furler	Germany	1956–1958	Christian Democrats

Presidents of the European Parliamentary Assembly

Name	Country	Term	Party
Robert Schuman	France	1958–1960	Christian Democrats
Hans Furler	Germany	1960–1962	Christian Democrats

Presidents of the European Parliament (prior to direct elections)

Name	Country	Term	Party
Gaetano Martino	Italy	1962–1964	Liberals and allies
Jean-Pierre Duvieusart	Belgium	1964–1965	Christian Democrats
Victor Leemans	Belgium	1965–1966	Christian Democrats
Alain Poher	France	1966–1969	Christian Democrats
Mario Scelba	Italy	1969–1971	Christian Democrats
Walter Behrendt	Germany	1971–1973	Socialists
Cornelis Berkhouwer	The Netherlands	1973–1975	Liberals and allies
Georges Spenale	France	1975–1977	Socialists
Emilio Colombo	Italy	1977–1979	Christian Democrats

Presidents of the Directly Elected European Parliament

Name	Country	Term	Party
Simone Veil	France	1979–1982	Liberal and Democratic Group
Piet Dankert	The Netherlands	1982–1984	Socialists
Pierre Pflimlin	France	1984–1987	Group of the European People's Party
Lord Plumb	UK	1987–1989	Group of the European Democrats
Enrique Barón Crespo	Spain	1989–1992	Socialists
Egon A. Klepsch	Germany	1992–1994	Group of the European People's Party and European Democrats
Klaus Hänsch	Germany	1994–1997	Group of the Party of European Socialists
José María Gil-Robles	Spain	1997–1999	Group of the European People's Party and European Democrats
Nicole Fontaine	France	1999–2002	Group of the European People's Party and European Democrats
Pat Cox	Ireland	2002–2004	Group of the European Liberal, Democratic and Reformist Party
Josep Borrell Fontelles	Spain	2004–2006	Group of the Party of European Socialists

Source: Official Website of the European Parliament: The President of the European Parliament, www.europarl.eu.int/president.

Appendix E
European Parliament, 2004–2009

Country	Total MEPs	Political Groups
Austria	18	EPP-ED (6), PES (7), Greens/EFA (2), NI (3)
Belgium	24	EPP-ED (6), PES (7), ALDE (6), Greens/EFA (2), NI (3)
Cyprus	6	EPP-ED (3), ALDE (1), GUE/NGL (2)
Czech Republic	24	EPP-ED (14), PSE (2), GUE/NGL (6), IND/DEM (1), NI (1)
Denmark	14	EPP-ED (1), PES (5), ALDE (4), Greens/EFA (1), GUE/NGL (1), IND/DEM (1), UEN (1)
Estonia	6	EPP-ED (1), PES (3), ALDE (2)
Finland	14	EPP-ED (4), PES (3), ALDE (5), Greens/EFA (1), GUE/NGL (1)
France	78	EPP-ED (17), PES (31), ALDE (11), Greens/EFA (6), GUE/NGL (3), IND/DEM (3), NI (7)
Germany	99	EPP-ED (49), PES (23), ALDE (7), Greens/EFA (13), GUE/NGL (7)
Greece	24	EPP-ED (11), PSE (8), GUE/NGL (4), IND/DEM (1)
Hungary	24	EPP-ED (13), PES (9), ALDE (2)
Ireland	13	EPP-ED (5), PES (1), ALDE (1), GUE/NGL (1), IND/DEM (1), UEN (4)
Italy	78	EPP-ED (24), PES (16), ALDE (12), Greens/EFA (2), GUE/NGL (7), IND/DEM (4), UEN (9), NI (4)
Latvia	9	EPP-ED (3), ALDE (1), Greens/EFA (1), UEN (4)
Lithuania	13	EPP-ED (2), PES (2), ALDE (7), UEN (2)
Luxembourg	6	EPP-ED (3), PES (1), ALDE (1), Greens/EFA (1)
Malta	5	EPP-ED (2), PES (3)
The Netherlands	27	EPP-ED (7), PES (7), ALDE (5), Greens/EFA (4), GUE/NGL (2), IND/DEM (2)
Poland	54	EPP-ED (19), PES (10), ALDE (4), IND/DEM (10), UEN (7), NI (4)
Portugal	24	EPP-ED (9), PES (12), GUE/NGL (3)
Slovakia	14	EPP-ED (8), PES (3), NI (3)
Slovenia	7	EPP-ED (4), PES (1), ALDE (2)

Country	Total MEPs	Political Groups
Spain	54	EPP-ED (24), PES (24), ALDE (2), Greens/EFA (3), GUE/NGL (1)
Sweden	19	EPP-ED (5), PES (5), ALDE (3), Greens/EFA (1), GUE/NGL (2), IND/DEM (3)
United Kingdom	78	EPP-ED (28), PES (19), ALDE (12), Greens/EFA (5), GUE/NGL (1), IND/DEM (10), NI (3)

Political Groups

EPP-ED: Group of the European People's Party (Christian Democrats) and European Democrats
PES: Socialist Group in the European Parliament
ALDE: Group of the Alliance of Liberals and Democrats for Europe
Greens/EFA: Group of the Greens/ European Free Alliance
GUE/NGL: Confederal Group of the European United Left–Nordic Green Left
IND/DEM: Independence/Democracy Group
UEN: Union for Europe of the Nations Group
NI: Non-attached Members

Source: Official Website of the European Union: EUROPARL, Members of the European Parliament, www.europarl.eu.int.

Appendix F

Presidents of the Court of Justice of the European Communities

Name	Country	Term
Massimo Pillotti	Italy	1952–1958
Andreas Matthias Donner	The Netherlands	1958–1964
Charles Léon Hammes	Luxembourg	1964–1967
Robert Lecourt	France	1967–1976
Hans Kutscher	Germany	1976–1980
Josse J. Mertens de Wilmars	Belgium	1980–1984
Lord Mackenzie Stuart	United Kingdom	1984–1988
Ole Due	Denmark	1988–1994
Gil Carlos Rodríguez Iglesias	Spain	1994–2003
Vassilios Skouris	Greece	2003–

Source: Iberian Section, Press and Information Division, Court of Justice of the European Communities, Luxembourg.

Appendix G

Members of the Court of Justice
of the European Communities, 2005

Name	Country	Position/Years
Arestis, George	Cyprus	Judge since 2004
Bahr, Stig von	Sweden	Judge since 2000
Borg Barthet U.O.M., Anthony	Malta	Judge since 2004
Colneric, Ninon	Germany	Judge since 2000
Cunha Rodrigues, José Narciso da	Portugal	Judge since 2000
Geelhoed, Leendert A.	The Netherlands	Advocate-general since 2000
Grass, Roger	France	Registrar since 1994
Gulmann, Claus Christian	Denmark	Advocate-general 1991–1994; judge since 1994
Ilešič, Marko	Slovenia	Judge since 2004
Jacobs, Francis Geoffrey	UK	Advocate-general since 1988
Jann, Peter	Austria	Judge since 1995
Juhász, Endre	Hungary	Judge since 2004
Klučka, Ján	Slovakia	Judge since 2004
Kokott, Juliane	Germany	Advocate-general since 2003
Kūris, Pranas	Lithuania	Judge since 2004
Léger, Philippe	France	Advocate-general since 1994
Lenaerts, Koen	Belgium	Judge since 2003
Levits, Egils	Latvia	Judge since 2004
Lõhmus, Uno	Estonia	Judge since 2004
Makarczyk, Jerzy	Poland	Judge since 2004
Malenovský, Jirí	Czech Republic	Judge since 2004
Ó Caoimh, Aindrias	Ireland	Judge since 2004
Pergola, Antonio Mario La	Italy	Judge in 1994; advocate-general 1995–1999; judge since 1999

Name	Country	Position/Years
Poiares Pessoa Maduro, Luís Miguel	Portugal	Advocate-general since 2003
Puissochet, Jean-Pierre	France	Judge since 1994
Rosas, Allan	Finland	Judge since 2002
Ruiz-Jarabo Colomer, Dámaso	Spain	Advocate-general since 1995
Schiemann, Konrad Hermann Theodor	UK	Judge since 2004
Schintgen, Romain	Luxembourg	Judge since 1996
Silva de Lapuerta, Rosario	Spain	Judge since 2003
Skouris, Vassilios	Greece	Judge since 1999; president since 2003
Stix-Hackl, Christine	Austria	Advocate-general since 2000
Timmermans, Christiaan	The Netherlands	Judge since 2000
Tizzano, Antonio	Italy	Advocate-general since 2000

Source: Official Website of the Court of Justice of the European Communities: The Members, http://curia.eu.int.

Appendix H

Select Regional Integration Associations around the World

Andean Community: Established 1969. Members: Bolivia, Colombia, Ecuador, Peru, Venezuela.

Arab Cooperation Council: Established 1989. Members: Egypt, Iraq, Jordan, Yemen.

Arab Maghreb Union: Established 1989. Members: Algeria, Libya, Mauritania, Morocco, Tunisia.

Asia-Pacific Economic Cooperation (APEC): Established 1989. Member economies: Australia, Brunei Darussalam, Canada, Chile, People's Republic of China, Hong Kong-China, Indonesia, Japan, Republic of Korea, Malaysia, Mexico, New Zealand, Papua New Guinea, Peru, Philippines, Russian Federation, Singapore, Chinese Taipei, Thailand, United States, Vietnam.

Association of Southeast Asian Nations (ASEAN): Established 1967. Members: Brunei Darussalam, Cambodia, Indonesia, Laos, Malaysia, Myanmar, Philippines, Singapore, Thailand, Vietnam.

Caribbean Community and Common Market (CARICOM): Established 1973. Members: Antigua and Barbuda, Bahamas, Barbados, Belize, Dominica, Grenada, Guyana, Haiti, Jamaica, Montserrat, Saint Lucia, St. Kitts and Nevis, St. Vincent and the Grenadines, Suriname, Trinidad and Tobago.

Central American Common Market: Established 1960. Members: Costa Rica, El Salvador, Guatemala, Honduras, Nicaragua.

Commonwealth of Independent States (CIS): Established 1991. Members: Azerbaijan, Armenia, Belarus, Georgia, Kazakhstan, Kyrgyzstan, Moldova, Russia, Tajikistan, Turkmenistan, Uzbekistan, Ukraine.

Council of Arab Economic Unity: Established 1964. Members: Egypt, Iraq, Jordan, Kuwait, Libya, Mauritania, Palestine, Somalia, Sudan, Syria, Yemen.

East African Community: Established 1999. Members: Kenya, Uganda, Tanzania.

Economic Community of Central African States (ECCAS): Established 1983. Members: Angola, Burundi, Cameroon, Central African Republic, Chad, Congo-Brazzaville, Congo-Kinshasa, Equatorial Guinea, Gabon, Rwanda, Sao Tome and Principe.

Economic Community of West African States (ECOWAS): Established 1975. Members: Benin, Burkina Faso, Cape Verde, Côte d'Ivoire, Gambia, Ghana, Guinea, Guinea Bissau, Liberia, Mali, Niger, Nigeria, Senegal, Sierra Leone, Togo.

Latin American Integration Association (ALADI): Established 1980. Members: Argentina, Bolivia, Brazil, Chile, Colombia, Cuba, Ecuador, Mexico, Paraguay, Peru, Uruguay, Venezuela.

North American Free Trade Agreement (NAFTA): Established 1994. Members: Canada, Mexico, United States.

South Asian Association for Regional Cooperation: Established 1985. Members: Bangladesh, Bhutan, India, Maldives, Nepal, Pakistan, Sri Lanka.

Southern African Development Community: Established 1992. Members: Angola, Botswana, Congo, Lesotho, Malawi, Mauritius, Mozambique, Namibia, South Africa, Swaziland, Zambia, Zimbabwe.

Southern Cone Common Market (MERCOSUR): Established 1991. Members: Argentina, Brazil, Paraguay, Uruguay.

Sources: Official websites of ALADI (www.aladi.org), Andean Community (www.comunidadandina.org), APEC (www.apecsec.org.sg/apec.html), Arab Maghreb Union (www.maghrebarabe.org), ASEAN (www.aseansec.org), CARICOM (www.caricom.org), CIS (www.cisstat.com/eng/cis.htm), Council of Arab Economic Unity (www.caeu.org.eg/English/Intro), East African Community (www.eac.int), ECCAS (www.ceeac-eccas.org), ECOWAS (www.ecowas.int), MERCOSUR (www.mercosur.org.uy), NAFTA (www.nafta-sec-alena.org), South Asian Association for Regional Cooperation (www.saarc-sec.org), and Southern African Development Community (www.sadc.int/index.php).

Bibliography

CONTENTS

Introduction	226
General	227
Overview	227
History	229
Institutional Framework	231
Theory	231
European Union Institutions	232
Treaties	234
Community Law	235
Politics	236
Policies and Policy-Making	238
Single Market and Economic and Monetary Union	240
External Relations	243
Relations with Other Regions/Countries	245
ACP/Development	246
Security	247
Enlargement	248
Identity	251
Integration in the Americas	252
Member States of the European Union	253
Scholarly Journals	254
Websites	254
Official European Union Sites	254
Agencies of the European Union	255
Associations, Centers, Institutes, and Research	255
External Relations and Regional Organizations	256

INTRODUCTION

In recent years there has been an enormous proliferation of literature on the European Union. After the so-called Dark Ages of the integration process, from the early 1970s to the mid-1980s, the European Community began a process of steady reforms, whose most visible results were the Single European Act, the Treaties of Maastricht, Amsterdam, Nice, and more recently the Constitutional Treaty. Universities reacted to these persistent changes in Europe by boosting the creation of courses and programs at both undergraduate and graduate levels. As a result, while the number of scholars increased in Europe and throughout the world, the literature devoted to the study of European integration aimed to explain the EU as a whole as well as particular aspects of it.

The bibliography encompasses literature on general explanations of the EU as well as texts focusing on particular issues of European integration. The references are divided in three groups. The first is comprised of books that provide a comprehensive explanation of the integration process, which include the most useful books recommended in a considerable number of courses in universities and colleges. Two subdivisions are included in this section. The first overviews the EU; Dinan (*Ever Closer Union*), McCormick (*Understanding the European Union*), and Nugent (*The Government and Politics of the EU*) have written updated versions of introductory books on the EU. The second part of this section recommends references about the history of the EU; in addition to the memoirs of Monnet, Jenkins, and Thatcher, overviews of the historical development of the EU can be found in Vanthoor (*A Chronological History of the EU*) and Pagden (*The Idea of Europe*).

The second section of the bibliography is designed to provide more specialized references about integration theory, institutional framework, community law, evolution of the treaties, and current political debates. Within the theoretical mosaic, Diez and Wiener (*European Integration Theory*) and Rosamond (*Theories of European Integration*) offer general assessments of the current debates in the field. The literature has been prolific in the area of European institutions; Peterson and Shackleton (*The Institutions of the EU*) and Devuyst (*The European Union at the Crossroads*) are two examples of works that aim to explain the complexity of the institutional architecture of the EU.

The third section highlights the literature on the policy-making process and particular policies of the EU. Wallace and Wallace (*Policy-Making in the EU*) have written one of the most comprehensive books in the area of EU policy-making. This section pays particular attention to four policies widely debated in Europe in the 1990s: economic and monetary union, external relations (relations with other regions/countries, ACP/Development), security, and enlargement. This section also provides two themes that have raised some interest in the academic debates: identity and integration in the Americas.

As the process of European integration has accelerated, the number of sources of information on integration has grown exponentially. In order to deepen their knowledge of the EU, the readers will find it very useful to start by consulting the collection of official and academic sources of the network of libraries that the EU has established in universities across the United States (www.eurunion.org/infores/library.htm#f) and especially in EU member states. Likewise, readers are encouraged to make use of the content and resources of the official EU website (http://europa.eu.int/) and subscribe to several of the free newsletter services provided by the EU institutions and sponsored programs.

GENERAL

Overview

Archer, Clive. *The European Union: Structure and Process*, 3rd ed. London: Continuum, 2000.

Bomberg, Elizabeth, and Alexander Stubb. *The European Union: How Does It Work?* New York: Oxford University Press, 2003.

Burgess, Michael. *Federalism and the European Union: The Building of Europe, 1950–2000*. London: Routledge, 2000.

Caporaso, James A. *The European Union: Dilemmas of Regional Integration*. Boulder, Colo.: Westview Press, 2000.

Cowles, Maria Green, and Desmond Dinan, eds. *Developments in the European Union*, 2nd ed. Basingstoke, U.K.: Palgrave Macmillan, 2004.

Cowles, Maria Green, and Michael Smith, eds. *The State of the European Union. Vol. 5: Risks, Reforms, Resistance, or Revival?* Oxford: Oxford University Press, 2001.

Dagtoglou, P. D. *Basic Problems of the European Community*. Oxford: Basil Blackwell, 1975.

Dinan, Desmond, ed. *Encyclopedia of the European Union*. Boulder, Colo.: Lynne Rienner, 2000.

———. *Ever Closer Union: An Introduction to European Integration*. Boulder, Colo.: Lynne Rienner, 2000.

Farrell, Mary, Stefano Fella, and Michael Newman, eds. *European Integration in the Twenty-first Century: Unity in Diversity?* London: Sage, 2002.

Fontaine, Pascal. *A New Idea for Europe. The Schuman Declaration 1950–2000*. Luxembourg: European Commission, 2000.

Gillingham, John. *European Integration, 1950–2003: Superstate or New Market Economy?* Cambridge: Cambridge University Press, 2003.

Hix, Simon. *The Political System of the European Union*. New York: St. Martin's Press, 1999.

Hurwitz, Leon, ed. *Contemporary Perspectives on European Integration: Attitudes, Nongovernmental Behavior, and Collective Decision Making*. Westport, Conn.: Greenwood, 1980.

Keating, Michael, ed. *Regions and Regionalism in Europe*. Northampton, Mass.: Edward Elgar, 2004.

Laffan, Brigid, Rory O'Donnell, and Michael Smith. *Europe's Experimental Union: Rethinking Integration*. New York: Routledge, 2000.

Landau, Alice, and Richard G. Whitman, eds. *Rethinking the European Union: Institutions, Interests and Identities*. New York: St. Martin's, 1997.

Lindberg, Leon, and Stuart Scheingold. *Europe's Would-Be Polity: Patterns of Change in the European Community*. Englewood Cliffs, N.J.: Prentice Hall, 1970.

McCormick, John. *Understanding the European Union: A Concise Introduction*. New York: Palgrave, 2002.

Monar, Jorg, and Wolfgang Wessels, eds. *The European Union after the Treaty of Amsterdam*. London: Continuum, 2000.

Nugent, Neil. *The Government and Politics of the European Union*, 5th ed. Durham, N.C.: Duke University Press, 2003.

Parsons, Craig. *A Certain Idea of Europe*. Ithaca, N.Y.: Cornell University Press, 2003.

Rodríguez-Pose, Andrés. *The European Union. Economy, Society, and Polity*. New York: Oxford University Press, 2002.

Schimmelfennig, Frank. *The EU, NATO and the Integration of Europe: Rules and Rhetoric*. New York: Cambridge University Press, 2003.

Tiersky, Ronald, ed. *Europe Today: National Politics, European Integration, and European Security*, 2nd ed. Lanham, Md.: Rowman & Littlefield, 2004.

Van Oudenaren, John. *Uniting Europe: European Integration and the Post–Cold War World.* Lanham, Md.: Rowman & Littlefield, 2000.

Wallace, Helen, ed. *Interlocking Dimensions of European Integration.* London: Palgrave, 2001.

Westlake, Martin, ed. *The European Union beyond Amsterdam: New Concepts of European Integration.* London: Routledge, 1998.

Wood, David Michael, and Birol A. Yesilada. *The Emerging European Union,* 2nd ed. New York: Longman, 2002.

Zeff, Eleanor, and Ellen B. Pirro, eds. *The European Union and the Member States: Cooperation, Coordination and Compromise.* Boulder, Colo.: Lynne Rienner, 2001.

History

Aron, Raymond, and Daniel Lerner, eds. *France Defeats EDC.* New York: Praeger, 1957.

Campbell, John. *Roy Jenkins: A Biography.* London: Weidenfeld & Nicolson, 1983.

Daddow, Oliver J. Harold. *Wilson and European Integration: Britain's Second Application to Join the EEC.* Portland, Ore.: Frank Cass, 2003.

Diebold, William. *The Schuman Plan.* New York: Praeger, 1959.

Dinan, Desmond. *Europe Recast: A History of European Union.* Boulder, Colo.: Lynne Rienner, 2003.

Di Nolfo, Ennio, ed. *Power in Europe? II: Great Britain, France, Germany and Italy and the Origins of the EEC, 1952–1957.* Berlin: Walter de Gruyter, 1992.

Duchene, Francois. *Jean Monnet: The First Statesman of Interdependence.* New York: W.W. Norton, 1994.

Dumoulin, Michel. *Spaak.* Brussels: Racine, 1999.

Fursdon, Edward. *The European Defense Community: A History.* London: MacMillan, 1980.

Gillingham, John. *Coal, Steel and the Rebirth of Europe, 1945–1955: The Germans and French from Ruhr Conflict to Economic Community.* Cambridge: Cambridge University Press, 1991.

Grant, Charles. *Delors: Inside the House That Jacques Built.* London: Nicholas Brealey, 1994.

Hallstein, Walter. *United Europe: Challenge and Opportunity.* Cambridge: Harvard University Press, 1962.

Jenkins, Roy. *European Diary, 1977–1981.* London: Collins, 1989.

———. *Life at the Center: Memoirs of a Radical Reformer.* New York: Random House, 1991.

Loth, Wilfried, William Wallace, and Wolfgang Wessels, eds. *Walter Hallstein: The Forgotten European?* Basingstoke, U.K.: Macmillan, 1998.

McAllister, R. *From EC to EU: An Historical and Political Survey.* London: Routledge, 1997.

Mahant, Edelgard. *Birthmarks of Europe: The Origins of the European Community Reconsidered.* Burlington, Vt.: Ashgate, 2004.

Marjolin, Robert. *Architect of European Unity: Memoirs 1911–1986.* London: Weidenfeld and Nicolson, 1989.

Mayne, Richard. *The Recovery of Europe: From Devastation to Unity.* New York: Harper & Row, 1970.

Milward, Alan S. *The Reconstruction of Western Europe, 1945–51.* London: Methuen, 1984.

Monnet, Jean. *Memoirs.* London: Collins, 1978.

Pagden, Anthony, ed. *The Idea of Europe: From Antiquity to the European Union.* New York: Cambridge University Press, 2002.

Rollat, Alain. *Delors.* Paris: Flammarion, 1993.

Ross, George. *Jacques Delors and European Integration.* New York: Polity Press, 1995.

Salmon, Trevor, and William Nicoll, eds. *Building European Union: A Documentary History and Analysis.* Manchester, U.K.: Manchester University Press, 1997.

Schuman, Robert. *Pour l' Europe.* Paris: Nagel, 1963.

Spierenburg, Dirk, and Raymond Poidevin. *The History of the High Authority of the European Coal and Steel Community: Supranationality in Action.* London: Weidenfeld & Nicholson, 1994.

Spinelli, Altiero. *The Eurocrats: Conflict and Crisis in the European Community.* Baltimore, Md.: John Hopkins University Press, 1966.

Stirk, Peter M. R. *A History of European Integration since 1914.* London: Pinter, 1996.

Stirk, Peter M. R., and David Willis, eds. *Shaping Postwar Europe: European Unity and Disunity, 1945–1957.* New York: St. Martin's, 1991.

Thatcher, Margaret. *Downing Street Years.* New York: Harper Collins, 1993.

Trachtenberg, Marc. *A Constructed Peace. The Making of the European Settlement 1945–1963.* Princeton, N.J.: Princeton University Press, 1999.

Trausch, Gilbert, ed. *The European Integration from the Schuman Plan to the Treaties of Rome.* Brussels: Bruylant, 1993.

Urwin, Derek W. *The Community of Europe: A History of European Integration since 1945.* London: Longman, 1995.

Vanthoor, Wim F. V. *A Chronological History of the European Union, 1946–2001.* Cheltenham, U.K.: Edward Elgar, 2002.

Zurcher, Arnold J. *The Struggle to Unite Europe: 1940–1958.* New York: New York University Press, 1958.

INSTITUTIONAL FRAMEWORK

Theory

Balassa, Bela. *The Theory of Economic Integration*. Homewood, Ill.: R.D. Irwin, 1961.

Christiansen, Thomas, Knud Erik Jørgensen, and Antje Weiner, eds. *The Social Construction of Europe*. London: Sage, 2001.

Chryssochoou, Dimitri. *Theorizing European Integration*. New York: Sage, 2001.

Cowles, Maria Green, James Caporaso, and Thomas Risse-Kappen, eds. *Transforming Europe: Europeanization and Domestic Change*. Ithaca, N.Y.: Cornell University Press, 2001.

Deutsch, Karl, ed. *Political Community and the North Atlantic Area: International Organization in the Light of Historical Experience*. Princeton, N.J.: Princeton University Press, 1957.

Diez, Thomas, and Antje Wiener, eds. *European Integration Theory*. Oxford: Oxford University Press, 2004.

Etzioni, Amitai. *Political Unification Revisited. On Building Supranational Communities*. Lanham, Md.: Lexington Books, 2001.

Haas, Ernst B. *The Uniting of Europe: Political, Social, and Economic Forces, 1950–1957*. Stanford, Calif.: Stanford University Press, 1958.

Hooghe, Liesbet, and Gary Marks, eds. *Multi-Level Governance and European Integration*. Lanham, Md.: Rowman & Littlefield, 2001.

Jeffery, Charlie, ed. *The Regional Dimension of the European Union. Towards a Third Level in Europe?* London: Frank Cass, 1997.

Kelstrup, Morten, and Michael C. Williams, eds. *International Relations Theory and the Politics of European Integration: Power, Security, and Community*. London; New York: Routledge, 2000.

Marks, Gary. *Governance in the European Union*. London: Sage, 1996.

Michelmann, Hans J., and Panayotis Soldatos, eds. *European Integration: Theories and Approaches*. Lanham, Md.: University Press of America, 1994.

Moravcsik, Andrew. *The Choice for Europe. Social Purpose and State Power from Messina to Maastricht*. Ithaca, N.Y.: Cornell University Press, 1998.

Nelsen, Brent F., and Alexander Stubb, eds. *The European Union: Readings on the Theory and Practice of European Integration*. Boulder, Colo.: Lynne Rienner, 2003.

Peters, Guy. *Institutional Theory in Political Science*. London: Continuum, 1999.

Pollack, Mark A. *The Engines of European Integration: Delegation, Agency, and Agenda Setting in the EU*. Oxford: Oxford University Press, 2003.

Rosamond, Ben. *Theories of European Integration*. New York: Palgrave, 2002.

Sandholtz, Wayne, and Alec Stone Sweet, eds. *European Integration and Supranational Governance*. Oxford: Oxford University Press, 1998.

European Union Institutions

Alter, Karen. "The European Court's Political Power." *West European Politics* 19, no. 3 (1996): 458–87.

Andenas, Mads, and Alexander Turk, eds. *Delegated Legislation and the Role of Committees in the EC*. The Hague: Klewer Law International, 2000.

Arnull, Anthony. *The European Union and Its Court of Justice*. Oxford: Oxford University Press, 1999.

Best, Edward, Mark Gray, and Alexander Stubb, eds. *Rethinking the European Union. IGC 2000 and Beyond*. Maastricht: European Institute of Public Administration, 2000.

Blondel, Jean, Richard Sinnott, and Palle Svennson. *People and Parliament in the European Union: Participation, Democracy and Legitimacy*. Oxford: Clarendon Press, 1998.

Bostock, David. "Coreper Revisited." *Journal of Common Market Studies* 40, no. 2 (2002): 215–34.

Brown, Neville L., and Tom Kennedy. *The Court of Justice of the European Communities*. London: Sweet & Maxwell, 2000.

Christiansen, Thomas, and Emil Kirchner, eds. *Committee Governance in the European Union*. Manchester: Manchester University Press, 2000.

Cini, Michelle. *The European Commission: Leadership, Organization and Culture in the EU Administration*. Manchester: Manchester University Press, 1996.

Coombes, David. *Politics and Bureaucracy in the European Community: A Portrait of the Commission of the E.E.C.* London: Sage, 1970.

Corbett, Richard. *The European Parliament's Role in Closer EU Integration*. Basingstoke, U.K.: Macmillian, 1998.

Corbett, Richard, Francis Jacobs, and Michael Shackleton, eds. *The European Parliament*. London: John Harper, 2000.

Cram, Laura, Desmond Dinan, and Niell Nugent, eds. *Developments in the European Union*. Basingstoke, U.K.: Macmillan, 1999.

de Bassompierre, Guy. *Changing the Guard in Brussels: An Insider's View of the EC Presidency*. New York: Praeger, 1988.

de Burca, Grainne, and J. H. H. Weiler, eds. *The European Court of Justice*. Oxford: Oxford University Press, 2001.

de Zwaan, Jaap W. *The Permanent Representatives Committee: Its Role in European Union Decision-Making*. Amsterdam: Elsevier, 1995.

Dehousse, Renaud. *The European Court of Justice*. Boulder, Colo.: Lynne Rienner, 1998.

Deighton, Anne, ed. *Building Postwar Europe. National Decision-Makers and European Institutions, 1948–63*. Basingstoke, U.K.: Macmillan, 1995.

Devuyst, Youri. *The European Union at the Crossroads: The EU's Institutional Evolution: From the Schuman Plan to the European Convention*, 2nd ed. Brussels: P.I.E.-Peter Lang, 2003.

Edwards, Geoffrey, and David Spence, eds. *The European Commission*. Harlow, U.K.: Catermill, 1997.

Eichengreen, Barry J., and Jeffry Frieden. *Politics and Institutions in an Integrated Europe*. New York: Verlag Springer, 1995.

Endo, Ken. *The Presidency of the European Commission under Jacques Delors: The Politics of Shared Leadership*. London: Palgrave Macmillan, 1999.

Eusepi, Giuseppe, and Friedrich Schneider, eds. *Changing Institutions in the European Union: A Public Choice Perspective*. Northampton, Mass.: Edward Elgar, 2004.

Hayes-Renshaw, Fiona, and Helen Wallace. *The Council of Ministers*. Basingstoke, U.K.: Macmillan, 1997.

Hix, Simon. "Elections, Parties, and Institutional Design: A Comparative Perspective on European Union Democracy." *West European Politics* 29, no. 3 (1998): 19–52.

Hooghe, Liesbet. *The European Commission and the Integration of Europe: Images of Governance*. Cambridge: Cambridge University Press, 2001.

Joerges, Christian, and Ellen Vos. *EU Committees: Social Regulation, Law and Politics*. Oxford: Hart Publishing, 1999.

Judge, David, and David Earnshaw. *The European Parliament*. Basingstoke, U.K.: Palgrave Macmillan, 2003.

Jupille, Joseph. *Procedural Politics: Issues, Influences and Institutional Choice in the European Union*. New York: Cambridge University Press, 2004.

Keohane, Robert O., and Stanley Hoffmann, eds. *The New European Community. Decision-Making and Institutional Change*. Boulder, Colo.: Westview Press, 1991.

Kreppel, Amie. *The European Parliament and Supranational Party System: A Study in Institutional Development*. Cambridge: Cambridge University Press, 2002.

Lodge, Juliet, ed. *The 1990 Elections to the European Parliament*. Basingstoke, U.K.: Palgrave, 2001.

Nugent, Neill. *The European Commission*. Basingstoke, U.K.: Palgrave, 2001.

Peterson, John, and Elizabeth Bomberg. *Decision-Making in the European Union*. London: Palgrave, 1999.

Peterson, John, and Michael Shackleton, eds. *The Institutions of the European Union*. Oxford: Oxford University Press, 2001.

Sherrington, Philippa. *The Council of Ministers: Political Authority in the European Union*. London: Pinter, 2000.

Skiadas, Dimitros. *The European Court of Auditors*. London: Kogan Page, 2000.

Smith, Julie. *Europe's Elected Parliament*. Sheffield, U.K.: Sheffield Academic Press, 1999.

Stevens, Anne, and Handley Stevens. *Brussels Bureaucrats. The Administration of the European Union*. Basingstoke, U.K.: Palgrave, 2001.

Warleigh, Alex. *Understanding European Union Institutions*. London: Routledge, 2002.

Wessels, Bernhard, and Richard S. Katz, eds. *The European Parliament, National Parliaments and European Integration*. Oxford: Oxford University Press, 1999.

Westlake, Martin, and David Galloway. *The Council of the European Union*, 3rd ed. London: John Harper Publishing, 2005.

Treaties

Baun, Michael J. *An Imperfect Union. The Maastricht Treaty and the New Policies of European Integration*. Boulder, Colo.: Westview Press, 1996.

Bond, Martin, and Kim Feus, eds. *The Treaty of Nice Explained*. London: Federal Trust, 2001.

Church, Clive, and David Phinnemore. *Understanding the European Constitution*. New York: Routledge, 2005.

Corbett, Richard. *The Treaty of Maastricht: From Conception to Ratification*. London: Longman, 1993.

Dehousse, Franklin. *Amsterdam: The Making of a Treaty*. London: Kogan Page, 1999.

Dobson, Lynn, and Andreas Follesdal. *Political Theory and the European Constitution*. New York: Routledge, 2004.

Devuyst, Youri. *EU Decision Making after the Treaty Establishing a Constitution for Europe*. Policy Paper No. 9. Pittsburgh, Penn.: University of Pittsburgh European Union Center and Center for West European Studies, 2004.

Duff, Andrew, ed. *The Treaty of Amsterdam: Text and Commentary*. London: Sweet & Maxwell, 1997.

Duff, Andrew, John Pinder, and Roy Pryce, eds. *Maastricht and Beyond: Building the European Union*. London: Routledge, 1994.

Eriksen, Erik Oddvar, John Erik Fossum, and Agustín Menéndez, eds. *Developing a Constitution for Europe*. New York: Routledge, 2004.

Fernández-Esteban, María Luisa. *The Rule of Law in the European Constitution*. The Hague: Kluwer Law International, 1999.

Fukuda, Koji, and Hiroyi Akiba, eds. *European Governance after Nice*. New York: Routledge, 2003.

Galloway, David. *The Treaty of Nice and Beyond. Realities and Illusions of Power in the EU*. Sheffield, U.K.: Sheffield Academic Press, 2001.

Joerges, Christian, Yves Meny, and J. H. H. Weiler, eds. *What Kind of Constitution for What Kind of Policy?* Florence: European University Institute, 2000.

Keller-Noellet, Macques, and Guy Milton, with Agnieszka Bartol-Saurel. *The European Constitution: Its Origins, Negotiation and Meaning.* London: John Harper Publishing, 2005.

Laursen, Finn, ed. *The Amsterdam Treaty. National Preference Formation, Interstate Bargaining and Outcome.* Odense: Odense University Press, 2002.

Laursen, Finn, and Sophie Vanhoonacker, eds. *The Ratification of the Maastricht Treaty: Issues, Debates and Future Implications.* Maastricht: EIPA, 1994.

Miccù, Roberto, and Ingolf Pernice, eds. *The European Constitution in the Making.* Baden-Baden: Nomos Verlagsgesellschaft, 2004

Neunreither, Karlheinz, and Antje Wiener, eds. *European Integration after Amsterdam: Institutional Dynamics and Prospects for Democracy.* Oxford: Oxford University Press, 2000.

Norman, Peter. *The Accidental Constitution: The Story of the European Convention.* Brussels: EuroComment, 2003.

Smith, Brendan P. G. *Constitution Building in the European Union. The Process of Treaty Reform.* The Hague: Kluwer Law International, 2002.

Stubb, Alexander. *Negotiating Flexibility in the European Union. Amsterdam, Nice and Beyond.* Basingstoke, U.K.: Palgrave, 2002.

Community Law

Alter, Karen. *Establishing the Supremacy of European Law. The Making of an International Rule of Law in Europe.* Oxford: Oxford University Press, 2001.

Arnull, Anthony, Alan Dashwood, Malcolm Ross, and Derrick Wyatt. *European Union Law.* London: Sweet & Maxwell, 2000.

Barents, René. *The Autonomy of Community Law.* The Hague: Kluwer Law International, 2004.

Bellamy, Christopher, and Graham Child with Peter M. Roth, eds. *European Community Law of Competition.* London: Sweet & Maxwell, 2001.

Biondi, Andrea, Piet Eeckhout, and James Flynn, eds. *The Law of State Aid in the European Union.* Oxford: Oxford University Press, 2004.

Borchardt, Klaus-Dieter. *The ABC of Community Law.* Luxembourg: Office for Official Publications of the European Communities, 1994.

Burley, Ann-Marie, and Walter Mattli. "Europe before the Court: A Political Theory of Legal Integration." *International Organization* 47, no. 1 (1993): 41–76.

Chalmers, Damian. *European Union Law. Vol. 1.* Aldershot, U.K.: Ashgate, 1998.

Craig, Paul, and Grainne de Burca. *EU Law: Texts, Cases and Materials*. Oxford: Oxford University Press, 2003.

Faull, Jonathan, and Ali Nikpay, eds. *The EC Law of Competition*. Oxford: Oxford University Press, 1999.

Hanlon, James. *European Community Law*. London: Sweet & Maxwell, 1998.

Hartley, T. C. *The Foundations of European Community Law: An Introduction to the Constitutional and Administrative Law of the European Community*. Oxford: Oxford University Press, 2003.

Kapteyn, P. J. G., and P. VerLoren van Themaat. *Introduction to the Law of the European Communities from Maastricht to Amsterdam*. London: Kluwer Law International, 1998.

Mathijsen, Pierre S. R. F. *A Guide to European Community Law*, 7th ed. London: Sweet & Maxwell, 2000.

Mengozzi, Paolo. *European Community Law: From the Treaty of Rome to the Treaty of Amsterdam*. The Hague: Kluwer Law International, 1999.

Shaw, J. *European Community Law*. Basingstoke, U.K.: Macmillan, 2000.

Weatherill, Stephen. *EU Consumer Law and Policy*. Northampton, Mass.: Edward Elgar Publishing, 2005.

Weatherill, Stephen, and Paul Beaumont. *EU Law*. London: Penguin, 1999.

Politics

Abromeit, Heidrun. *Democracy in Europe: Legitimizing Politics in a Non-State Polity*. New York: Berghahn, 1998.

Arnull, Anthony, and Daniel Wincott, eds. *Accountability and Legitimacy in the European Union*. Oxford: Oxford University Press, 2002.

Arter, David. *The Politics of European Integration in the Twentieth Century*. Aldershot, U.K.: Dartmouth, 1993.

Banchoff, T., and M. P. Smith. *Legitimacy and the European Union: The Contested Polity*. London: Routledge, 1999.

Bell, David Scott, and Christopher Lord, eds. *Transnational Parties in the European Union*. Aldershot, U.K.: Ashgate, 1998.

Bellamy, Richard, and Alex Warleigh, eds. *Citizenship and Governance in the European Union*. London: Continuum, 2001.

Búrca, Gráinne de, and Joanne Scott, eds. *Constitutional Change in the EU: From Uniformity to Flexibility?* Oxford: Hart, 2000.

Burgess, Michael. *Federalism and European Union: Political Ideas, Influences and Strategies in the European Community, 1972–1987*. London: Routledge, 1989.

Christiansen, Thomas, and Emil J. Kirchner, eds. *Committee Governance in the European Union*. Manchester: Manchester University Press, 2000.

Christiansen, Thomas, and Simona Piattoni, eds. *Informal Governance in the European Union*. Northampton, Mass.: Edward Elgar, 2004.

Chryssochoou, Dimitris. *Democracy in the European Union*. London: I. B. Taurus, 2000.

Conant, Lisa. *Justice Contained : Law and Politics in the European Union*. Ithaca, N.Y.: Cornell University Press, 2002.

Conti, Nicolo. *Party Analysis to European Integration: A Longitudinal Analysis of the Italian Case*. SEI Working Paper 70. Sussex, U.K.: Sussex European Institute, 2003.

Eder, Klaus, and Bernhard Giesen, eds. *European Citizenship between National Legacies and Postnational Projects*. Oxford: Oxford University Press, 2001.

Eriksen, Erik Oddvar, and John Erik Fossum, eds. *Democracy in the European Union. Integration through Deliberation?* London: Routledge, 2000.

George, Stephen, and Ian Bache. *Politics in the European Union*. Oxford: Oxford University Press, 2001.

Goetz, Klaus, and Simon Hix. *Europeanised Political European Integration and National Political Systems*. London: Frank Cass, 2001.

Greenwood, Justin. *Interest Representation in the European Union*. New York: Palgrave Macmillan, 2003.

Harlow, Carol. *Accountability in the European Union*. Oxford: Oxford University Press, 2002.

Hix, Simon, and Christopher Lord. *Political Parties in the European Union*. Basingstoke, U.K.: MacMillan, 1997.

Hug, Simon. *Voices of Europe: Citizens, Referendums, and European Integration*. Lanham, Md.: Rowman & Littlefield, 2002.

Jansen, Thomas. *The European People's Party: Origins and Development*. Basingstoke U.K.: MacMillan, 1998.

Johansson, Karl Magnus, and Peter Zervakis, eds. *European Political Parties between Cooperation and Integration*. Baden-Baden, Germany: Nomas, 2001.

Kelemen, R. Daniel. *The Rules of Federalism: Institutions and Regulatory Politics in the EU and Beyond*. Cambridge, Mass.: Harvard University Press, 2004.

Kelley, Judith. *Ethnic Politics in Europe: The Power of Norms and Incentives*. Princeton, N.J.: Princeton University Press, 2004.

Kirchner, Emil Joseph. *Decision Making in the European Community: The Council Presidency and European Integration*. Manchester: Manchester University Press, 1992.

Knill, Christoph. *The Europeanization of National Administrations: Patterns of Institutional Persistence and Change*. Cambridge: Cambridge University Press, 2001.

Kreppel, Amie. "Rules and Ideology and Coalition Formation in the European Parliament: Past, Present and Future." *European Union Politics* 1, no. 3 (2000): 340–62.

Kreppel, Amie, and George Tsebelis. "Coalition Formation in the European Parliament." *Comparative Political Studies* 38, no. 2 (1999): 933–66.

Lahav, Gallya. *Immigration and Politics in the New Europe: Reinventing Borders.* Cambridge: Cambridge University Press, 2004.

Lord, Christopher. *Democracy in the European Union.* Sheffield, U.K.: Sheffield Academic Press, 1998.

Marks, Gary, and Marco R. Steenbergen, eds. *European Integration and Political Conflict.* New York: Cambridge University Press, 2004.

Mazey, Sonia, and Jeremy Richardson. *Lobbying in the European Community.* Oxford: Oxford University Press, 1993.

Middelmas, Keith. *Orchestrating Europe: The Informal Politics of the European Union, 1973–95.* London: Fontana Press, 1995.

Norton, Philip, ed. *National Parliaments and the European Union.* London: Frank Cass, 1996.

O'Neill, Michael. *The Politics of European Integration: A Reader.* London: Routledge, 1996.

Rathbun, Brian. *Partisan Interventions: European Party Politics and Peace Enforcement in the Balkans.* Ithaca, N.Y.: Cornell University Press, 2004.

Raunio, Tapio. *The European Perspective: Transnational Party Groups in the 1989–94 European Parliament.* Aldershot, U.K.: Ashgate, 1997.

Sbragia, Alberta, ed. *Euro-Politics: Institutions and Policymaking in the "New" European Community.* Washington, D.C.: Brookings Institution, 1992.

Schmitter, Philippe C. *How to Democratize the European Union . . . and Why Bother?* Lanham, Md.: Rowman & Littlefield, 2000.

Tallberg, Jonas. *European Governance and Supranational Institutions: Making States Comply.* London: Routledge, 2003.

Vachudova, Milada Ann. *Europe Undivided: Democracy, Leverage, and Integration after Communism.* Oxford: Oxford University Press, 2005.

Warleigh, Alex, and Jenny Fairbrass, eds. *Influence and Interests in the European Union: The New Politics of Persuasion and Advocacy.* London: Europa, 2003.

POLICIES AND POLICY-MAKING

Ackrill, Robert. *The Common Agricultural Policy.* Sheffield, U.K.: Sheffield Academic Press, 2000.

Anderson, Malcom, et al., eds. *Policing the European Union.* Oxford: Clarendon Press, 1995.

Anderson, Svein, and Kjell Eliassen. *Making Policy in Europe*. London: Sage, 2001.

Andonova, Liliana B. *Transnational Politics of the Environment: The European Union and Environmental Policy in Central and Eastern Europe*. Cambridge, Mass.: MIT Press, 2004.

Baldassari, Mario, and Francesco Busato. *Full Employment and High Growth in Europe*. London: Palgrave Macmillan, 2003.

Caloghirou, Yannis, Nicholas S. Vonortas, and Stavros Ionides, eds. *European Collaboration in Research and Development: Business Strategy and Public Policy*. Northampton, Mass.: Edward Elgar, 2004.

Cini, Michelle, and Lee McGowan. *Competition Policy in the European Union*. Basingstoke, U.K.: Macmillan, 1998.

Cram, Laura. *Policy-Making in the European Union: Conceptual Lenses and the Integration Process*. London: Routledge, 1997.

Cox, Aidan, and Antonique Koening. *Understanding European Community. Aid Policies, Management and Distribution Explained*. London: Overseas Development Institute, 1997.

Goodman, Joseph W. *Telecommunications Policy-Making in the European Union*. Northampton, Mass.: Edward Elgar Publishing, 2005.

Grant, W. *The Common Agricultural Policy*. London: Macmillan, 1997.

Hayes, J. P. *Making Trade Policy in the European Community*. New York: St. Martin's, 1993.

Heisenberg, Dorothee. *Negotiating Privacy: The European Union, the United States, and Personal Data Protection*. Boulder, Colo.: Lynne Rienner, 2005.

Hennis, Marjoleine. *Globalization and European Integration: The Changing Role of Farmers in the Common Agricultural Policy*. Lanham, Md.: Rowman & Littlefield, 2005.

Heritier, Adrienne. *Policy-Making and Diversity in Europe: Escape from Deadlock*. Cambridge: Cambridge University Press, 1999.

Hooghe, Liesbet. *Cohesion Policy and European Integration: Building Multi-Level Governance*. Oxford: Oxford University Press, 1996.

Jordan, A., and D. Liefferink, eds. *Environmental Policy in Europe: The Europeanization of National Environmental Policy*. London: Routledge, 2004.

Jordan, A. J., ed. *Environmental Policy in the European Union: Actors, Institutions and Processes*, 2nd ed. London: Earthscan, 2005.

Kassim, Hussein, Guy Peters, and Vincent Wright. *The National Co-ordination of EU Policy: The Domestic Level*. Oxford: Oxford University Press, 2000.

Kassim, Hussein, and Handley Stevens, eds. *Air Transport and the European Union: Europeanization and Its Limits*. Basingstoke, U.K.: Palgrave Macmillan, 2004.

McCormick, John. *Environmental Policy in the European Union*. New York: Palgrave, 2001.

——. *The European Union Politics and Policies*. Boulder, Colo.: Westview Press, 1999.

Majone, Giandomenico. *Regulating Europe*. London: Routledge, 1996.

Matlary, Janne H. *Energy Policy in the European Union*. Basingstoke, U.K.: Macmillan, 1997.

Meehan, E. *Citizenship and the European Community*. London: Sage, 1993.

Messerlin, Patrick A. *Measuring the Costs of Protection in Europe: European Commercial Policy in the 2000s*. Washington, D.C.: Institute for International Economics, 2001.

Mortenson, Jorgen. *Improving Economic and Social Cohesion in the EC*. New York: St. Martin's, 1994.

Occhipinti, John D. *The Politics of EU Police Cooperation: Toward a European FBI?* Boulder, Colo.: Lynne Rienner Publishers, 2003

Peterson, J., and M. Sharp. *Technology Policy in the European Union*. Basingstoke, U.K.: Macmillan, 1998.

Richardson, Jeremy John, ed. *European Union: Power and Policy Making*. London: Routledge, 1996.

Slodka, Anna. *Eco Labeling in the EU: Lessons for Poland*. SEI Working Paper 75. Sussex, U.K.: Sussex European Institute, 2004.

Springer, Beverly. *The European Union and Its Citizens: The Social Agenda*. Westport, Conn.: Greenwood, 1994.

Stavridis, Stelios, ed. *New Challenges to the European Union: Policies and Policy Making*. Aldershot, U.K.: Dartmouth Publishing, 1997.

Wallace, Helen, and William Wallace, eds. *Policy-Making in the European Union*. Oxford: Oxford University Press, 2000.

SINGLE MARKET AND ECONOMIC AND MONETARY UNION

Apel, Emmanuel. *European Monetary Integration: 1958–2002*. London: Routledge, 1998.

Armstrong, Kenneth, and Simon Bulmer. *The Governance of the Single European Market*. Manchester: Manchester University Press, 1998.

Barzanti, Sergio. *The Underdeveloped Areas within the Common Market*. Princeton, N.J.: Princeton University Press, 1965.

Brown, Brendan. *Euro on Trial: To Reform or Split Up?* New York: Palgrave Macmillan, 2004.

Carchedi, Guglielmo. *For Another Europe: A Class Analysis of European Economic Integration*. New York: Verso, 2001.

Cockfield, Arthur. *The European Union: Creating the Single Market*. London: Wily Chancery Law, 1994.

Collignon, Stefan. *Monetary Stability in Europe*. London: Routledge, 2002.

Collignon, Stefan, and Daniela Schwarzer. *Private Sector Involvement in the Euro: The Power of Ideas*. New York: Routledge, 2003.

Crouch, Colin, ed. *After the Euro: Shaping Institutions for Governance in the Wake of European Monetary Union*. New York: Oxford University Press, 2000.

Dosenrode, Søren, ed. *Political Aspects of the Economic and Monetary Union*. Abingdon, U.K.: Ashage, 2002.

Dyson, Kenneth, ed. *European States and the Euro: Europeanization, Variation, and Convergence*. Oxford: Oxford University Press, 2002.

Dyson, Kenneth, and Kevin Featherstone. *The Road to Maastricht. Negotiating Economic and Monetary Union*. Oxford: Oxford University Press, 1999.

Egan, Michelle. *Constructing a European Market. Standards, Regulation, and Governance*. Oxford: Oxford University Press, 2001.

Grauwe, Paul De. *The Economics of Monetary Integration*. Oxford: Oxford University Press, 1994.

Grauwe, Paul De, and Vladimir Lavrac, eds. *Inclusion of Central European Countries in the European Monetary Union*. Boston, Mass.: Kluwer Academic, 1998.

Gros, Daniel, and Niels Thygesen. *European Monetary Integration: From the European Monetary System to European Monetary Union*, 2nd ed. London: Longman, 1997.

Hallerberg, Mark. *Domestic Budgets in a United Europe: Fiscal Governance from the End of Bretton Woods to EMU*. Ithaca, N.Y.: Cornell University Press, 2004.

Harrop, Jeffrey. *The Political Economy of Integration in the European Union*. Northampton, Mass.: Edward Elgar, 2000.

Heisenberg, Dorothee. *The Mark of the Bundesbank: Germany's Role in European Monetary Cooperation*. Boulder, Colo.: Lynne Rienner, 1999.

Henning, C. Randall. *Cooperating with Europe's Monetary Union*. Washington, D.C.: Institute for International Economics, 1997.

Hosli, Madeleine. *The Euro: A Concise Introduction to Europe's Single Currency*. Boulder, Colo.: Lynne Rienner, 2005.

Jacquemin, Alexis, and André Sapir, eds. *The European Internal Market: Trade and Competition*. Oxford: Oxford University Press, 1990.

Jones, Erik. *The Politics of Economic and Monetary Union*. Lanham, Md.: Rowman and Littlefield, 2000.

Keating, Michael, John Loughlin, and Kris Deschouwer. *Culture, Institutions and Economic Development: A Study of Eight European Regions*. Northampton, Mass.: Edward Elgar Publishing, 2005.

Kenen, Peter B. *Economic and Monetary Union in Europe: Moving beyond Maastricht*. Cambridge: Cambridge University Press, 1995.

Kettell, Steven. *The Political Economy of Exchange Rate Policy-Making: From the Gold Standard to the Euro*. New York: Palgrave Macmillan, 2004.

Levitt, Malcolm, and Christopher Lord. *The Political Economy of Monetary Union*. London: Palgrave, 2000.

Lindberg, Leon. *The Political Dynamics of European Economic Integration*. Stanford, Calif.: Stanford University Press, 1963.

Ljungberg, Jonas, ed. *The Price of the Euro*. New York: Palgrave Macmillan, 2004.

Lucarelli, Bill. *The Origin and Evolution of the Single Market in Europe*. Aldershot, U.K.: Ashgate, 1999.

Ludlow, Peter. *The Making of the European Monetary System*. London: Butterworths, 1982.

McDonald, Frank, and Stephen Dearden, eds. *European Economic Integration*. Boston, Mass.: Addison-Wesley Longman, 1999.

McNamara, Kathleen. *The Currency of Ideas: Monetary Politics in the European Union*. Ithaca, N.Y.: Cornell University Press, 1997.

Maes, Ivo, ed. *Economic Thought and the Making of European Monetary Union: Selected Essays of Ivo Maes*. Northampton, Mass.: Edward Elgar, 2002.

Magnusson, Lars, and Bo Strath, eds. *From the Werner Plan to the EMU: In Search of a Political Economy for Europe*. New York: Peter Lang, 2001.

Martin, Andrew, and George Ross, eds. *Euros and Europeans: Monetary Integration and the European Model of Society*. New York: Cambridge University Press, 2004.

———. *Monetary Integration and the European Model of Society*. Cambridge: Cambridge University Press, 2004.

Molle, Willem. *The Economics of European Integration*. Aldershot, U.K.: Dartmouth, 1990.

Moss, Bernard, ed. *Monetary Union in Crisis: The European Union as Neo-Liberal Construction*. London: Palgrave MacMillan, 2005.

Overturf, Stephen Frank. *Money and European Union*. London: Palgrave, 2000.

Padoa-Schioppa, Tommaso. *The Euro and Its Central Bank: Getting United after the Union*. Cambridge, Mass.: MIT Press, 2004.

Savage, James. *Making the EMU: The Politics of Budgetary Surveillance and the Enforcement of Maastricht*. Oxford: Oxford University Press, 2005.

Swann, Dennis. *The Economics of the Common Market*, 7th ed. London: Penguin, 1992.

Thompson, Grahame, ed. *Governing the European Economy*. London: Sage, 2001.

Tsoukalis, Loukas. *The New European Economy Revisited*. Oxford: Oxford University Press, 1997.

Ulst, Ingrid. *Linkages of Financial Groups in the European Union: Financial Conglomeration Developments in the Old and New Member States*. New York: Central European University Press, 2005.

Ungerer, Horst. *A Concise History of European Monetary Integration: From EPU to EMU*. Westport, Conn.: Quorum, 1997.

Verdun, Amy, ed. *The Euro: European Integration Theory and Economic and Monetary Union*. Lanham, Md.: Rowman & Littlefield, 2002.

EXTERNAL RELATIONS

Batt, Judy, et al. *Partners and Neighbors: A CFSP for a Wider Europe*. Paris: EU Institute for Security Studies, 2003.

Bretherton, Charlotte, and John Vogler. *The European Union as a Global Actor*. London: Routledge, 1999.

Cameron, Fraser. *The Foreign and Security Policy of the European Union*. Sheffield, U.K.: Sheffield Academic Press, 1999.

Carlsnaes, Walter, Helene Sjursen, and Brian White, eds. *Contemporary European Foreign Policy*. London: Sage, 2004.

——. *The General Law of E.C. External Relations*. London: Sweet & Maxwell, 2000.

Christainsen, Thomas, and Ben Tonra, eds. *Rethinking European Union Foreign Policy*. Manchester, U.K.: Manchester University Press, 2004.

Dannreuther, Roland. *European Union Foreign and Security Policy: Towards a Neighbourhood Strategy*. London: Routledge, 2004.

Duke, Simon, ed. *Between Vision and Reality. CFSP's Progress on the Path to Maturity*. Maastricht: European Institute of Public Administration, 2000.

Eliassen, Kjell A., ed. *Foreign and Security Policy in the European Union*. London: Sage, 1998.

Gasteyger, Curt. *An Ambiguous Power: The European Union in a Changing World*. Gütersloh: Bertelsmann, 1996.

Gilson, Julie. *Japan and the European Union*. Basingstoke, U.K.: Palgrave, 2000.

Gilson, Julie, and P. W. Preston, eds. *The European Union and East Asia: Inter-Regional Linkages in a Changing Global System*. Cheltenham, U.K.: Edward Elgar, 2001.

Ginsberg, Roy. *The European Union in International Politics: Baptism by Fire*. Lanham, Md.: Rowman and Littlefield, 2001.

Granell, Francesc. "Conflicto y Cooperación Entre Europa y EE.UU." *Política Exterior XI, no. 60* (November–December 1997): 35–53.

Griller, Stefan, and Birgit Weidel, eds. *External Economic Relations and Foreign Policy in the European Union.* Vienna: Springer Verlag, 2002.

Guttman, Robert, ed. *Europe in the New Century. Visions of an Emerging Superpower.* Boulder, Colo.: Lynne Rienner, 2001.

Hill, Christopher, ed. *The Actors in Europe's Foreign Policy.* New York: Routledge, 1996.

Hoffman, Stanley. "Toward a Common European Foreign and Security Policy?" *Journal of Common Market Studies* 38, no. 2 (June 2000): 189–98.

Holland, Martin, ed. *Common Foreign and Security Policy: The Record and Reforms.* Washington, D.C.: Pinter, 1997.

Knodt, Michele, and Sebastiaan Princen, eds. *Understanding the European Union's External Relations.* London: Routledge, 2003.

Koutrakou, Vassiliki N., ed. *Contemporary Issues and Debates in EU Policy: The European Union and International Relations.* Manchester, U.K.: Manchester University Press, 2004.

Macleod, Iain, Ian Hendry, and Stephen Hyett. *The External Relations of the European Communities.* Oxford: Clarendon Press, 1996.

Manners Ian, and Richard Whitman, eds. *The Foreign Policy of the EU Member States.* Manchester: Manchester University Press, 2001.

Nuttall, Simon J. *European Foreign Policy.* Oxford: Oxford University Press, 2000.

———. *European Political Cooperation.* Oxford: Clarendon Press, 1992.

Padoa-Schioppa, Tommaso. *Europe, A Civil Power: Lessons from EU Experience.* London: The Federal Trust, 2004.

Paemen, Hugo, and Alexandra Bensch. *From the GATT to the WTO: The European Community in the Uruguay Round.* Leuven, Belgium: Leuven University Press, 1995.

Peterson, John, and Helene Sjursen, eds. *A Common Foreign Policy for Europe?* London: Routledge, 1998.

Piening, Christopher. *Global Europe: The European Union in World Affairs.* Boulder, Colo.: Lynne Rienner, 1997.

Regelsberger, Elfriede, Phillipe de Schoutheete, and Wolfgang Wessels, eds. *Foreign Policy of the European Union: From EPC to CFSP and Beyond.* Boulder, Colo.: Lynne Rienner, 1997.

Rhodes, Carolyn, ed. *The European Union in the World Community.* Boulder Colo.: Lynne Rienner, 1998.

Rummel, Reinhardt, ed. *Toward Poltical Union. Planning a Common Foreign and Security Policy in the European Community.* Boulder, Colo.: Westview Press, 1992.

Schimmelfennig, Frank, and Ulrich Sedelmeier, eds. *The Europeanization of Central and Eastern Europe*. Ithaca, N.Y.: Cornell University Press, 2005.

Smith, Hazel. *European Union Foreign Policy. What It Is and What It Does*. London: Pluto Press, 2002.

Smith, Karen E. *European Union Foreign Policy in a Changing World*. Cambridge: Polity, 2003.

——. *The Making of European Union Foreign Policy: The Case of Eastern Europe*. London: Macmillan, 1999.

Smith, Michael E. *Europe's Foreign and Security Policy: The Institutionalization of Cooperation*. Cambridge: Cambridge University Press, 2004.

Soetendorp, Ben. *Foreign Policy in the European Union: Theory, History and Practice*. New York: Longman, 1999.

White, Brian. *Understanding European Foreign Policy*. London: Palgrave, 2001.

Zielonka, Jan, ed. *Paradoxes of European Foreign Policy*. The Hague: Kluwer Law, 1998.

Relations with Other Regions/Countries

Balis, Christina, and Simon Serfaty, eds. *Visions of America and Europe: September 11, Iraq, and Transatlantic Relations*. Washington, D.C.: The CSIS Press, Significant Issues Series Vol. 26/3, 2004.

Dashwood, Alan, and Christophe Hillion, eds. *Western European Union 1954–1997. Defense, Security, Integration*. Oxford: St. Antony's College, 1997.

Egan, Michelle, ed. *Creating a Transatlantic Marketplace: Government Policies and Business Strategies*. Manchester, U.K.: Manchester University Press, 2004.

Featherstone, Kevin, and Roy Ginsberg, eds. *The United States and the European Union in the 1990s: Partners in Transition*. New York: St. Martin's, 1996.

Gardner, Anthony Laurence. *A New Era in US–EU Relations?: The Clinton Administration and the New Transatlantic Agenda*. Aldershot, U.K.: Ashgate, 1997.

Joffé, George, and Álvaro Vasconcelos. *The Barcelona Process: Building a Euro–Mediterranean Regional Community*. London: Frank Cass, 2000.

Kagan, Robert. *Of Paradise and Power. America and Europe in the New World Order*. New York, N.Y.: Alfred A. Knopf, 2003.

Kramer, Steven Philip, and Irene Kyriakopoulos, eds. *U.S.–European Union Relations: Economic Change and Political Transition*. Washington, D.C.: National Defense University, Institute for National Strategic Studies, 1999.

Levine, Norman. *The United States and the European Union: Economic Relations in a World of Transition*. Lanham, Md.: University Press of America, 1996.

Lewis, William H. *The European Union–Maghrebian Dialogues: Echoes of Disappointments Past*. Washington, D.C.: Center for Strategic and International Studies, 2001.

Lindstrom, Gustav, ed. *Shift or Rift: Assessing US–EU Relations after Iraq*. Paris: EU Institute for Security Studies, 2003.

Mayhew, Alan. *Recreating Europe. The European Union's Policy towards Central and Eastern Europe*. Cambridge, Cambridge University Press, 1998.

Müller-Jentsch, Daniel. *Deeper Integration and Trade in Services in the Euro–Mediterranean Region: Southern Dimensions of the European Neighborhood Policy*. Washington, D.C.: World Bank, 2005.

Nye, Joseph, Jr. "The US and Europe: Continental Drift?" *International Affairs* (2000): 51–60.

Peterson, John, and Mark A. Pollack, eds. *Europe, America, Bush: Transatlantic Relations in the Twenty-first Century*. New York: Routledge, 2003.

Pollack, Mark A., and Gregory C. Shaffer, eds. *Transatlantic Governance in the Global Economy*. Lanham, Md.: Rowman & Littlefield, 2001.

Roy, Joaquín, ed. *Cuba, the United States and the Helms–Burton Doctrine: International Reactions*. Gainesville, Fla.: University of Florida Press, 2000.

———. *The Reconstruction of Central America: The Role of the European Community*. Coral Gables, Fla.: Institute of Iberian Studies/European Community Project, 1991.

Smith, Karen. *The Making of EU Foreign Policy. The Case of Eastern Europe 1988–95*. Basingstoke, U.K.: MacMillan, 1998.

Xuereb, Peter G., ed. *Euro–Mediterranean Integration: The Mediterranean's European Challenge*. (Vol. III). Msida, Malta: European Documentation and Research Center, 2002.

ACP/Development

Babarinde, Olufemi. A. "The Lomé Convention: An Aging Dinosaur in the European Union's Foreign Policy Enterprise." In *The State of the European Union: Integration in Perspective*, eds. Carolyn Rhodes and Suzan Mazey. Boulder, Colo.: Lynne Rienner, 1995.

———. *The Lomé Conventions and Development: An Empirical Assessment*. Brookfield, Vt.: Avebury, 1994.

Cosgrove-Sacks, Carol, ed. *Europe, Diplomacy and Development: New Issues in EU Relations with Developing Countries*. Basingstoke, U.K.: Palgrave, 2001.

———, ed. *The European Union and Developing Countries: The Challenge of Globalization*. Houndmills, U.K.: Macmillan, 1999.

Grilli, E. *The European Community and the Developing Countries*. Cambridge: Cambridge University Press, 1993.

Holland, Martin. *The European Union and the Third World*. Basingstoke, U.K.: Palgrave, 2002.

Lister, Marjorie. *The European Union and the South: Relations with Developing Countries*. London: Routledge, 1997.

———, ed. *European Union Development Policy*. New York: St. Martin's, 1998.

———, ed. *New Perspectives on European Development Cooperation*. Boulder, Colo: Westview Press, 1999.

Thorp, Teresa. *Regional Implications for the ACP-EU Economic Partnership Agreements*. The Global Trade Negotiations, Center for International Development, http://www.cid.harvard.edu/cidtrade/Papers/thorp.pdf, August 30, 2003 (accessed January 10, 2005).

Security

Apap, Joanna, ed. *Justice and Home Affairs in the EU: Liberty and Security Issues after Enlargement*. Northampton, Mass.: Edward Elgar, 2004.

Aus, Jonathan. *Supranational Governance in an "Area of Freedom, Security and Justice": Eurodac and the Politics of Biometric Control*. SEI Working Paper 72. Sussex, U.K.: Sussex European Institute, 2003.

Cogan, Charles G. *The Third Option: The Emancipation of European Defense, 1989–2000*. Westport, Conn.: Praeger, 2001.

Cottey, Andrew, and Anthony Forster. *Reshaping Defense Diplomacy: New Roles for Military Cooperation and Assistance*. Oxford: Oxford University Press, 2004.

Duke, Simon. *The Elusive Quest for European Security. From EDC to CFSP*. Basingstoke, U.K.: MacMillan, 2000.

Gordon, Philip H. "Their Own Army? Making European Defense Work." *Foreign Affairs* (2000): 12–17.

Henderson, Karen. *The Area of Freedom, Security and Justice in an Enlarged Europe*. Basingstoke, U.K.: Palgrave Macmillan, 2004.

Howorth, Jolyon. *European Integration and Defense: The Ultimate Challenge?* Paris: Institute for Security Studies of WEU, 2000.

Howorth, Jolyon, and John T. S. Keeler, eds. *Defending Europe: The EU, NATO and the Quest for European Autonomy*. New York: Palgrave, 2003.

Ruane, Kevin. *The Rise and Fall of the European Defence Community. Anglo–American Relations and the Crisis of European Defence, 1950–55*. London: MacMillan, 2000.

Salmon, Trevor C., and Alistair J. K. Shepherd. *Toward a European Army: A Military Power in the Making?* Boulder, Colo.: Lynne Rienner, 2003.

Timmins, Graham, and Martin Smith, eds. *Uncertain Europe: Building a New European Security Order?* London: Routledge, 2001.

Vanhoonacker, Sophie. *The Bush Administration (1989–1993) and the Development of a European Security Identity.* Burlington, Vt.: Ashgate, 2001.

Walker, Neil, ed. *Europe's Area of Freedom, Security and Justice.* Oxford: Oxford University Press, 2004.

Youngs, Richard. "The European Security and Defense Policy: What Impact on the EU's Approach to Security Challanges?" *European Security* 11, no. 2 (Summer 2002): 95–125.

Enlargement

Andenas, Mads, and John Usher, eds. *The Treaty of Nice. Enlargement and Constitutional Reform.* Oxford: Hart, 2002.

Arikan, Harun. *Turkey and the EU: An Awkward Candidate for EU Membership?* Burlington, Vt.: Ashgate, 2003.

Avery, Graham, and Fraser Cameron. *The Enlargement of the European Union.* Sheffield, U.K.: Sheffield Academic Press, 1998.

Baun, Michael J. *A Wider Europe: The Process and Politics of European Union Enlargement.* Oxford: Rowman & Littlefield, 2000.

Cameron, Fraser, ed. *The Future of Europe—Integration and Enlargement.* London: Routledge, 2004.

Christou, George. *The European Union and Enlargement: The Case of Cyprus*, 2nd edition. Basingstoke, U.K.: Palgrave Macmillan, 2004.

Cremona, Marise, ed. *The Enlargement of the European Union.* Oxford: Oxford University Press, 2003.

Croft, Stuart, et al. *The Enlargement of Europe.* Manchester: Manchester University Press, 1999.

Cutrini, Eleonora. "Evolution of Local Systems in the Context of Enlargement." SEI Working Paper 67. Sussex, U.K.: Sussex European Institute, 2003.

Dimitrova, Antoaneta L. *Driven to Change: The European Union's Enlargement Viewed from the East.* Basingstoke, U.K.: Palgrave Macmillian, 2004.

Elvert, Jurgen, and Wolfram Kaiser, eds. *European Union Enlargement: A Comparative History.* London: Routledge, 2004.

Falkner, Gerda. "How Pervasive Are Euro-Politics? Effects of EU Membership on a New Member State." *Journal of Common Market Studies* (2000): 223–50.

Fierke, Karin, and Antje Weiner. "Constructing Institutional Interests: EU and NATO Enlargement." *Journal of European Public Policy* 6, no. 5 (December 1999): 721–42.

Gorman, Lyn, and Marja-Liisa Kiljunen. *The Enlargement of the European Community: Case Studies of Greece, Portugal, and Spain*. London: Macmillan, 1977.

Grabbe, Heather, and Kirsty Hughes. *Enlarging the EU Eastwards*. London: Royal Institute of International Affairs, 1998.

Henderson, Karen, ed. *Back to Europe: Central and Eastern Europe and the European Union*. London: Routledge, 1999.

Henderson, Karen. "The Challenges of EU Eastward Expansion." *International Politics* 37, no.1 (2000).

Ingham, Hilary and Mike, eds. *EU Expansion to the East: Prospects and Problems*. Northampton, Mass.: Edward Elgar, 2002.

Jacoby, Wade. *The Enlargement of the European Union and NATO: Ordering from the Menu in Central Europe*. Cambridge: Cambridge University Press, 2004.

Kaiser, Wolfram, and Jurgen Elvert, eds. *European Union Enlargement: A Comparative History*. London: Routledge, 2004.

Lannon, Erwan, and Marc Maresceau. *The EU's Enlargement and Mediterranean Strategies*. Basingstoke, U.K.: Palgrave, 2001.

Lewis, Paul G. *The Impact of the Enlargement of the European Union on Central European Party Systems*. SEI Working Paper 71. Sussex, U.K.: Sussex European Institute, 2003.

McLaren, Lauren. "Turkey's Eventual Membership of the EU: Turkish Elite Perspectives on the Issue." *Journal of Common Market Studies* (2000): 117–29.

Mair, Peter, and Jan Zielonka, eds. *The Enlarged European Union*. London: Frank Cass, 2002.

Mannin, Mike, ed. *Pushing Back the Boundaries: The European Union and Central and Eastern Europe*. Manchester, U.K.: Manchester University Press, 1999.

Mayhew, Alan. *Recreating Europe: The European Union's Policy Towards Central and Eastern Europe*, 2nd ed. Cambridge: Cambridge University Press, 2002.

Miles, Lee, ed. *The EU and the Nordic Countries*. London: Rouledge, 1996.

Moravcsik, Andrew, and Milada Vachudowa. "National Interests, State Power, and EU Enlargement." *East European Politics and Societies* 17, no. 1 (February 2003): 42–57.

Preston, Christopher. *Enlargement and Integration in the European Union*. London: Routledge, 1997.

Redmond, John. *The 1995 Enlargement of the European Union*. Aldershot, U.K.: Ashgate, 1997.

Redmond, John, and Glenda G. Rosenthal, eds. *The Expanding European Union: Past, Present, Future*. Boulder, Colo.: Lynne Rienner, 1998.

Rollo, Jim. "Agriculture, the Structural Funds, and the Budget after Enlargement." SEI Working Paper 68. Sussex, U.K.: Sussex European Institute, 2003.

Rometsch, Dietrich, and Wolfgang Wessels, eds. *The European Union and Member States: Towards Institutional Fusion?* Manchester: Manchester University Press, 1996.

Ross, Cameron, ed. *Perspectives on the Enlargement of the European Union.* Leiden: Brill, 2002.

Schimmelfennig, Frank. "The Double Puzzle of EU Enlargement: Liberal Norms, Rhetorical Action, and the Decision to Expand to the East." *ARENA Working Papers* no. 15 (1999) at www.arena.uio.no/publications/wp99_15.htm (accessed 5 July 2004).

———. "International Socialization in the New Europe: Rational Action in an Institutional Environment." *European Journal of International Relations* 6, no. 1 (March 2000): 109–39.

Schimmelfennig, Frank, and Ulrich Sedelmeier. "Theorizing EU Enlargement: Research Focus, Hypotheses, and the State of Research." *Journal of European Public Policy* 9, no. 4 (August 2002): 500–28.

Scholl-Latour, Peter. "EU Membership for Turkey: Con: Loss of Identity." *Internationale Politik* 2 (2000): 61–64.

Senior Nello, S., and K. E. Smith. *The European Union and Central and Eastern Europe: The Implications of Enlargement in Stages.* Burlington, Vt.: Ashgate, 1999.

Sjursen, Helene. "Enlargement and the Common Foreign and External Policy: Transforming the EU's External Policy?" *ARENA Working Papers* no. 18 (1998) at www.arena.uio.no/publications/wp98_18.htm (accessed 5 July 2004).

———. "Why Expand? The Question of Justification in the EU's Enlargement Policy." *Journal of Common Market Studies* 40, no. 3 (September 2002): 491–513.

Soetendorp, Ben, and Kenneth Hanf. *Adapting to European Integration: Small States and the European Union.* London: Longman, 1998.

Sperling, James, ed. *Europe in Change: Two Tiers or Two Speeds? The European Security Order and the Enlargement of the European Union and NATO.* Manchester: Manchester University Press, 1999.

Stankovsky, Jan, Fritz Plasser, and Peter A. Ulram. *On the Eve of EU Enlargement: Economic Development and Democratic Attitudes in East Central Europe.* Vienna: Signum, 1998.

Steinbach, Udo. "EU Membership for Turkey: Provider of Stability." *Internationale Politik* 2 (2000): 57–61.

Torreblanca, Jose I. *The Reuniting of Europe: Promises, Negotiations, and Compromises*. Aldershot, U.K.: Ashgate, 2001.

Van Oudenaren, John. "The Changing Face of Europe: EU Enlargement and Implications for Transatlantic Relations." *AICGS Policy Report #6, The American Institute for Contemporary German Studies*, (2003).

Viñas, Angel. "La ampliación de la Unión Europea: percepciones desde la UE." *Anuario Internacional CIDOB* (1998–1999): 165–175.

Warleigh, Alex. *Flexible Integration: What Model for the European Union?* London: Continuuum, 2002.

Weiler, J. H. H., Iain Begg, and John Peterson, eds. *Integration in an Expanding European Union. Reassessing the Fundamentals*. Malden, Mass.: Blackwell, 2003.

Zielonka, Jan, ed. *Europe Unbound: Enlarging and Reshaping the Boundaries of the European Union*. London: Routledge, 2002.

Identity

Cederman, Lars-Erik. "Nationalism and Bounded Integration: What It Would Take to Construct a European Demos." *European Journal of International Relations* 7 (2001): 139–74.

Checkel, Jeffrey. *Norms, Institutions and National Identity in Contemporary Europe*. Arena Working Paper, WP 98/16, 1998.

———. "Why Comply? Social Learning and European Identity Change." *International Organization* 55, no. 3 (September 2001): 553–88.

Delanty, Gerard. *Inventing Europe: Idea, Identity, Reality*. New York: St. Martin's Press, 1995.

Diez Medrano, Juan. *Framing Europe: Attitudes to European Integration in Germany, Spain, and the United Kingdom*. Princeton, N.J.: Princeton University Press, 2003.

Habermas, Juergen. *Post-National Constellation*. Cambridge: Polity Press/MIT: 2001.

Imig, Doug, and Sidney Tarrow, eds. *Contentious Europeans. Protest and Politics in an Emerging Polity*. Lanham, Md.: Rowman & Littlefield, 2001.

Loth, Wilfried. "Identity and Statehood in the Process of European Integration." *Journal of European Integration* 6, no. 1 (2000).

Menendez-Alarcon, Antonio. *The Cultural Realm of European Integration: Social Representations in France, Spain and the United Kingdom*. Westport, Conn.: Praeger, 2004.

Moxon-Browne, Edward, ed. *Who Are the Europeans Now?* Burlington, Vt: Ashgate, 2004.

Muench, Reinhard. *Nation and Citizenship in the Global Age*. New York: Palgrave, 2001.

Niedermayer, Oscar, and Richard Sinnott. *Public Opinion and Internationalized Governance*, from the series Beliefs in Government, Vol. 2. New York: Oxford University Press, 1995.

Risse, Thomas. "A European Identity? Europeanization and the Evolution of Nation-State Identities." In Cowles, Maria G., James Caporaso, and Thomas Risse, eds. *Transforming Europe. Europeanization and Domestic Change*. Ithaca, N.Y.: Cornell University Press: 2001: 198–216.

Smith, Anthony. "National Identity and the Idea of European Unity." *International Affairs* 68, no.1 (1992): 55–76.

Wintle, Michael. *Culture and Identity in Europe. Perceptions of Divergence and Unity in Past and Present*. U.K.: Ashgate, 2002.

Integration in the Americas

Anderson, Sarah, and John Cavanagh. *Lessons of European Integration for the Americas*. Washington, D.C.: Institute for Policy Studies, 2004.

Deere, Carolyn L., and Daniel C. Esty, eds. *Greening the Americas: NAFTA's Lessons for Hemispheric Trade*. Cambridge, Mass.: MIT Press, 2002.

Hakim, Peter, and Robert E. Litan, eds. *The Future of North American Integration: Beyond NAFTA*. Washington, D.C.: Brookings Institution Press, 2002.

Hall, Kenneth O., ed. *Re-inventing CARICOM: The Road to a New Integration: A Documentary Record*. Kingston: I. Randle, 2003.

Jaguaribe, Helio, and Álvaro de Vasconcelos, eds. *The European Union, MERCOSUL, and the New World Order*. London: Cass, 2003.

Miles, Lee, ed. *Sweden and the European Union Evaluated*. London: Continuum, 2000.

O'Keefe, Thomas A., and Jerry Haar. *The Impact of MERCOSUR on the Automobile Industry*. Coral Gables, Fla.: Dante B. Fascell North-South Center, University of Miami, 2001

Orphée, Gray. *Economic Implications of CARICOM for Haiti*. New York: Edwin Mellen Press, 2003.

Pastor, Robert. *Toward a North American Community: Lessons from the Old World for the New*. Washington, D.C.: Institute for International Economics, 2001.

Philip Arestis, Luiz Fernando de Paula Cheltenham, eds. *Monetary Union in South America: Lessons from EMU*. Northampton, Mass.: Edward Elgar, 2003.

Phillips, Nicola. *The Southern Cone Model: The Political Economy of Regional Capitalist Development in Latin America*. New York: Routledge, 2004.

Pollard, Duke E. *The CARICOM System: Basic Instruments.* Kingston: Caribbean Law, 2003.

Roy, Joaquín, Alejandro Chanona, and Roberto Domínguez. *La Unión Europea y el TLCAN. Integración Regional Comparada y Relaciones Mutuas.* México: Miami European Union Center-UNAM, 2004.

Roy, Joaquín, Roberto Domínguez, and Rafael Velázquez. *Retos e Interrelaciones de la Integración Regional: Europa y América.* México: Plaza y Valdés–Miami European Union Center–UQROO, 2003.

THE MEMBER STATES OF THE EUROPEAN UNION

Almarcha Barbado, Amparo, ed. *Spain and EC Membership Evaluated.* New York: St. Martin's, 1993.

Archer, Clive, and Neil Nugent. "Small States and European Union." *Current Politics and Economics of Europe* 11, no. 1 (2002): 1–10.

Bischof, Gunter, Anton Pelinka, and Michael Gehler, eds. *Austria in the European Union.* New Brunswick, N.J.: Transaction, 2002.

Bulmer, Simon, Stephen George, and Andrew Scott, eds. *The United Kingdom and EC Membership Evaluated.* London: Pinter, 1992.

Crespo MacLennan, Julio. *Spain and the Process of European Integration, 1957–85: Political Change and Europeanism.* London: Macmillan, 2000.

Farrell, Mary. *Spain in the EU: The Road to Economic Convergence.* London: Palgrave, 2001.

Geddes, Andrew. *The European Union and British Politics.* Basingstoke, U.K.: Palgrave Macmillan, 2004.

George, Stephen. *An Awkward Partner: Britain in the European Union*, 3rd ed. Oxford: Oxford University Press, 1999.

——, ed. *Britain and the European Community: The Politics of Semi-Detachment.* Oxford: Clarendon Press, 1992.

Gstöhl, Siglende. *Reluctant Europeans: Norway, Sweden, and Switzerland in the Process of Integration.* Boulder, Colo.: Lynne Rienner, 2002.

Guyomarch, Alain, Howard Machin, and Ella Ritchie. *France in the European Union.* Basingstoke, U.K.: Macmillan, 1998.

Hansen, Lene, and Ole Waever. *European Integration and National Identity: The Challenge of the Nordic States.* London: Routledge, 2002.

Jakobson, Max. *Finland in the New Europe.* Washington, D.C.: CSIS Press, 1998.

Kazakos, Panos, and P. C. Ioakimidis. *Greece and EC Membership Evaluated.* New York: St. Martin's, 1994.

Keatinge, Patrick. *Ireland and EC Membership Evaluated.* New York: St. Martin's, 1991.

Kuosmanen, Antti. *Finland's Journey to the European Union*. Maastricht: European Institute of Public Administration, 2001.

Luif, Paul. *On the Road to Brussels: The Political Dimension of Austria's Finland's and Sweden's Accession to the European Union*. Vienna: Austrian Institute for International Affairs, 1995.

Magone, Jose M. *European Portugal: The Difficult Road to Sustainable Democracy*. London: Macmillan, 1997.

Maher, D. J. *The Tortuous Path: The Course of Ireland's Entry into the EEC, 1948–73*. Dublin: Institute of Public Administration, 1986.

O'Donnell, Rory. *Ireland and Europe: Challenges for a New Century*. Denver, Colo.: Academic Books, 2000.

Quaglia, Lucia. *Euroscepticism in Italy and Center-Right and Right-Wing Political Parties*. SEI Working Paper No. 60. Sussex, U.K.: Sussex European Institute, 2003.

Rees, Nicholas, and Michael Holmes. "Capacity, Perceptions and Principles: Ireland's Changing Place in Europe." *Current Politics and Economics of Europe* 11, no. 1 (2002): 49–60.

Silva Lopes, Jose da. *Portugal and EC Membership Evaluated*. New York: St. Martin's, 1994.

Thorhallsson, Baldur. *The Role of Small States in the European Union*. Aldershot, U.K.: Ashgate, 2000.

Young, John W. *Britain and European Unity, 1945–1999*. New York: St. Martin's, 2000.

SCHOLARLY JOURNALS

Foreign Affairs
Foreign Policy
Journal of Common Market Studies
Journal of European Integration
International Affairs
International Organization
International Studies Quarterly
World Policy

WEBSITES

Official European Union Sites

Committee of Regions: www.cor.eu.int
Council of the European Union: http://ue.eu.int

Economic and Social Committee: www.esc.eu.int
European Central Bank: www.ecb.int
European Commission: www.europa.eu.int/comm
European Court of Auditors: www.eca.eu.int
European Court of Justice: www.curia.eu.int
European Ombudsman: www.euro-ombudsman.eu.int/
European Parliament: www.europarl.eu.int
European Union: www.europa.eu.int
European Union Delegation to the United States: www.eurunion.org/
EU External Relations: www.europa.eu.int/comm/external_relations/index.htm
Portal to EU Law: www.europa.eu.int/eur-lex/
The EU: A Guide for Americans: www.eurunion.org/infores/euguide/euguide.htm

Agencies of the European Union

Community Plant Variety Office (CPVO): http://europa.eu.int/agencies/cpvo/
    index_en.htm
European Agency for Reconstruction: www.ear.eu.int
European Agency for Safety and Health at Work: http://agency.osha.eu.int/
    agency/index_en.htm
European Aviation Safety Agency (EASA): www.easa.eu.int
European Centre for the Development of Vocational Training (CEDEFOP):
    www.cedefop.eu.int
European Environment Agency (EEA): www.eea.eu.int
European Food Safety Authority (EFSA): www.efsa.eu.int
European Foundation for the Improvement of Living and Working Conditions:
    www.eurofound.eu.int
European Maritime Safety Agency (EMSA): www.emsa.eu.int
European Medicines Agency (EMEA): www.emea.eu.int
European Monitoring Centre for Drugs and Drug Addiction (EMCDDA):
    www.emcdda.eu.int
European Monitoring Centre on Racism and Xenophobia (EUMC): http://eumc
    .eu.int
European Network and Information Security Agency (ENISA): http://europa
    .eu.int/agencies/enisa/index_en.htm
European Training Foundation (ETF): www.etf.eu.int
European Union Institute for Security Studies (EUISS): www.iss-eu.org
European Union Satellite Centre (EUSC): www.eusc.org
Office for Harmonization in the Internal Market (Trademarks and Designs)
    (OHIM): www.oami.eu.int
Translation Centre for the Bodies of the European Union: www.cdt.eu.int

Associations, Centers, Institutes, and Research

Archivos del Presente (Buenos Aires): www.forosur.com.ar/pag_publicaciones
.htm
Association Jean Monnet: www.jean-monnet.net
Centre for European Policy Studies (CEPS): www.ceps.be/index.php
Centre d'Informacio I Documentacio a Barcelona (CIDOB): www.cidob.es
Challenge Europe (Belgium): http://www.theepc.be/en/default.asp?TYP=CE
&LV=177&PG=CE/en/listing&see=y
College of Europe: www.coleurop.be
Council of European Studies: www.europanet.org/frames/overall
Economic and Social Research Council (ESRC): www.one-europe.ac.uk
Euractiv: www.euractiv.com
European Community Studies Association: www.ecsanet.org
European Integration Online Papers: www.eiop.or.at/eiop
The European Journal of International Law: www.ejil.org
The European Policy Centre: www.theepc.be
European Research Papers Archive: www.eiop.or.at/erpa
European Union Studies Association (EUSA): www.eustudies.org/home.html
European University Institute: www.iue.it
Foundation Robert Schuman: www.robert-schuman.org
The Interuniversity Research Centre on Southern Europe: www.cires-ricerca.it
Journal of Common Market Studies (UK): www.blackwellpublishing.com/
journals/JCMS/
Konrad Adenauer Foundation: www.kas.de
Notre Europe: www.notre-europe.asso.fr
Revista de Derecho Comunitario Europeo (Spain): www.cepc.es
The Trans-European Policy Studies Association: www.tepsa.be

External Relations and Regional Organizations

Actors and Processes in EU-ACP Cooperation: www.ue-acp.org
Africa, Pacific, Caribbean (ACP): http://europa.eu.int/comm/development/
body/cotonou/index_en.htm
Andean Community: www.comunidadandina.org
Arab Maghreb Union: www.maghrebarabe.org
Asia-Pacific Economic Cooperation (APEC): www.apecsec.org.sg/apec.html
Association of Southeast Asian Nations (ASEAN): www.aseansec.org
Caribbean Community and Common Market (CARICOM): www.caricom.org
Commonwealth of Independent States (CIS): www.cisstat.com/eng/cis.htm
Council of Arab Economic Unity: www.caeu.org.eg/English/Intro

East African Community: www.eac.int
Economic Community of Central African States (ECCAS): www.ceeac-eccas.org
Economic Community of West African States (ECOWAS): www.ecowas.int
Latin American Integration Association (ALADI): www.aladi.org
North American Free Trade Agreement (NAFTA): www.nafta-sec-alena.org
Secretariat of the African, Caribbean, and Pacific States: www.acpsec.org
South Asian Association for Regional Cooperation: www.saarc-sec.org
Southern African Development Community: www.sadc.int/index.php
Southern Cone Common Market (MERCOSUR): www.mercosur.org.uy

About the Authors

Joaquín Roy (Lic. Law, University of Barcelona, 1966; Ph.D, Georgetown University, 1973) is Jean Monnet Professor of European Integration, founding director of the European Union Research Institute, and director of the European Union Center (www.miami.edu/eucenter/) of the University of Miami. He is the author of over 200 articles and reviews and 25 books, among them *The Reconstruction of Central America: The Role of the European Community* (North-South Center, 1991); *The Ibero-American Space/El Espacio Iberoamericano* (U. Miami/University of Barcelona, 1996); and *Cuba, the U.S. and the Helms-Burton Doctrine* (University of Florida Press, 2000). He is co-editor of *Las relaciones exteriores de la Unión Europea* (México: UNAM, 2001); *Retos de la integración regional: Europa y América* (México: UNAM, 2002); and *La Unión Europea y el TLC* (México: UNAM, 2004). His over 1,200 columns and essays have appeared in newspapers and magazines in Spain, the United States, and Latin America. Among his honors received is the "Encomienda al Mérito Civil," awarded by King Juan Carlos I of Spain.

Aimee Kanner (B.A. in International Relations, George Washington University, 1995; M.A. in Inter-American Studies, University of Miami, 1997; Ph.D. in International Studies, University of Miami, 2001) is assistant professor of political science at Florida Atlantic University, where she teaches courses on the politics of Western Europe, the politics of the European Union, the politics of Latin America, and comparative politics. She is the former associate director of the Miami European Union Center, serving also as an editor, research associate, and program consultant. Dr. Kanner's interests include European studies, particularly the European Union, Latin American studies, and regional studies. She has published several works related to these interests, including "La

Convención Europea: ¿Una Constitución para Europea?" in Alejandro Chanona, Roberto Domínguez, and Joaquín Roy (coordinators), *La Unión Europea y el TLCAN* (México: UNAM, 2003); "La institucionalidad del MERCOSUR" in Roberto Domínguez Rivera, Joaquín Roy, and Rafael Velázquez Flores (coordinators), *Retos e Interrelaciones de la integración regional: Europa y América* (México: Plaza y Valdés, 2003); and (with Joaquín Roy) "Spain and Portugal: Partners in Development and Democracy" in Eleanor E. Zeff and Ellen B. Pirro (eds.), *The European Union and the Member States: Cooperation, Coordination and Compromise* (Boulder: Lynne Rienner, 2001); and *España y Portugal en la Unión Europea* (México: UNAM, 2001).